Garden On, Vashon!

Garden On, Vashon!

A year-round,
years-back look
at how
we have gardened,
farmed, and cultivated
our Island Paradise

by Karen Dale
2013

Dedicated to Bob, who laughs at my Latin, helps make our stone walls, points to the weeds and the chores I've missed, and pads after me through many a garden.

And to Bill, my garden mentor

Front cover: calla lilies and arbor at the garden of Sherene Zolno & Rick Skillman; a scabiosa; members of Shoulder-to-Shoulder Farm; Bill Green eating the first ripe tomato, a 'Stupice', at GreenDale; a bowl of ripe 'Siletz' tomatoes from my garden.

Portions of this book may have been included in the author's blog, "Gardening On, Vashon!" that is offered online by the *Vashon Beachcomber*, a newspaper published by Sound Publishing. All writing by the author on that blog are the property of the author. It can be found at http://blogs.vashonbeachcomber.com/gardenon.

Printed in the United States of America.
Published & distributed by Garden On Publications
ISBN #978-0-9896837-0-8

Contents

4

How-To Sidebars

Garden on, Vashon!

I've been gardening for 25 years, but it was the hard winter of 2008/09 that turned me into a garden writer.

During those three snow-bound weeks, I kept sane by burrowing into the Always Green, Always June World of my gardening books. Shortly before Christmas, I unwrapped Michael Pollan's *The Omnivore's Dilemma,* and let him persuade me how much better it is for us and for the planet if we produce more of our food close to home. A mantra in my head grew: *"Grow more vegetables. Learn to cook. Grow a bigger garden."* I was so eager to get started that, on Christmas Day, I put on my boots, grabbed a shovel, and carved myself a new kitchen garden out of snow. Talk about cabin fever...

I wasn't the only one. By February, when a class on vegetable gardening was offered, 60 people registered. They scheduled a second class, and ANOTHER 60 people showed up. The local nursery found it was paying its bills by installing raised beds for clients eager to start new gardens.

People have always come to Vashon to grow things. The early homesteaders from the 1860s on couldn't "prove up" without growing a food garden. Once land was cleared, farmers put in crops, and strawberries, currants, cane fruit, peaches, even marijuana, all had their years of popularity. But with WWII, the forced removal of the Japanese berry farmers, and more non-agricultural jobs on-Island and off, farming as a primary livelihood declined on the Island.

But did growing things fade from Island self-identity? I doubt it. The "Back to the Land" hippie movement of the 70s brought a big infusion of newbie Islanders eager to break sod (including for backwoods marijuana, which gained a certain regional notoriety.) My husband and I came here on the tail-end of the "exurbia" out-migration from cities that started in the late 1980s, when people with technology skills and Internet access could move to the hinterlands, taking their living with them. No one trades a 40'-wide city lot for five acres unless you want to dig in the dirt.

After that December snow of 2008—one we'll long remember for its three weeks of snowcover—I phoned our local newspaper and volunteered to write a gardening article. That year, I wrote on how Islanders start seeds, grow tomatoes, plant a winter garden. That fall when Sound Publishing decided to jump on the blogging bandwagon, they asked me to write a gardening blog. Thus was born "Garden On, Vashon!" (www.blogs.vashonbeachcomber.com/gardenon)

We have wonderful resources here for gardening. We can gather all kinds of natural amendments: leaves, seaweeds, barnyard poo. We can get gravel, stones, and concrete cheaply, close by. We have good nurseries, plant clubs, garden tours, and a farmers' market full of Island-grown produce. And, most important for this book, we have plenty of experienced, plant-mad gardeners who can show us what wonders can be done on our land. "We're a learning species," says Abel Eckhardt of the Vashon Land Trust. Fellow Islanders have a lot to teach us.

To write this book, I've talked to and visited nearly 100 Vashon gardeners to find out what makes Vashon such a Garden of Eden. The Island has many scientists who were happy to explain Vashon & Maury Island soils, weather conditions and water systems, what fruit varieties do best here, what bees stand the best chance of survival. In telling this Island story about us and our land, I have delved into what was, and what's still happening. I've walked the fields, snooped the gardens, asked my fellow growers all the questions I can think of so we can learn something about Island gardening—and I've shared plenty of my own dumb mistakes along the way. Gardening, for me, isn't about achieving perfection—one look at my garden and you'll know THAT'S true. It's about the wonders you can grow and discover on your piece of our rocky Island Paradise.

So—let's garden on, Vashon!

What I mean when I say "the Island"

I'll use the term "the Island" with a capital "I" if I'm referring to the combination of Vashon and Maury Islands. (sometimes, V-MI for short). If I need to be specific, I'll use "Vashon Island" or "Maury Island."

Thanks—

To all the Islanders who answered my questions, shared their experiences in their gardens, and let me poke around their heads and their land.

For their experience as growers: Jenn Coe, Margaret Hoeffel, Nancy Lewis-Williams, James Dam, Colleen James, Rob Peterson, Jasper Forrester, Michelle Crawford, Leda Langley, Zilla Copper, and Rebecca Wittman.

For their knowledge of our environment: Susie Calhorn, Tom DeVries, Kevin Freeman, Robert Fuerstenberg, Mike Wolczko, Ann Spiers, Michael Laurie, Beth Bordner and Tom Dean of the V-MI Land Trust,

For their memories: Mary Jo Barrantine, Tom Beall, Helen Brocard, Hal Green, Mary Matsuda Gruenewald, Greg Harmeling, Matthew Mosteller, Gene Sherman, Frank Shride, Barbara Steen, Jim Stewart, Katy Jo Steward & Merilee Runyan, Kathy Wheaton, and VAA Garden Tour coordinators.

For letting me in: Anita Halstead, Sally Fox & Steve Brown, Roy Haase, Sherene Zolno & Rick Skillman, Mary Bruno & Kate Thompson, Mary Ann Roberts, Carol & Chuck Ahlfors, Delinda McCann & Noni Morrison, Whit & Mary Carhart, Bonnie MacAllister & Dean Haugen, the folks at the quarry, to Diane Inman for her archiving for VAA, and especially to Bill Green for inviting me to share his vegie patch.

For their areas of expertise: Ron Irvine of Vashon Winery, Wes & Laura Cherry of Dragon's Head Cider, Ken Miller, Carolina Nurik, Mary Robinson, Dan Carlson, Cheryl Grunbock, Steve Rubicz, Bill Riley, Joe Curiel & Tony Raugust and all the wine guys, Cathy Fulton, Elizabeth Sullivan, Michelle Ramsden, and especially Dr. Bob Norton.

For shoving me forward: Kathy Bosler, Julia Lakey, Jack Remick.

To Leslie Brown of the *Vashon-Maury Island Beachcomber,* who gave me a platform for garden articles and my blog, "Garden On, Vashon!"

For Kickstarting the first printing of this book: Karen Biondo, Amy Bogaard, Kathy Bosler, Shirley Brown, Judi Burwell, Lyn Buscaglia, Cathie

Crouse, Arden Dale, Bob Dale, James & Edna Dam, Rick Edwards, Jerry Gehrke, Hal Green, Penny Grist, Bruce Haulman, Amy Huggins, Susan Kutscher, Sharon Masek Lopez, Lotus, Cathy MacNeal, Teresa McFall, Leslie McIntosh, Glenna Mileson, Mark Musik, Dorothy Napoli, Pat Neslund, Carolina Nurik, Jeff Pierce, Molly Reed, Nancy Roehm, Nancy & Steve Rose, Steve Rubicz, Christel Stierle, Bill Stroebel, Susan Sullivan, Catholine & Stu Tribble, and Dr. Al Watts. And all the rest of you KickStarters, too.

There's more of you than I can name here. For all your generosity and openness to the curiosity of this nosy amateur—thank you.

Picture this Island...

You're on the ferry heading to Vashon Island, leaving the mainland of Washington behind. The boat chugs toward a tree-dark mound of land 13 miles long, its shoulders undulating in and out into blue distance. If, ferrying from Seattle, you see a bump east into the shipping channel, you're probably looking at Pt. Robinson on Maury Island, Vashon Island's companion island that's barely attached by a ribbon of land. If you're coming on the Tacoma ferry, you see the southern ends of both islands that bookend the mouth of Quartermaster Harbor. And then the bluff behind the dock looms high above the boat, and you're here.

Closer in, and particularly in autumn, you'll also notice layers of color revealing the preferred environments of our native trees. Dark evergreens—douglas fir, western hemlock, and western red cedar—dominate the island's crown. Cloaking the slopes are gray-barked alders and big-leaf maples—chartreuse in spring with their yellow catkin flowers, soft green in summer, golden-leafed in fall. On the drier slopes of Maury and Vashon's south end, orange-trunked madrones twist forward, leaning into the sunlight.

Unlike the urban shores of Seattle and Tacoma, our Island isn't carpeted with human habitation. 73% of Vashon is in forest, and only 11% is developed land. Thanks to rural zoning and no bridge, Vashon still looks like country; suburbia only exists on the northend and in a few subdivisions that got in before King County in the 1970s imposed the five-acre minimum lot size. Population booms have been few—the "Back to the Land" movement and talk of a bridge in the '70s started a burst of subdivision and migration, while a walk-on ferry in the '90s attracted commuters who had jobs in downtown Seattle. For the most part, the Island has stayed rustic, lightly populated, and trending back into forest since it was homesteaded 150 years ago.

But that's our story. For The Rock, the story began a long time ago...

Prologue: Ice, Water, Rock

For our bucolic garden of an Island, you can thank a layer of stones and a thousand-foot ice cube driven by climate change a long time ago

Around 25,000 years ago, our region's glaciers started to grow. The planet was in one of its periodic cooling phases, and the glaciers of the Canadian Cascades, with growing burdens of ice, began to slip downhill, meet, and creep south. Advancing a few hundred yards a year, a finger of this ice that geologists would later call "the Puget Lobe" reached the Fraser River Lowlands around 21,000 years ago, slowly pushed into Northern Washington, and 5000 years later plugged up the Strait of Juan de Fuca. In our area, the ice was about 1000 feet thick and so heavy that, from its source in Canada to Puget Sound, the earth's crust and underlying mantle sagged beneath it.

The terrific force generated by the ice's movement ripped bedrock from the sides of mountains, breaking and grinding the rocky material like a gigantic tumbler. As the glacier advanced from the mountains to the lowlands, sub-glacial erosion carved deeply into the land, while meltwater gauged 1000 feet deep into lowland sediments, creating deep channels that moved enormous quantities of gravel and sand. As this meltwater spewed from beneath the glacier, its rocky load settled around the glacier in a debris fan called "the great advance outwash plain." Once the advancing ice cut off the land's key drainage point to the sea (what we call today the Straits of Juan de Fuca), that meltwater gathered around the glacier's toe in a vast lake. Greased by this glacial lake and a slime trail of its own creation—silt, clay, sand, and rock flour pulverized by the great weight above—the ice slowly advanced south over its own advance outwash plain, ever so gradually heading toward where we live today.

Sounds very destructive and dramatic, this restless old ice cube. But why, should it matter to us? I put that question to Kevin Freeman, a geologist who once taught a geology section for that series of classes called "Vashon 101" held in 2006-2008. By the time I called him in 2011, I'd read all about the "Puget Lobe" of the "Vashon Glacier" and the "Vashon Stade." My first question: why a gardener on Vashon Island would care?

He chuckled and said, "Because it's ALL geology. What gardeners deal with on Vashon Island IS what the glacier left behind."

By the time the ice sheet reached this far south, it was advancing about 400-500 feet a year. It took another 600 years to grind to a halt north of the Chehalis River. As the lake water rose during the glacier's advance, it eventually reached a notch in the coastal foothills near Black Lake and started to drain toward the ocean. This far south, the glacier met its tipping-point: as melt-off exceeded replacement snowfall, the glacial advance stopped. "And now, the whole process goes in reverse," said Freeman. As in present-day climate change, glaciers don't retreat so much as disintegrate. Waters already running through the ice fractured it even more, excelerating the purging of sands and gravels, depositing them in ribbons and layers on top of the glacer's till layer. "That compressed stuff we call the Vashon Till, that just stays where it is. The meltwater runs on top, carving channels in the till and depositing more outwash on it—a looser, uncompressed mix that we call 'recessional outwash.' The ice disintegrates, the sands and gravels settle downward, boulders come to rest on the earth."

As the glacier retreated, its glacial lake retreated as well, all the way back to the north end of Olympic Peninsula where another notch in the coastal mountains—the Leland Creek Spillway—allowed the lake water to escape toward the ocean. And as the grip of ice eased, this region underwent complex interactions from now-floating ice sheets to the north, melting glaciers to the south, waters from the ocean reconnecting with drainage in the Puget Sound Basin, tectonic shifts, rising sea levels, and rising land as the earth's crust rebounded from under that once-vast weight. As ice cleared and water drained, a new land's form was revealed: big slugs of layered glacial deposits, mostly running north/south, that we know as the landmass of Puget Sound and all the islands in it.

Our Island—or at least the raw piles of glacial debris that will be named Vashon-Maury Islands—emerged from this last Ice Age between 11,000-13,500 years ago. One might ask, why does the Puget terrain feature these humps of land at all—why not one vast, thick plain of debris? The theoretical answer is, says Freeman, is that meltwater had already established channels underneath the glacier, which only became deeper once water began draining north again. When we visualize Puget Sound, its north-south waterways and long narrow hills, we're seeing forms carved by that northward flow of water. And it cut into rising land: no longer suppressed by the weight of the glacier, the land is rising with the return of magna flowing back under the once-depressed crust of the earth.

And so, it appeared: Vashon-Maury Island—a glacier's dump site, lakebeds topped by compressed sand and pebbles, lidded by hardened till, dusted by looser sands and pebbles. Layer cakes in the rain.

"After the Island emerged, then the forces of weathering and reforestation took over," said Freeman. "As we saw after the eruption of Mt. St. Helens, vegetation reestablishes incredibly quickly. Forest soils aren't very deep: we don't have deep soils like they do in the Midwest in the flood plains of the Missouri or Mississippi Rivers. We have this shallow forest duff, and underneath it's Vashon Till. Once that forest is gone, that thin layer that loggers clear-cut and farmers plow easily weathers away."

I mention to Freeman that I've seen the maps showing locations dominated by Vashon till, advance outwash, or recessional outwash. In general, Vashon Till mantles the Island's top, advance outwash is exposed along the Island's steeper sides, while recessional outwash sits in upland depressions and in canyon drainages such as Judd Creek. He explains, "The center of the island is primarily Vashon Till. It's essentially a ridge: the sands, gravels, and cobbles of the recessional outwash are found in just a few depressions where they were protected from eroding away downhill."

So what did the glacier leave us?

My Very Own Recessional Outwash Soil

I'm digging in my potato patch. It's at elevation 400 feet, nearly as high as Island elevations go, and within the clearing made for our house overlooking outer Quartermaster Harbor. With a forested ravine to my right, another to my left, it's a typical Island "hole in the forest."

The topsoil in the ravines is forest duff: a thin crust of maple and madrone leaves over decaying bits of hemlock and fir. Roots stop my shovel whenever I try to dig. But on the slope cleared for a view, the soil is mostly sand and pebbles so loose that my gloved hands can claw it up easily.

My fingertips touch something round and cool: a potato? Nope: it's our dead common, coin-of-the-realm cobble, a little pocket-sized spud of a stone. I pitch it over the fence. Presumably, like thousands of its unearthed ancestors, it will roll a ways downhill.

Just another moment of erosion for the Island's recessional outwash.

Recessional outwash are the deposits of pebbles, gravel, and sand that the glacier dropped or purged during its meltdown. On Vashon Island, it's found on flat terraces such as those of Dilworth, upper Burton into Misty Isles Farm, and a large area between Cemetery and Cove Roads, from K2 north to the airport. The lowest elevations within the Judd Creek watershed—and probably other deeper ravines of the Island—are also filled with recessional outwash, collected there as the slopes eroded.

Because the siting of our houses and gardens, our septic systems, and our access to water depend on the composition of the soil below, the Island has a number of professionals who spent their days poking holes into Island soil. Mike Wolczko is one: he's a geo-tech engineer who's dug his share of "perk holes" to gauge whether a patch of land can be used as a septic system's drainfield. "Near Cove Road where I live, we have what's been described as 'ice contact deposits': places where there might have been either water with ice in it or a huge chunk of ice sitting on the soil. As that ice melted or was pushed around by wind, it slowly carved out a depression that filled up with the junk the ice contained—sand, gravel, cobbles, even boulders."

Some of these pockets still have water in them today. Look on a map that shows glacial deposits and island waterways, and you'll see that Fisher Pond, Whispering Firs Bog, and other upland ponds lie in recessional outwash areas. The theory goes that water bottoms out on the hardpan, then spreads out underground until it backfills one of these natural depressions or reaches an outlet like a seep, stream, or man-made water system.

High school science teacher Tom DeVries told me a local story of this process in action. "The recessional outwash most famous on the Island is across the middle of Misty Isle Farm. Near 232nd is a long Misty Isles field that slopes into a basin near the gate at 115th Road. This shallow basin is filled with sand above hardpan: it's recessional outwash. All the water that falls on that field, now covered with grass and once cattle, runs downhill toward 232nd, where Burton Water Company has its wells. The claim was once made that Misty Isles' cattle operation contaminated the water. They did a lot of tests, but nothing was ever proved."

Digging in my ground that's in a recessional advance area, I can see their point. Water can travel through loose sand and gravel 10-10,000 times faster than through clay. Water drains fast here, TOO fast, and the soil is easily leached of nutrients. The best thing about it is that it's easy to dig.

But under my old garden on Beall Road—and most of the old farmlands on the upper terraces of Vashon Island—there lies a natural, underground barrier. It keeps pollutants out of our drinking water, holds our buildings secure during earthquakes, and keeps groundwater within reach of the roots of our crops. Gardeners call it hardpan and rue its presence. Geologists call it Vashon Till.

Our notorious Vashon Till

Vashon Till starts about 2-10' below ground and keeps going 5' to 125' down. It mantles the upland of Vashon Island, as it does most of the Puget Sound landscape. It's a compressed mosaic of sand, silts, clays, cobbles, seashells, fish skeletons, and probably a few drowned mastodons—anything that sank to the bottom of the glacial lake and was overrun by the glacier. Our Island's name came to be associated with this obdurate earthwork in the 1890s, when geologist Bayley Willis, sent here by the U.S. Geologic Survey, found traces of this layer in most Puget Sound bluffs. He named this hardpan layer, and the glacier that formed it, after "Vashon, where the gravelly till characteristic of the episode occurs typically, if not heavily."

After the fourth edition of the Park District's Trails book came out, I asked the co-author, Ann Spiers, where I could find the best exposure of Vashon Till. Her husband David Frank, a geologist, recommended the bluff at the north end of KVI Beach, so I organized a field trip.

Four rock-mad friends and I walked past the KVI marsh and around the bluff at the northeast corner. Here the bluff turns into a 60' cliff, and we stared up its sheer face dotted and seamed with cobbles, topped by scraggly grass and tree roots reaching into thin air. I grasped one of the largest cobbles sticking halfway out, tried in vain to pry it loose. Not a chance—might as well been stuck in concrete.

June Niece, who used to design septic fields for Islanders, was along for the love of geology; I asked about her encounters with Vashon Till. "When we were searching a property for a drain-field, we did not want to find this stuff," she said. "No bulldozer can get its teeth into it, and nobody has enough money to dig through it."

Till is bad news for septic fields and plowing farm fields in spring, and for the same reason: an underlayment of hardpan keeps soil waterlogged. Till only lets water perk through about 1-1.5" inches per month, but a good winter storm can dump that much rain in a day—40" during the whole year. Water builds up on the hardpan faster than it can perk through, so water backfills toward the surface, ponding on the land, making fields and gardens too wet to work. If there's a low point anywhere, water will find it: filling ponds, wetlands, springs, streams, drainage ditches, seeping down through cracks in the till, squirting out the sides of the Island from seeps, springs, or creeks. Water might even perch in depressions in the till; scrape through the muck of many a summer pond and you'll probably find it has a silt-slicked floor of Vashon Till.

Advance Outwash and Lawton Clay

As we geology buffs strolled north toward the beach houses of Klahanie, the bluff face changed: June pointed out the small streaks of rust oxide mottling where water had leached from the rock. Had we reached a layer of "advance outwash"—that sand and gravel layer that stores our island's water supply—or was this just erosion? The surface was loose enough for somebody to scrape "Geri" into its sandy face, sticky enough to squeeze scrapings into a ball. We debated: silt? clay? Certainly not till.

"As you walk north on that beach, you're actually walking back in time," Ann's geologist husband later told me. "The till layer rises higher because the land uplifted once the glacier's weight melted away. Nearing Klahanie, you'll find 'advance outwash.' These sands and gravels are pretty clean, and while compressed, they weren't cemented together. There's actually quite a bit of space around the rock and cobble, and that's where water collects, that's where our drinking water comes from. And it's kept pure and clean thanks, in part, to that lid of Vashon Till on top."

"At beach level, you might see a layer of Lawton Clay: a dark grayish layer of fines that sank to the bottom of the lake in front of the advancing glacier. And in the beach itself, did you see a layer of what we geologists call 'woody peat?' It's made of twigs and old trees from the period before the Vashon glacier. That stuff's REALLY old."

We don't find the Lawton Clay here, but I knew what he meant. A rainstorm the winter before had sent a landslide of sand and gravel over the highway on Shawnee Beach south of Burton. Once the road crews cleared off the landslide, a layer of dark gray clay was revealed just above the road, water weeping down its face. These clay-beds weep because they are "aquitards"—they are so thick with clay, they retard the passage of water. So water backs up into the spaces around the sands and gravels above it, spreading sideways until it finds a release point—here, the weeping slope. This stiff, black-brown clay not far above today's sea-level can be seen around the north-end ferry dock, exposed after landslides or erosion, or near the base of the Wingehaven cliff face, where the clays, Kevin Freeman told me, are the oldest sediments on the island—somewhere north of 780,000 years old. It's as stiff as clay comes; the early settlers used it to make bricks. Around Quartermaster Harbor, the beach is still studded by chunks of red brick manufactured in shoreline shops during the early years of the 20th century. Their sharp corners are as rounded as cobbles by decades of tidal action tumbling them over the gritty sand.

We can't walk any farther back in time: June's got an appointment, and our lower backs are starting to ache. So we return, filling our pockets with beach trophies: cobbles of Canadian granite transported here by the glacier, chips of red brick from old brickworks, seashells brought here by the tide.

Back home, I put a granite cobble on the garage windowsill, next to the chunk of Lawton Clay I took from the 2010 landslide. I should add one of my stone "potatoes" and fill a jar with advance outwash from Maury Island's gravel yard (once named, appropriately, Glacier NW). Then I'd see a full representation of Vashon's geology every time I drive in the garage.

It fires my imagination, deepens my understanding, knowing my bit of ground was formed by grinding ice, the power of water to sort and rearrange, the decaying of wood and leaves, the finger-scratchings of individuals. We garden on ground that gave its name to an Ice Age. How grand is that?

In mid-winter... ༄

Dark woolly clouds hang over the Island. It's chilly, barely reaching mid-40s by mid-afternoon. Wind scrapes white-caps off the water in Quartermaster Harbor and tosses around crows and seagulls trying their best to fly. It's late January on the Island.

Oregon grape's towering flowers, bright yellow on the slope above Shawnee Beach, advertise to Anna's Hummingbirds one of the few nectar sources available now. On the water, the wintering-over scoters, goldeneyes, and buffleheads are still dipping, bums-up, for mussels and whatever else they can find in the gravels and sands of the harbor.

Driving north up the highway, I notice dull yellow catkins dangling from the shrub hazels—the first signs of a new season rising. Clumps of heather pink a few front yards and rockeries. Across from the athletic club, the autumn-flowering cherry (always running late) blooms its lacy cloud of cool pink.

The drainage ditches along the highway run full. In the flooded field of the Country Store, ducks paddle among the blueberry shrubs, cruising amongst the clouds in the sky-reflecting waters held high by hardpan.

At the Lutheran Church, the parking lot is full as the ladies of the garden club are meeting, soon to be recruited to grow on plants for their big sale in May. At Kathy's Corner, her crews are sowing lettuce, tomatoes, onions, and annuals. The winter-sown pansies are starting to set flowers, halfway to their bloom in March.

Up here on the Island's top, the clouds are breaking. It might become a nice day after all. And as cabin fever grabs hold of me, I go forth for my shovel, wanting badly to dig. Surely somewhere on my sloped land, I can make a place to plant.

A Soil for Strawberries

Readying the land for planting, soil prep (especially for a berry patch), and what kind of soil do we have here?

I wanted a strawberry patch. Doesn't FEEL right to live on this Island and NOT grow strawberries.

Vashon's Strawberry Festival, held in mid-July, was probably the first public event I attended here. I saw fair goers enjoying strawberry shortcake, searched up and down, found the shortcake truck at last. But when I dug into this "local" treat, was I disappointed—nothing fresh or local about those red blobs! I remember asking, "Where are the local strawberries?"

I come from a Oregonian tradition of berry-picking: my mom is famous among her friends for pies made of blueberries, boysens, marions, logans. We kids earned our first pocket change picking strawberries east of Portland. So when I first moved here in 1995 and started exploring this rural place on bicycle, I assumed I would find some berry fields. I would wander out onto those big, unused fields behind K2, Vashon Market, at Center, on Sunrise Ridge, above Dockton, and wonder what once grew there. The only u-pick I could find was a few weed-infested rows at Pete Svinth's farm on Maury (now Pacific Crest Farm). Not even the local small farmers carried berries: "They grow out of sync with our other crops... they're too much trouble... we haven't got the time," they told me.

I soon realized that if I wanted to enjoy this Island tradition, I would have to carry it on myself in my own backyard. The question was, did I have the kind of place that berries could love?

There's no question that berries have loved growing on Vashon soil. And Vashon farmers loved growing them—at least in the first decades of farming. Within the first ten years of white settlement, farmers were lifting crates of strawberries into boats to be sold in Seattle, Tacoma, up to Alaska and out to the Midwest. 6595 crates by 1893. 15,000 by 1901. 100,000 crates by 1908 and two years later, 165,000. A local booster printed a pamphlet in

1909 that claimed Vashon Island, "Home of the Big Red Strawberry...is the most fertile spot in the Puget Sound region. That 300-500 crates of strawberries to the acre are considered common yields is a pretty good testimony for its soil...producing the largest and best-flavored berry in the world." Local farmers organized themselves into a canning company to ship fresh and frozen berries off boats docked at Vashon Landing at the end of Soper Road. That same year, local boosters began planning the first Strawberry Festival.

Most Vashon farms were on the Island's more-or-less flat plateau, from Judd Creek up through town and north to the Norwegian settlements of Colvos. Once cleared of trees, these fields were open to sunlight and the plow. The nearness of the ocean kept temperatures moderate, with cold air draining down the sides of "the rock." The glacial soil seemed to drain well and was (like most newly cleared land) quite fertile. And since it was easier to get products to market via boat than it was to move it overland, Vashon berry farmers could easily compete with farmers in Bellevue, Puyallup, and the river valleys.

When you look at agricultural soil maps, these cultivated lands largely correspond to two types of soils: "alderwood" and a related soil called "everett-alderwood." Named for locales with the most typical example, these labels provide a "handle," in trucker-speak, for a longer description of what's in each soil. For instance: when you say "alderwood soil," a soil scientist (and possibly nobody else) knows you are referring to a gravelly, sandy loam soil of marine climates that formed under conifer forests and above till. About a third of it is sand, gravel and/or cobbles, with an acidity of 6.0-6.5. With all that sand, it is moderately well-drained, with rapid perk in the upper inches but slow perk below, with a high water table from January to March.

Alderwood soil covers about 30% of the Puget Sound land-mass and about half of Vashon Island. Proceeding from the north end, one finds it in a narrow corridor on either side of the highway, spreading south of the John L. Scott/Cedarhurst turnoff to cover the uplands of Vashon Island before the terrain drops into the Judd Creek and Ellisport Creek drainages. Most of these lands contained the big berry fields and orchards of the mid 20th century. (Maury Island is a far more jumbled picture: only the cleared fields of Dockton and the acreages around Pete's Picks/Pacific Crest Farm are alderwood soils of any extent.)

When King County did a land use assessment in 1975, they considered these areas of alderwood soils "best used for pasture and timber" and gave them the "Class 4" designation. (The best soils in King County are class 2 soils, suitable for growing berries or truck crops, but there are only a few tiny pockets, the largest locked up behind the gates of Misty Isle Farm where the late millionaire and Republican supporter Tom Stewart ran his herd of Black Angus cattle. One of the larger pockets of #3 soil is under Vashon High School, once a strawberry field). The land use report does go on to say that "crops respond well to applications of manure and fertilizer" in class 4 soils, and so it seemed to, as farmers made use of the natural fertilizer available from the Island's many chicken-n-egg operations.

Winter alderwood is an entirely different creature than summer alderwood. In winter when it's waterlogged, it can look and behave like dense dark fudge—and can stay that way for months. I once helped rescue a stranded visitor to the local garden tour who had backed her car into the grip of a muddy road verge off Cemetery Road—and that was in June. Because of its gooey, saturated grip, a lot of gardeners may be assuming they have a predominantly clay soil, when what they really have is a high water-table that makes a soil with *a little* clay drain as poorly as one predominantly clay. But as spring rains end and the water table recedes, the soil literally lightens up—it drains, becomes easier to work, horse and plow (or tractor and tiller) can move across the field. Left to dry out completely, by August alderwood soil may become as pale brown as a latte—as you can see in farmers' hoophouses just a few inches from drip-tapes.

Mary Matsuda Gruenewald, a second-generation Japanese-American whose family farmed strawberries in the big field west of the old K2 campus, describes the soil & water predicament in her book about her family before and during WWII. In *Looking Like the Enemy,* she writes—

> During the months when it rained daily, we donned our boots and raingear and trudged outdoors anyway. There were times when we had to take shovels and pick axes and make trenches or dig ditches to redirect excess water. ... During overly rainy summers, the strawberries didn't have a chance to ripen properly, and we lost much of the potential crop to mold and fungus. Other years when rain was scarce, the plants dried up and the berries, though sweet, were small and withered."

So once again, the problem for farmers on alderwood soil is the water near their plants' roots—except by July, it's a matter of bringing water to the plants instead of wishing the water would go away. Islanders came up with ingenious ways to manage water. Some tiled their fields with drain-pipes or ditches. Yoneichi Matsuda, Mary's brother who returned to the farm after his service with the 442nd Regimental Combat Team during WWII, directed his water toward a natural pond that, in summer, he used for piped irrigation; this practice earned him the 1957 "Conservation Farmer of the Year" award from King County Soil Conservation District. Other farmers around Paradise Valley installed hydraulic rams that pumped creek water uphill to their fields. Craig Harmeling, whose family homesteaded Sunrise Ridge, told me you once could hear those rams thumping underground all along 204th as it descends into the valley.

The challenges of growing berries on alderwood soil became clearer over time. In November 1957, a *Seattle Times* writer in an interview with Mr. Matsuda wrote—

"The Matsudas know from the rude experience of several strawberry growers on Vashon that water is critical... These soils, apparently open and porous at the surface, are underlaid with a hardpan that stops proper drainage. In many places on the Island, water stands free in the soil during winter and spring months. *During dry spells, the light surface layer of soil does not hold sufficient moisture for the crop. These are anything but ideal moisture conditions for plants, esp. berry plants.* *Free water standing at the root zone of strawberry encourages the development of a root rot disease called red stele. Entire fields of strawberries have been wiped out by this disease during a cool, wet season."*

Red stele, root weevils, strawberry maggots, long cold springs. Add to this difficulties restrictive labor laws, lack of pickers, easier and better-paying jobs both on- and off-island—and particularly the removal and internment during WWII of Vashon's talented Japanese farmers—and you have an island that slowly transitioned out of berry-farming. By the 1970s, the berry fields briefly became U-picks, then hayfields or subdivided properties, passed to children or developed for homes. Today, the Island's alderwood soil grows mostly what King County thought it should: grass.

Still, a headstrong gardener will dig in anything. When I started digging into the soil of my first Island garden, it seemed to pop more cobbles than a potato field. My land there, on Beall south of the greenhouse ruins, is part of a transition zone beyond the Vashon Till and into something called "everett-alderwood soil." East of Vashon Highway, this zone goes from the Beall Road greenhouses southeast to Ellisport; west of the highway, the zone extends south from Judd Creek to Tahlequah.

The chief difference between the soils is that underneath everett-alderwood soil isn't hardpan, but glacial outwash. The soil, free of hardpan, drains water "excessively" (according to the soil description) and lets the cobbles of the underlaying glacial outwash rise to the surface (particularly during freeze/thaw cycles). As an agricultural designation, "everett-alderwood" is class 6, considered best for growing forests, as the lack of a hardpan means trees can root deeply, without drowning in a high water table. In fact, the soil is so gravelly, allows rainwater to run so freely, that erosion can become a problem on steeper slopes—another reason to leave trees in place.

That doesn't mean that it's loose soil: oh no, not on the flat. My first garden on Beall had soil so compacted, I had to attack it with a pick-ax, then shovel the dirt into a milk-crate I'd rock back and forth to sift the pebbles out of my future vegie beds. But those darn spud-stones came back every year, fooling my fingers whenever I went pawing for potatoes.

Strawberries now and then, with Kathy Wheaton

Just a few months after I broke ground on that first garden, a friend thrust on me a box of 'Tri-Star Everbearing" divisions from her strawberry patch. Like many traditions, strawberries impose themselves on others: they shoot out new plants like Topsy, and anybody who grows them will soon have give-aways. More recently, when I mentioned in yoga class that I wanted strawberries, a fellow student said, "I'm going to divide mine—how many will you want?" I would argue that the island tradition of strawberries is just this passing-down of divisions, one friend or neighbor to another.

A lot of references advise that strawberries only last four years; by year three, you'd better pinch off the runners and plant them in a new row because the following year the original plants' productivity will drop way off.

In fact, the big Skagit Valley grower Sakuma Brothers, suppliers of both grocery berries and nursery plants, is now flogging day-neutral plants grown as annuals to big growers: after they fruit the first year, the plants are plowed under and the fields reset with ready-to-go Sakuma starts.

Although our largest nursery does sell strawberry bundles from Sakuma Brothers, Kathy Wheaton, the owner of Kathy's Corner, doesn't believe that strawberries have to be a burden. When I stopped by in late winter to get advice about a new berry patch of my own, she was revising her flyer on growing strawberries. before placing her spring order. "JUST FEED THEM," she said, claiming she'd kept her own patch of strawberries going for 15 years without division, feeding them every March with compost and an all-purpose fertilizer like 5-5-5, repeated in May before the plants flower.

"Back in the 1970s when my family was running the Ace Hardware franchise, we hauled in 10-20 tons of fertilizers at a time, strong 20-20-20 fertilizer. For berries, it was 10-20-20. Some of the ol' timers STILL come every spring and order that stuff and dolomite lime for their berries."

She told me about picking strawberries here as a kid, back in the 1960s. "We were picked up at 5am in flat-bed trucks to go pick for Augie Takatsuka or Tok Otsuka, the last guys who were still farming berries then. I was paid 25 cents a flat, plus a bonus for so many flats. Hoods were the biggie back then. We still sell a lot of Hoods for nostalgic reasons; they're not as prolific, but they do have sweet, big fruit. Strawberry picking started a couple days before my birthday, June 21, and some years it was still so cold in the mornings, they fired up bonfires in big cans so we could warm our fingers."

This early in February, it was too early to plant, but it was the perfect time to prepare a bed for strawberries. She told me to choose a site that would receive at least six hours of sunshine and had sandy, well-drained soil within reach of my garden hose. Strawberries like a soil with a pH from 5.5–6.2, but since my soil is closer to neutral (pH 7), she suggested adding peat moss to acidify it a bit. "And you'll need protection from slugs, birds—and are raccoons a problem?" and she talked about the foot-high, 2-strand electric barrier her husband had put around her berry patch. "The raccoons get a jolt when they try to drag themselves over or under, so we hadn't had any problems with coons since putting in that little fence.

"When you're ready to plant strawberries, you make a little hill of soil, spread the roots down the side of the hill, then cover the roots with soil and firm lightly, so the base of the crown sits just above the soil." And if I hadn't already done so, to fertilize with 5-5-5. "And don't bother to de-flower if you get plants from me—my stock is ready to fruit the first year."

On the next nice day, I dug my shovel into a bit of risen ground with a good morning exposure. I grubbed out the grass and sheep's dock, added compost, bonemeal, coconut coir (a good substitute for peat moss, which isn't a renewable resource), and some 5-5-5 all-purpose fertilizer. After I surrounded the newly-fluffy soil with boards of pressure-treated lumber, I sprinkled Sluggo liberally, covered the soil with a blanket of plasti-mulch, and stuck in two hoops to hold a web of bird-netting, pinning it with clothes-pins to the hoops.

A week later, my fellow yoga student Annie handed me that flat of her 'Tri-star' everbearers, and I heeled them in. Ever-bearers don't actually bear all the time (like day-neutrals); they crop in spring and again in late summer. At Kathy's Corner, I bought some June-bearing 'Shuksan' berries, and because she crowed "It couldn't be a better berry!" some 'Albion' day-neutrals, which bear the first year and set fruit throughout the season.

Back home, I sliced Xs on 12' centers into the plasti-mulch in two rows down the bed, made the little dirt hills, spread the roots over them, then covered the roots with soil and the black blanket. I made a hoophouse out of bird-netting and bamboo poles, ground stapled down the netting, and hoped the raccoons couldn't get in. (Three years later, they did, showing me that a stouter cage made of wire or thicker plastic-mesh is a much better bet against birds, coons, and the chipmunks & squirrels that will surely wiggle through your bird-netting the very morning the berries are perfectly ripe.)

Though they didn't bear much, by July my new plants bore just enough red berries to top my cereal for one weekend. The next June, I had enough berries to make a couple of pies. And by that August, I had more than enough running daughter plants to give away to... let's see... surely I know SOMEBODY who wants to start a Vashon Island strawberry patch...

Gardening on a Slope

Retaining walls, the gravel yard, landslides, and planting on slopes

On our hilltop homestead, we've installed many a retaining wall. You have to if you want any level places on a 20° slope. Some walls are made with railroad ties, some with pressure-treated lumber, but most are made of concrete rubble. Rubble is by far the least expensive, as you can scavenge it off demolition sites or get truckloads at our local quarry. It can be quite attractive: one of our walls looks (to us, anyway) like high-priced granite, but is really chunks of a custom-tinted patio that the original client didn't like. Once the moss takes hold within a couple years, a wall of rubble or natural stone will look like it's been there forever.

I had a sun-catching slope that I thought might make a decent site for raspberries. I was given a bucketful of canes the year before, and I had just heeled them into a future perennial bed thinking I'd move them soon… months later, they were sprawling all over my flowers, their thorns snagging at every passersby. Clearly they needed their own space, along with some training—and the sun-catcher slope would work fine if it wasn't so steep.

Yay! An excuse to build a new wall!

So husband and I got into tough, grubby clothes and stout boots, threw shovel, mallet, and buckets into the back of the truck, and headed for Maury Island. Crossing the isthmus at Portage, we continued south on Dockton Road along what King County now considers a "heritage corridor." This landscape has barely changed over the last 100 years: it's still shorelines, marsh, pastures, a few truck farms, forest and grass reclaiming what's unused. The few houses are old farmhouses or mossy-roofed bungalows; anything newer than Ranch look much too moderne. The hyper-groomed golf course on the right like the Invasion of Suburbia.

At the southeast corner of the golf course we turned left, went another 100 yards on, turned right. Good-bye green countryside, hello Geology. Around us on three sides rise 400' foot ramparts of nothing but gravel. This is Vashon Sand & Gravel, here since the 1940s, the last of at least three gravel mines that tapped a huge deposit of advance outwash gravel from the top of Maury to the water, from Gold Beach north to Pt. Robinson. In the late 2000s the quarry's parent company (then Glacier NW, now CalPortland) battled with local environmentalists to reopen a much larger mine on the water-side of the Maury ridge, but that controversy ended with a conservationist win. Today's lease with King County stipulates that any mined material remains on the Island. So this quarry still serves only Islanders.

Consider this: our Island community is webbed together by this gravel, as it underlies every road and building, makes up every gravel drive and walkway. The quarry sells rock of all sizes, from sand to pea gravel, crushed rock and smaller screenings for roads, aggregate and concrete for pouring, and what manager Todd Gateman calls "pretty rocks" set aside for stone wall building and garden boulders. Plus they have rubble—so much rubble—a mountain of unused concrete made from slurry left over in the concrete trucks after their jobs. They dump it into settling basins; when hard, the concrete's broken up, then piled on what we call "Rubble Mountain."

I parked on the weight scale and went in to say hello to Karen, their short, jovial secretary. She had a new pal, a white toy poodle she's fostering for Vashon Island Pet Protectors. "We named him Crusher..." pause..."You know, after our rock crusher?" laughed, then handed us orange hard hats and safety vests. There's a warning sign outside that proclaims hundreds of days without an accident: we didn't want to be next on the casualty list.

After Karen waved us off the scale, we drove to Rubble Mountain slowly so the dozer drivers would notice us. A front-loader rumbled over; I pointed to the pile, the driver scooped in, then spread out his scoopful for us to pick over. There's broken-up pieces from the settling pans, demolition from contractor jobs, pieces of old patio concrete or brick, leftover flagstones from paving projects. No one seems to want the stuff but us.

We're looking for "two-man rocks" that aren't too heavy for Bob and me to lift to the truck-bed. To make good walling material, each piece must be flat on both faces and equally thick, without bumps to make it rock after it's laid. Sometimes pebbles stuck in the concrete can be tapped free with a heavy hammer, but if the rock has a belly, it can only be used bump-side down in a cavity tailor-made in the foundation coarse. If I find a whole family of untypical but equal thickness, I'll use them all in one coarse.

We loaded up small pieces for backfill, some long tie-back pieces, big fellas for the top coarse. In last went buckets of pea-gravel, plus chinks and tapered flats for wedging. Then we slammed the tail-gate home, headed to the weight scale to shed the bright-orange clothes, settle up, see how close we got to our truck's half-ton limit. Then we slowly drove the truck laden with glacier leavings and manmade blocks down the road and up our hill toward the Island's next Shaping-the-Land project.

Building a Retaining Wall

Back at our sun-catcher slope, the first task was to cut across the slope to make space for the wall and its backfill. I used a sharp shovel to shave off soil, straight down, to create a cliff about 16' long and 2 feet tall, tossing the soil above for later backfilling. Then I dug a foundation trench at its feet about one rubble-thickness below grade and a few inches in front of the "cliff;" in it would go an inch of pea-gravel, then the first coarse of stones down its length. Since these stones will be underground, I used the ugly pieces or custom-tailored a hole for an odd-shaped stone. As I built, I tried to keep the tops even across so the next coarse would lay down easy.

There's one other adjustment that starts in the foundation trench: to tilt each piece so that the outer lip is slightly higher than the back. That's to give the wall a backward lean—masons call it "batter" —that will resist the earth's outward thrust. Unfortunately, that tilt also pulls rainwater into the wall, and unless you give that wall drainage, the water can get hydraulic on you and blow out your wall (as I saw happen, once, to a wall project on Bank Road after a rainstorm). So on this project, I threw plenty of gravel around the rocks and as backfill to create drainage. The rocks settle better, anyway, with gravel tucked into their joints. (Another way to gain this batter is to set each coarse back a bit to create a 2" setback per foot of height, which will put your wall's center of balance nearer the earth you want to retain.)

This yard-high wall is as tall as one should build without professional consultation. Once the first course was set correctly, the rest went faster: two stones meeting over one or one covering the joint between two, with gravel thrown in between and behind. How secure, how anchored, a well-graveled wall feels. I tested its stability by walking across the top. Why, it'll last the Ages (oh, I can dream, can't I...).

As the coarses rose and the wall turned into a bench, I took a break to sit and soak up some of this winter sun. Leaning back, squinting, my fingers curled into the loose dirt I tossed uphill. How lucky I am to have a good project outside during this late winter thaw. How lucky I am to have soil that drains so well... And I thought about my neighbors downslope, who have built as many walls as I have. They didn't have much choice.

Hillside terraces: hold the earth, make space for plants

My neighbors Rick Skillman and Sherene Zolno garden just 100 feet below me, on a steep slope of firs and maples, hemlocks and madrones. With both clay and sand pockets, the soil has slid around their house at least three times, and so a garden has been built to hold the earth in place.

Several years ago, the ravine that starts just below their driveway was gouged out by a falling Big-Leaf Maple. To heal and hold the ripped earth, Sherene planted hill-holding natives like salal, elderberry, Oregon grape, red-flowering currant, Indian plum, vine maple, rhodies, nootka rose, and snowberry, using large, well-rooted plants from local nurseries.

At the bottom of the stairs near their greenhouse, the hill is held in by a style of pipe-n-beam terracing used throughout the garden. Shortly after they moved here in 1995, my neighbors noticed sand eroding into their garage from the slope above. They were referred to Al Bradley, rock and retaining wall specialist; he and crew drove rows of steel pipe 10-14 feet down, sinking it into hardpan. Behind the pipes they stacked, on edge, 4"x12" planks of pressure-treated lumber 3-4' high, depending on need.

Al told them, "you need walls like this in front of your house, too." So they built a staircase down the south side of the house, wrapped more pipe/ stack walls around the south-to-east sides of the slope. Walls supported paths or planting beds, held vines or artworks. Different levels meant more steps to install, railings to commission, artworks set among the flowers, benches so one could rest and meditate upon the magnificent water view.

Rick became a skillful woodworker who built pergolas, terraces, and arches to mark the rest stops along the paths. Sherene became a Master Gardener, planting hostas, native bleeding hearts and piggy-back plants, hardy geraniums, and lush maidenhair ferns, and in the sunny patches calla lilies, senecio, lambs' ears, honeysuckle, barberries. Foxgloves seeded themselves, sweeping the gaze ever up in this vertical landscape.

The trail ends on the north side of the house with a bellflower-lily-astilbe garden. And here, within a stone's throw of the house, is another sluff-off that let loose in a January rainstorm, sliding downhill about 100 feet. My neighbors nervously replanted as quickly as possible, crawling down 25' ladders laid on the slope and sticking in native plants every couple of feet. Nurseryman John Browne, who runs Judd Creek Native Plant Nursery, loaned them his huge leather satchel to carry plants and dirt to the areas they were replanting. Those opportunistic foxgloves soon seeded themselves into the exposed dirt and, by the following summer, turned the torn slope into a cascade of foxglove beauty.

Every slope has the potential to slide

You can find the gougings of these sluffs and slides all over the steep sides of the Island. It's not so much the earth moving as it is water, moving down, sideways, and out—and carrying the soil along with it.

Geologist Kevin Freeman explained that one of the reasons we're vulnerable to slides is our layered sequence of soils. Rainwater sinks into the layer-cake geology and drains down until it finds an aquitard—an impervious layer like Vashon till or a deep clay layer—then moves sideways seeking an outlet. When the Island gets two inches of rain within two days, that's when we're at greatest risk of slides.

But what causes a landslide is ultimately gravity: the more weight on it, the more likely it is to fail. Freeman said, "Pick up a one-gallon bucket of water, then imagine that bucketful in a slope, multiplied many times over. As water pressure and weight build up, that contact between sand & clay layers becomes a ready-made failure plane." If the slope is close to that soil type's angle of repose, the force of gravity alone on all that weight can get the earth moving. Or a catalyst, like a a top-heavy tree tipping over or runoff concentrated toward a vulnerable place, can set things in motion.

The least damaging (though impressive to the eye) are superficial sluffs that start from the top and scrape off the saturated surface just a few inches deep. The most damaging slides are when the toe of a slope releases and brings down everything with it. It will look like a giant scoop-out and can cut back a hillside quite deeply. In fact, many cliffs around the Island, said Freeman, are hillsides that have failed in the past.

Freeman said, "The highest risk place to build is on the beach with a steep slope behind you. If that slope gives, your house is no match for moving soil." Island lore tells many tales of beach homes being shoved into the Sound by landslides. In her Island history, *Search for Laughter,* Marjorie Stanley tells of a slide at Wingehaven Park, of a "K.W. Klose, who in 1907 built a cement plant in the area. Just after getting all of his machinery set up, a landslide wiped it out in one fell swoop. Disheartened, he sold to Harold Cunliffe (hence Cunliffe Road) in 1911."

"Indian Point, an old recreational community on Quartermaster Harbor south of Burton, has to win the prize for spectacular slide stories," Stanley wrote. "According to Magnolia Beach resident Bob Gordon, Grandpa Haddow's beautiful two-story log house slid into the bay in 1936. Then, about 25 years ago, the house owned by 'Young' Haddow just off the Indian Point dock also was pushed off its foundation." In one of these stories, captured in Bob Gordon's memoirs of Magnolia Beach, a resident had to jump out a side window to escape sliding into the drink with his house.

After a 1997 storm, a *Beachcomber* article reported that 17 homes had been yellow-tagged—considered too vulnerable to live in after heavy rains had moved earth behind them. "The two hardest hit neighborhoods, Hake and Bachelor Road, were actually built on the debris of previous slides."

In time lost to memory, the quasi-mythical "Lost Lake" on Vashon's south end was created when a massive "slide block" of land pulled away from the main landmass, leaving a trough that backfilled with water. It's now a hard-to-find swamp deep in the woods behind Pacific Potager.

A homeowner with a hillside at his back might think it's a good idea to put a retaining wall there, but chipping at the slope's toe to make room for a wall may be exactly what NOT to do. "You don't want to cut away the toe of a steep slope," said Freeman. "A retaining wall on the bottom of a slope should be done only by a trained geo-tech. Get some professional advice if your house is in such a situation. You want some toe support for your slope;

it doesn't eliminate the risk, but it can help."

For those on a hilltop, Freeman advised keeping weight off the slope. Don't plant trees, tall shrubs, or bamboo that could become top-heavy, but plant shrubs with good root systems and a low center of gravity. Don't put an inpervious surface like a road, wall, deck, or patio on a slope that would add weight or concentrate run-off. And though he thought it's safer to be over Vashon Till (more stable), Freeman in his professional opinion claims "there's no slope that doesn't have the potential to slide."

I didn't think my little three-foot wall was in any danger of washing out, but then, I was also glad to be working with such drainy recessional outwash soil. Would my little raspberry bed would thrive here? Only the months ahead and some good advice from more experienced Islanders would tell.

Strategies and Plants for Slopes

A mixture of strategies work on a slope:
— lots of groundcovering plants to shield exposed soil from erosion
— deep-rooting, but relatively short plants
— plant in layers so that rain is slowed before it hits the ground
— use plants with a low center of gravity: no top-heavy bamboo!

NATIVES—
red-flowering currant   serviceberry   Indian plum   Nootka rose
salal   huckleberry   vine maple   sword fern
kinnick-kinnick   snowberry   Oregon grape   red elderberry

ORNAMENTALS—
rugosa rose   ceonothus   pyracantha   St. John's Wort
boxwood   rock roses   cotoneaster horizontalis   creeping rosemary
pachysandra   genista pilosa (prostrate broom)

Starting Seeds

Tips from growers and serious hobby gardeners on starting vegetable seedlings indoors in early spring

In late winter when it's still cold and wet, what a relief to have garden tasks you can do indoors. I've sown seeds in flats as early as January 30, sliding them into my plastic-sheathed "start cart" that hangs out in our kitchen all spring. With a heat-mat beneath and light tubes above, seedlings don't take long to germinate in these tropical conditions.

But as bad weather drags on, those seedlings may sit in the flat for a month. They get leggy, stretching for the light tubes and whatever sun straggles in through the window. They're slow to put out true leaves. They are a far cry from the short, lush seedlings I remember my Victory Garden neighbor used to grow under lights. Is there a better way?

When I consulted Jasper Forrester, gentlewoman farmer of GreenMan Farm, one of the Island's longest-running CSA farms, I received the most wonderful answer: "When the frogs start singing, I know it's time to sow my cool-season crops." Apparently Pacific tree frogs emerge from winter dormancy when they feel there's no longer any danger of freezing. The boys find their own spring mud-puddle for egg-laying and then put out the call: "Hey lady: I've got a nice pond, so come down and see me sometime!" When the frogs sing, you can bet that winter's retreating and spring's on the way.

Then there's the theory that one should plant by lunar phases. PNW garden guru and seedsman Ed Hume claims in his seed booklet that you get better results if you garden in sync with the moon. When the moon's on the increase and its gravitational pull is stronger, it's a good time to sow seeds of leafy plants, groom perennials, graft fruit trees, or fertilize. When the moon's on the wane and its energy sinking, one sows root crops. When the moon is at its lowest ebb, so is its pull on water, so soil will be drier and pruned wood will not drip with sap. Sounds like moonshine? I sowed cole crops during a Supermoon phase (occasional periods when the moon's orbit brings it closest to earth) and they were up within two days.

Growing good seedlings

In my search to make better seedlings, I talked to over 15 market farmers and hobby gardeners to find out their best techniques.

A cluster of them farm in Paradise Valley. On a frosty morning in March 2009, I met Chandler Briggs, farm manager at Island Meadow Farm on the upper slopes of the valley off Cemetery Road. Island Meadow is a small market farm of the post-60s generation. It was planted in hazelnuts by the Shane Brothers in the early 1970s, then run by Bill Iles who sold icelandic poppies as cut flowers in Seattle's Pike Place Market. Bob & Bonnie Gregson farmed here through the 1990s and wrote a book about their experience setting up the Island's first CSA farm. After selling to Greg Kruse and Julie Thielges, the farm has since been run by a succession of farm managers like Briggs with the help of seasonal WOOFers (Workers on Organic Farms).

Chandler had his germinating benches set up in a small barn, its south wall and roof glazed with plexiglass to let in sunlight. But that didn't make the space quite warm enough for quick germination, so Chandler was warming the flats with heating coils. He stuck a thermometer in one flat: the soil was 70°, perfect for germination. "I cover the trays with plastic domes to keep humidity and warmth in," he said, "but once the seeds germinate, they're uncovered and moved to the unheated benches for a few weeks." His seedlings were short and stocky—not a bit of "leg" showing, their leaves spread wide just above the soil. As we talked, he scooped up flats of 1" lettuce he'd started a few weeks before and walked them to outdoor benches to spend a couple of hours "hardening off" in the cool sunshine.

Most growers repeated this "sprout warm, grow cool" advice, especially for starts of cool-hardy crops like lettuce, peas, and coles. Too much moisture on the soil surface can encourage growth of a fungus that can cause tender stems to rot, a disease known as "damping off."

At Plum Forest Farm next door, Rob Peterson told me, "Light is key: keep your environment on the cool side, but bright." When I described the two-inch stems on my pak choi seedlings, he explained that "if your growing situation is warm and not very light, the warmth will push seedlings to grow, while your gro-lites encourage them to stretch."

Even within glazed greenhouses, several growers also used artificial lights.

Jasper at GreenMan Farm hung eight fluorescent tubes over seed-flats, checking daily to make sure seedlings didn't dry out. (Though fluorescents are cool, their ballasts can warm a space upward of 80°.)

Several gardeners combined gro-lites with a sunny window. Gardener (writer and Tango instructor) March Twisdale hung eight gro-lites an inch above her seedlings, staged against south-facing glass doors. "The trick is, never have the light more than an inch from the plants." Over and over, gardeners said to do whatever you can to bring light to the seedlings, such as wash windows or remove the screens. At Kathy's Corner, they power-wash their hoophouses inside and out to remove pollen, fungus, and insect eggs.

Sowing—and growing on

Though the farmers were sowing greens and alliums indoors by early February, experienced home gardeners seemed to wait until mid-March, about four weeks before our last frost date in late April.

Leda Langley, whose Langley Fine Gardens sells seedlings as far away as Portland, said "Many gardeners start too early, then end up nursing seedlings along. Plants only need 2-4 weeks before going outdoors." William Forrester of GreenMan Farm agreed, "If you start things too early and then plant them out too early, they'll just sit there."

The quality seedlings I saw, whether grown in greenhouses or on windowsills, seemed to grow 1/4" a week and, after a month, had one-two pairs of true leaves and were 1-2" high. You'll know it's time to transplant when the plants stall, turn yellow, or roots grow out the bottom of cells. At that point, especially if it's a warm-season plant like, basil, or peppers, you transplant to larger pots, but keep them indoors until late April or May. Cool-season plants like brassicas, lettuce, or peas can be moved outside for a few hours a day, then planted outdoors 7-10 days later. This hardening-off process— giving baby plants a little more exposure to the outdoors each day —will toughen up their tender tissues. They'll be less shocked when you do plant them in the ground, especially if you transplant on a moist, gray spring day. Plants so prepared will size up quickly, said Peterson.

When to start what, indoors

February: alliums, tomatoes, cauliflower, sweet peas, artichokes, brussel sprouts, all on heat coils. All will benefit from augmented light.

March: cool-season crops like broccoli, cabbages, kale, chard, parsley, lettuce. Peppers, tomatillos, eggplant, basil on 60-70° heat coils.

Late March: arugula, spinach, greens, bush peas

April: bush beans. In larger pots on heat, cukes, squashes, melons.

May: chit corn, cucurbits, beans indoors mid-month, then plant when there's a little tongue of plant emerging, in a deep flat if weather's still cool, outdoors if temperatures reach 60°.

When and what to direct-seed outdoors

Soil nutrients are "locked up" until temps reach 45-50°, and most seeds germinate best within a preferred range. You can gain a few degrees of heat with reemay cloth or clear plastic, or by covering the soil with black plasti-mulch (Sluggo underneath!) and planting through holes.

February: plant peas once your soil is no longer wet—which may be now, may not be until May.

Mid-March: peas again, potatoes on St. Paddy's Day. In full-sun areas, direct-sow cool-season crops with protection such as Reemay. Plant lots of radish to mark rows of slower germinating seeds and to attract flea beetles away from other leafy crops like lettuce, cabbages.

Late April: By now, we've free of frost danger. All cool-season crops, plus carrots, beets, spinach. In full-sun spots, transplanted tomatoes.

May: tomato transplants and chitted beans early in the month. Later, direct-sow beans, New Zealand spinach.

June: pepper, eggplant, corn, cilantro, squashes, melons.

July: fall garden crops (see "It's July: plant for winter" chapter)

Other Tips for Starting Seedlings

• **Use fresh seed:** last year's seed, stored at room temperature, may germinate poorly. This is particularly true for allium seed.

• **Use sterile soil** to prevent fungal diseases

• **Temperature matters:** plants have optimum temperatures at which they germinate fastest. I once grew seed flats of tomatoes on heating coils that were unevenly heating: the front half of the flat on 68° cables germinated 10 days before the back half on 58° cables.

• **Little or no fertilizer at first:** too much nitrogen makes seedlings spindly and soft. Even compost slows growth at first.

• **Dilute fertilizer in proportion to the seedling's size:** I use a 1/10 dilution of liquid fertilizer after the first pair of true leaves appear. For fish fertilizer, that's a capful per 2 gallons. Increase the proportion of fertilizer in stages as the seedlings grow.

• **Try "chitting" to jump-start corn & beans:** soak seeds for a day, then set between damp paper; plant when a little "tongue" of root peeks out.

• **Be realistic about your land's "grow-ability:"** if your land offers less than six hours of direct sunlight on the plants through the growing season, you might get better vegetables by buying them from local growers through the VIGA market, farm stands, or CSA subscriptions.

• **Just try it:** explore what your own micro-climate has to offer.

Early Spring ❧

*We swing from rain, to freak outbreaks of snow, to mild days of 50.°
Dull red catkins dangle from every alder branch, gold from willows,
maples, and hazels. Rockeries bloom pink with bergenia and heather.
Crocuses and snowdrops pop. Anna's Hummingbirds are working red
currant shrubs. Indian plum perks up its white rabbit-ear flowers.
The forsythia shrieks in yellow that it's time to prune the roses.*

*When the weather's mild, honeybees will make their first foraging
trips to gather pollen. Fans of the mason bee are ordering new cocoons
and tubes, and cleaning out the bee condos near the orchards that the
bees will pollinate this spring.*

*At Kathy's Corner, pansies are starting to bloom; they'll be out for sale
by mid-March. In donated greenhouses, volunteers are sowing for
plant sales put on by the Garden Club, VIPP, and the high school horticulture program later this spring. Seed packets are flying off racks,
torn open at kitchen tables, sprinkled across flats, placed on heat mats
or windowsills or anywhere the anxious grower can find warmth.
If the ground's not too wet, pea seeds are dusted with inoculant and
stuck into the earth. Potatoes go into the ground on St. Patrick's Day.*

*It's time to divide perennials that bloom after June, such as asters,
shasta daisies, hostas, sedums, alliums, anemones, campanulas, hardy
geraniums, kniphofia, nepeta, or violas. Garden beds need a light first
feeding and a heavy dose of Sluggo. If cover crops were sown last fall,
it's time to hoe them under to give the green stuff time to decompose.
It's also the last days to install or transplant bare-root roses, shrubs,
and trees—including those still heeled in from the Land Trust's
native plant sale in early February—and to give fruit trees a light
pruning and dormant spray.*

And then, one sunny day, you see it—Leaf-Break! Spring!

Apple Trees and a Fruit Club

Restoring old orchard trees. Apples in Island history. Winter pruning techniques, learned from experts in the Vashon Fruit Club

Nothing like a storm to get people telling tales. After an ice-storm had knocked out power in January 2011, a bunch of us were standing around in the Vashon Athletic Club lobby, offering up our horror stories of fallen trees and cooking dinner in the dark. Joe Curiel, a money manager with salt-n-pepper hair, a young man's build and a boy's big grin, cut into the talk. "We lost the tire-swing King."

We all wailed "NOOO!" This old apple tree dangling a car tire has long been a landmark at the intersection of Harbor Drive and Monument Road. It still produced many bushels of apples every fall. But Joe wasn't just concerned about losing all that fruit. It was possible this old tree was Island legacy, planted by a member of our first homesteading family.

Joe and his partner Tony Raugust live and garden at Monument Farm, on the sun-soaked slope north of Quartermaster Harbor. Their place, long ago, was once part of the Sherman family's land, first claimed by Salmon D. Sherman in the 1870s. According to Gene Sherman, 90-year-old descendent who still lives on the Island, that tree may have been planted by his great-grandfather Christopher in the 1880s. "He planted the cherry trees along the drive, so I bet he planted those apple trees as well."

Shortly after Salmon and Eliza Sherman arrived on the shores of Quartermaster in 1877, Salmon wrote to his papa Christopher in New York to "come out and get some of this free land." In those days, to claim land you had to make "improvements"—planting fruit trees, digging a well, putting up buildings to show you were serious about developing the land. Then, after two years you could run to the local land office to "pre-empt" your property for 12.5 cents an acre, or you could wait out the five years required by the 1862 Homestead Act to get your land for free. Christopher Sherman came west, developed his land then pre-empted it, conveyed it to son Salmon, and returned to New York, where he died ten years later.

It's just possible that, like the tire-swing King, fruit trees from our first decades of white settlement still survive and bear fruit. Apple trees can last well into their second century. Ron Irvine, owner of Vashon Winery and author of *The Wine Project*, a history of Washington state wine-making, compiled a timeline on apple cultivation on the Island. Apple trees came west in 1857, brought by Henderson Luelling who set up Luelling & Meek nursery in Oregon; three nurseries supplied by L & M set up around Puget Sound in the 1850s, including one in Steilacoom. In 1878 on Vashon, the Miner family planted an orchard that included Rhode Island Greening, King of Tompkins County, Wagener, Wealthy, Winter Banana, and Gravenstein. By 1883, the *Tacoma News* reported that nine orchards had been established on the Island, including a mixed orchard of 400 trees planted by a Reverend John A. Banfield "at the Three Corners."

When the state's first Horticultural Society met in 1892, they chose as Secretary a C. A. Tonneson, whose father, a Danish immigrant, had planted an orchard on the Burton Peninsula with King, Russet, Transparent, Gravenstein, and other apple varieties. Two years later, Philip McCormick arrived on the Island and started selling fruit trees door-to-door; by 1917 he had an orchard of 700 fruit trees on the present site of K2 and reportedly shipped out 1000 boxes of Duchess, Baldwin, Spitzenberg, Gravenstein, and Transparent apples. In 1902, Steven Harmeling established a nursery just east of Vashon-town. In 1914, the state's horticultural inspector told Islanders, "There are not better apples raised in the state than on Vashon... the soil here is ideal"—even while chiding locals for their "lack of interest, failure to introduce modern methods, and inefficiency in spraying."

When I started asking around about old island apple trees, the years around 1900 came up often. Sharon Munger, who through the 1980s-2012 hosted the art show known as "Barnworks" in her rustic barn on Cove Road, was visited in the 1970s by two elderly brothers who reminisced about their father planting 'Hood River Kings' on her property around 1900. At 100-year farm Triplebrook Farm on Westside Highway, Hal Green conjectures that his King, Baldwin, Esopus Spitzenberg and Gravenstein trees were planted by the original homesteader just before 1900.

Doug Ostrom, who grew up on Burton Peninsula where many of the first orchards were established, inherited an old orchard that once numbered over 50 trees—mostly old varieties then considered good for cider or storage in the days before refrigeration. "We now have fewer than half the trees we had 60 years ago, which is one of the reasons we are planting more this year. Some of them are [grafted using] scions from a Sultan, Washington orchard that received scions from our family's orchard about 1975—including from trees that died in our orchard after that."

After a century of productivity, the tire-swing King nearly joined the ranks of trees brought down by time and nature. The morning after the storm, Joe and Tony found their old tree so burdened with ice, the weight had tipped the tree on its side, half its rootmass lifted into the freezing air. But the guys had a fix: they called in heavy equipment guy Stew Nelson. For five hours, Stew and his daughter Alex worked on the tree, first pruning limbs to lighten it and balance what must have been heavy root-loss. They opened up the root-hole so the roots would have somewhere to land, then threaded long cables through pieces of garden hose, wrapped those around the tree and secured the opposite free ends to an excavator and a back-hoe. With the machines forming a triangle with the tree at the apex, Stew shouted "HEEEEAVE" and the cables slowly pulled the King upright. Three eight-foot fence posts pounded 6 feet deep held the tree steady, as everybody crossed their fingers. Would the King show appreciation for all this hard work? Would it live, leaf out, bear fruit again? Only time would tell.

Restoring an Old Orchard

All over the Island these old apple trees stand—carpeted with green moss, shagged over with lichen and mistletoe, into their second century but still bearing fruit. Sometimes they've been cared for, carefully pruned into widely-spaced scaffold branches, their heavy limbs propped up by 2x4s jammed against the earth. Sometimes they bear the scars of bad pruning: shaved down to bare stubs that become tufted with water-sprouts. Sometimes they've been laid low or broken by bad weather or rot. Or they've been abandoned, covered over in blackberries until somebody busting trail discovers apples hanging in the forest.

My community has a mixed orchard that was planted in the mid-1970s: two English walnuts, several cherries, plums, a fig, a standard apple, and two dwarf apple trees planted some time later. Neglected for years, the trees had grown tall and tangled, fruit way beyond reach. But a new generation moved in, saw these old trees, and wanted to return the trees to fruitfulness.

When I started asking around for a tree expert, absolutely everybody told me to call Dr. Bob Norton. Back in 1964, Dr. Norton ran a research program and field station devoted to hobby fruit up in Mt. Vernon for WSU Extension. After a field trip to Wax Orchard Farm owned by Robert & Betsy Sestrap, he, the Sestraps and others decided to form the Western Cascade Tree Fruit Society to teach about fruit tree cultivation in our maritime climate. Then after he had retired to Vashon Island, he helped set up the Vashon Fruit Club in 2004. What a resource for the Island!

When I told him that our community did work parties, he suggested I call in an arborist, Michelle Ramsden, to guide us. She came early to look over the trees. Straight and slim in her 30s, with a strawberry blonde's complexion and a stub-nosed chain-saw dangling from her belt, Michelle struck me as a no-nonsense, get the job done person: she went straight to a plum tree and sawed off the suckers rising from its base. We agreed on a late February pruning session: she would teach, the work party would prune. "And get a 10-foot orchard ladder—the 3-legged kind that doesn't wobble."

On a brilliant late winter Saturday, eight of us met Michelle in the orchard. She gave us a short how-to: "Cut off criss-crossed branches, suckers from the base, any broken limbs, and those water sprouts that shoot straight up. Then stand back and look at the branch structure: you want to leave a central leader, then secondary branches at around a 45° or greater angle to the main leader, spaced far enough for a bird to fly through without its wings touching any wood."

"When cutting a good-sized limb, you want to cut just beyond a branch's collar—that's where it thickens at the trunk. Flush with the trunk is too much. If it's a big branch, remove weight first by cutting 12" up the branch from the trunk, then trim off the stub just above the collar. But don't try to cut back today everything you want to remove: the tree's preparing to start growth and if you cut off too much, it may respond with lots of water-sprouts and suckers. Stop when you've removed about 30%"

With three ladders, two chain-saws, sunshine, and plenty of 30-something manpower, we may have pruned a little beyond 30%. The guys went at the job like a crew of monkeys, climbing into the trees to prune—one knocked the ladder out from under and swung one-handed until I got his ladder back under him. Jason climbed into the Rainier cherry and sawed off half its towering trunk. Michelle did the same to the pie cherry trees, her chain-saw dangling by several feet of rope until she'd pull it up and start it once in position. Inspired, I climbed up and tried to fire up my saw, but my neighbor Roland said, "PLU-EEZE! You're making me nervous." Remembering how a friend, trying to prune in a big birch, had fallen and ended up in a wheelchair, I thought, "He's right: leave the climbing to the pro."

I asked Michelle whether late winter was the best time to prune. "Now is fine for removing winter damage and badly placed branches. But for pruning a mature tree, late summer is better: the tree is slowing growth then and won't be so likely to respond to pruning by pumping out water sprouts. And since fruit's developing, you can remove the unproductive wood and thin excess fruit (if you're lucky enough to have any) at the same time. You learn this stuff from the Fruit Club," she said. "You really ought to join."

Winter Pruning with the Vashon Fruit Club

A year later, I did join. In February 2013, I met 20 other members at Pacific Crest Farm for one of the club's winter pruning workshops. Typically, members meet on a Saturday at an established orchard; Dr. Bob and other experienced hands teach how to prune, and members practice on the trees. This farm on Maury Island has grown fruit trees for decades; part of it was planted in nut trees by the Shane Brothers (they developed the old orchard still growing at Island Meadow Farm). Between 1973-2000 it was Pete Svinth's, a Danish-Nisqually grower who trialed fruit trees (especially Asian pears), grew giant pumpkins, and sold produce on the honor system. He sold the farm to the Pacific Crest Montessori School of Seattle in 2000.

Farm manager Bob Keller met us at a stand of 15 Jonagold apple trees—the variety Pete promoted as best for the Island—each only 10' high with a relatively shallow fruiting zone. "I'd like to increase their height by leaving about 5-6 of the 40-or-so water sprouts to grow on into productive limbs," he said. "Another reason is that I'd like room to run my riding mower underneath without scraping off my hat." We all laughed.

Ever prepared, Dr. Bob took the mobile mic and waved a laminated card at us. "Everybody got this '10 Steps for Winter Pruning Apple Trees' Good!

So let's look at this first tree here. Step 1: Read it for Vigor. This tree is pretty well-formed with some vertical water-sprouts, but we'll leave the few that are leaning so that they'll become productive. You can snip the end to a down-facing bud: that'll grow out more horizontal. There aren't any suckers growing from the base of the trunk, but there ARE shaded lower branches…" He marked it with a squirt from a paint can. "You don't want to remove more than 30% of the tree. By marking what I plan to remove, I can see when I'm coming close to that 30% BEFORE cutting anything."

It was easy to spot the water-sprouts—so vertical, so bare of leaf nodes or fruit spurs. Ditto the criss-crossing branches or those angled toward the ground. What was harder to visualize was the future weight of fruit on the end of a branch. But Michelle Ramsden, here to help, had a good tip. She draped a forearm over a branch-end bristling with fruit spurs, weighting the limb down. "See how the tree is rocking a bit when I'm putting the equivalent weight of what could be 10-20 apples out here? See how the crotch of this branch is widening? With a lot of fruit, that could split. So let's cut back to… let's see…this upper branch the main limb pumped out a couple years ago. We'll lose some fruit, but that's better than losing the whole limb."

After a half-hour of snipping at these small trees, Bob Keller led us to an older orchard. "There are 100 trees in here, but we couldn't see them because blackberries covered them. It took us three years of tractor-work to clear the berries. These trees probably haven't been pruned in 10-15 years."

"Right—this will be renovation pruning," said Dr. Bob. "Keep to the 30% rule: take water sprouts, criss-crossers, and suckers, and head back by half the overly long branches. And remove dead wood: you'll know it because it's darker, with no leaf or fruit spurs."

After a half-hour's work, we left Pacific Crest Farm for a property around the corner. This too had once been Pete Svinth's land, and here he'd planted 125 Jonagolds and other apple trees—way too much for the present owners. "We have a cider party, invite friends over to harvest, freeze cider and make applesauce—and there'd still be trees to pick," owner LuAnne Branch told me. She'd offered the club an ownership stake: by adopting and pruning a tree each, the members could return in October to harvest "their" apples.

I chose the tree at the NW corner (figured I could always find it) and tied my name-tag to a branch. Dr. Bob took the tree next to mine, so I got some free advise: "Don't remove THOSE; they're fruit spurs!" he said as I lifted my felcos to what I thought were claw-like "hangers" growing well below a horizontal plane. "Don't forget to clean your snips: these trees are full of anthracnose fungus. See that open blister with what look like fiddle-strings? That's the fungus. It can girdle your branch and kill it, eventually. Endemic to the Maritime Northwest—it's on the ground—nothing to do but cut off as many branches with the disease as you can."

Dr. Bob said this winter pruning could be done right through March when the leaves break out, though for stone fruits like peaches and apricots, he liked to wait until bloom to see how plentiful that year's fruit might be.

Would our newly-pruned trees burst with bloom, with leaf, and finally with plenty of fruit? We'd done our work. Now we had to wait for a good spring and, hopefully, a good season of pollination from local bees.

10 Steps for Winter Pruning Apple Trees

compiled for the Fruit Club by Dr. Bob Norton. Printed by permission

1) Read the tree for vigor and fruiting potential

2) Remove suckers from base and ground

3) Remove branches that will be shaded by upper branches

4) consider creating a ladder bay (for pruning, light, harvesting)

5) Remove surplus and/or crossing branches

6) Cut back "hangers" — branches that dip below horizontal

7) Cut branches with excess spurs to half their length

8) Top of tree—reduce height (if applicable).

9) Remove watersprouts (follow up in late spring or summer)

10) Step back and evaluate the tree for balance.

Clubs For Fruit and Bee Lovers

Vashon Island Beekeepers

This is a casually organized group of Island beekeepers, and most are also members of the fruit club. They compare notes, make presentations to the fruit club, and in some cases move their hives to bee-friendly sites not their own. If you are interested, contact founder Elizabeth Vogt, Steve Rubicz, or Elizabeth Sullivan.

Vashon Fruit Club

Begun in 2004 by Dr. Bob Norton, Carolina Nurik, Ron Weston, and other hobby fruit growers on the Island, this club meets monthly at the Land Trust Building. Focusing on the cultivation of all kinds of backyard fruit, the group holds workshops and work parties year round on winter pruning, grafting, pollination, summer pruning, and harvest. They also run a CiderFest in October and a Fruit Show in November where you can bring mystery fruit for identification by experts. They are also developing a demonstration orchard on Sunrise Ridge next door to the Food Bank Garden. Membership is $20 paid annually.

Vashon Fruit Club relies heavily on volunteerism to put on its labor-intensive but extremely fun programs. They also are always looking for orchards that could be used for pruning demonstrations and workshops.

Western Cascade Fruit Club

Vashon Fruit Club is one of eight chapters in this non-profit, which was founded by Dr. Bob Norton, Robert & Betsy Sestrap of our own Wax Orchard Farm, and others in 1979. Their mission is to bring together people, amateur and commercial, interested in all phases of tree fruit production, processing, and marketing, with special attention to varieties, rootstocks, high-density planting, spray programs and cider, and to offer this information to the public.

This club's website (wcfs.org) has links to articles, archives, and the websites of other chapters—including the excellent website of the Seattle Tree Fruit Society (www.seattletreefruitsociety.com) that includes a list of "The Best 25" and "Bob's 100." Once you join the Vashon Fruit Club, you're automatically part of WCFS and will get their quarterly e-newsletter, "The BeeLine."

Beeeeee Good to Our Bees

We've got a challenging environment for honeybees, but there's grow-ing awareness of how to help them. Plus the Mason Bee Conspiracy

The weather that spring was ten degrees cooler than usual—clinging clammily to the upper 40s instead of the mild 50s. Such cool has conse-quences for fruit: you don't get fruit without pollination, you don't get pol-lination without bees, and bees don't emerge from their hives until the out-side temperature reaches the high 40s for bumblebees and mason bees, the mid-50s for honeybees. Even the local newspaper rang with complaints from orchardists that their trees were blooming without any bees to pol-linate them. No bees—no fruit set.

It's not just cool springs that keep bees hive-bound. Our long, wet win-ters can threaten their very survival. In the spring of 2012, the *Beachcomber* asked me to look into declining honeybee populations on the Island— whether honeybees were suffering from Colony Collapse Disorder that has decimated honeybee hives worldwide, or whether it was something else.

So I talked to a few of the Island's 30-odd beekeepers. First to respond was Margot Boyer, who writes, teaches, and markets husband Bob Powell's Meadow Creature broadfork. They'd gotten their first honeybee colony four years ago, but none of their colonies had come through winter well. "My goal is to get them through the second year. Last year I had 100% dead. I've opened the hive in the spring and found a wet mess of dead bees, mold, and honey. I think it's a moisture problem: if the hive is closed up too tight, their breathing condenses and drops on them in the hive."

"Everyone does okay the first year—it's that second year that confounds folks," confirmed Elizabeth Vogt, an entomologist, President of the Vashon Fruit Club, leader in an informal beekeepers group, and keeper of four hives. "On Vashon, we have a short nectar flow—from mid-April to mid-July if we're lucky. And our long, chilly, damp winters are real killers, when all the dwinding and disappearances happen. Bees can drown, get chilled, or suffer from viruses and molds."

And then there are those nasty parasites. Tracheal mites and Varroa mites, both of which suck vital life fluids from bees, entered the U.S in the 1980s and have since grown epidemic across the world. After the invasion hit and bees started dying, Vogt (then living in Oregon near the big agriculture valleys of Yamhill and Tualatin) set up a kind of bee forensic lab for commercial beekeepers—literally digging into bees' guts looking for tracheal mites or for nosema, a gut disease bees get when, during a long winter, they can't get outside to eliminate.

"There's a synergy among all those causes that's part of the problem," says Steve Rubicz, who has raised honeybees on the Island since the 1970s. "The mites are compromising the health of the hives. What the varroa mite did was pretty dramatic: it arrived in 1987, and by 1990-2004 probably about 25% of U.S. bee colonies and most feral populations all disappeared. I experienced that here on Vashon in the early 90s: I had downsized from 85

Problem Pesticides for Bees

NEONICOTINOIDS

Bayer Advanced Complete Insect Killer
Bayer Advanced 12 Month Tree & Shrub Protect & Feed
Ortho Tree & Shrub Insect Control

—With Acetamiprid— Ortho Flower, Fruit & Veg Insect Killer, Ortho Rose & Flower Insect Killer

CARBARYL & MALATHION

Sevin
Bonide Fruit Tree Spray
Corry's Slug-killer
Ortho Basic Solutions,
Ortho Malathion Plus
Orthos Mosquito-B-Gone

PYRETHRINS (recognize them by ingredients ending in "thrin")

Green Thumb: Flying Insect Killer, Insect Control, and Home Insect Killer.
Lily Miller Multi-Purpose Insect Spray
Safer Products: Tomato & Veg Insect Killer, Yard & Garden Insect Killer
Bayer Advanced Lawn PowerForce Multi-Insect Killer
Bonide Delta Eight Insect Control
many RAID products

colonies to just 24 hives, then one winter I lost them all. Lots of honey in the hives, but most of the bees just disappeared. I looked at a few crawlers under a magnifying glass and could see the mites on them. At the time, the bee inspectors in the state thought that nosema disease associated with the mite was the actual cause-of-death. When I have re-nuc'ed (getting a nucleus hive of some frames, a queen, and worker bees) I have received packages with bees that had mites."

Raising bees in an inhospitable, parasite-infested environment seems quite the challenge. Yet the Island is better off than most places, said Rubicz: "We're really fortunate to not be in an agri-business area because our bees don't suffer from the pesticide load." He knows, perhaps better than any keeper on the Island, that bees at least on the south end used to suffer under a chemical shadow. In the 1980s, Rubicz got involved with a study lead by Dr. Jerry Bromenshenk that used bees to detect the spread of pollutants from ASARCO's copper smelter in Ruston, home to the south-end ferry. By sampling from honeybee colonies (including some of Steve's hives) at increasing north/south distances from south Vashon, Dr. Bromenshenk was able to show a correlation between the northern drift of the smelter's plume and the presence of its contaminants (cadmium, arsenic, and fluoride) in Vashon hives. (Since that 1985 experiment, Dr. Bromenshenk, now at University of Montana, has become a leader in using bees as biomonitors to track pollutants, other chemicals, even the location of landmines.) "That plume was over the southern end of Vashon for 100 years, and it definitely had a suppressing effect on honeybee populations," said Rubicz. "The plume went as far north as Wax Orchard; I had a friend who tried to keep bees there. Despite all those fruit trees, he never did very well with those hives."

Asarco's smelter closed in 1985, but pesticides are still an issue because Islanders are such avid buyers of chemicals. Beekeepers bitingly referred to the "The Aisles of Death" in local hardware and garden stores, where aisles stink from bags and cans of pesticides, herbicides, and dusts. Many of these plants are toxic to bees, either quickly or by cumulative effects. When the weather warms and bees fly, these chemicals also go flying off shelves and presumably onto garden plants where bees are likely to land. These products, particularly the dusts, can be picked up by bees' furry bodies much like pollen grains are carried—and as easily transferred back to the hive, where through body-to-body contact and feeding of young, exposure to the chemical spreads throughout the colony.

Pesticides have been much studied for bee toxicity and their contribution to Colony Collapse Disorder, and certain chemicals have been found problematic enough to warrant warning labels and even country-wide bans in some cases. For instance, Sevin, one of the country's most widely-used, broad-spectrum insecticides, uses carbaryl and malathion to kill any insect it touches—and that can include bees if the product is put on flowering plants. (Its maker, Bayer CropScience, made a formulation, Sevin XLR Plus, that was ground fine enough to not resemble pollen, then balked at displaying the EPA's requested warning language because it felt the product came with warnings enough.)

Then there's pyrethrin and its more potent derivatives: these potions paralyze a bug's nervous system so that it literally falls from the air. The first pyrethrins were developed in the 1800s and were much used against mosquitoes until they developed resistance. Today's stronger, longer-lasting formulations have names that always end with "thrin"—deltamethrin, cypermethrin, permethrin, bifenthrin, and cyfluthrin.

What sounds like a good idea—put the poison IN the plant instead of UPON it, as in the case of systemic chemicals—turns out to be perhaps the very worse of the lot. Commercial agriculture has widely adopted systemic neonicotinoids such as imidacloprid, clothianidin, or acetamiprid because the grower need not spray as much: you apply it once on the field or orchard and the plants take it up. However, the plant still exudes these chemicals from their leaves in what's called guttations—water is exuded out the edges of leaves—and bees imbide the chemical when they drink from these droplets. "Neo-nics" as they're called for short have been found to affect bee's nervous system: they get confused, don't collect pollen, even lose their way back to the hive. Neo-nics have been have been banned in France and nearly so in Germany, and in the State of California their maker, Bayer Crop-Science, has quietly asked the state ag department to stop recommending their use in the huge almond orchards of central California.

Unfortunately, these "Kills in a Can" are tempting to the home gardener whose plants have being chewed to pieces. To counter our very human tendency to want a quick fix, in 2007 a group of Islanders led by environmental educator Susie Kalhorn, water consultant/conservationist Michael Laurie, and the VMI Groundwater Protection Committee initiated a project called "Garden Green/Drink Clean" to caution Islanders about the dangers of using pesticides and inorganic fertilizers willy-nilly. With funding from the Puget Sound Action Team, the group created colorful hang-tags that listed products from Least Environmental Impact to High Impact, using as their source the "Grow Smart, Grow Safe" publication written by Dr. Philip Dickey of the Washington Toxics Coalition. Then they persuaded local stores to hang these awareness tags right on the shelves next to the product.

When I read through the list, some products surprised me: something called "Green Light Biorganic" was still quite toxic. Even "Safer" products still used pyrethrins. In response to the program, some vendors, like Kathy's Corner, pulled some of the worst products off their shelves, and other stores saw a slight boost in sales of "greener" products. But the group wasn't entirely happy: the program was run in late winter when sales in garden sections are still slow; as of 2012, they're seeking funding to rerun the program.

Lifting the lid on a honeybee hive in Paradise Valley

That spring, as March developed some balmy weekends, Elizabeth Sullivan of Paradise Valley decided to open her hives to check out her bees' health. She invited me to tag along, and there I saw signs and techniques that could give any Island beekeeper fresh hope, not just for the coming season, but for the better survival of their bees.

We donned bee suits in her garden, surrounded by alder groves flushed ruddy with spring catkins. She walked up to the first hive, removed several covers (tin, foam, and burlap), passed her smoker over the hive to calm the bees, then pried up a frame from the topmost hive. "Look: they're making honey," she pointed at capped honeycomb cells under a crowd of bustling bees. "These are my Italians: I caught them in a swarm on Beall Road a few years ago," she said. "I left them most of their honey last fall so they'd go into winter happy, healthy, and with enough food to get them to spring."

Given enough honey and protection from winter's wet, a hive may start winter with a couple pints' worth of bees. By July it will have grown to over 60,000 bees and may hold nearly 100 pounds of honey.

A few bees head-butt my veil, and one lands on my sleeve, her legs loaded with saddlebags of yellow pollen. I'm not worried: unlike wasps or yellow jackets, honeybees sting only as a last resort. These bees get their bearings, then zip away toward what's blooming: alders, hazels or maple, red currant, Oregon grape, Indian Plum. Once loaded up with nectar, water, or pollen (each forager has her specialty), they'll bee-line back into the hive and and there do a "wiggle-dance" that signals to sister bees the directions to and size of the motherlode.

Elizabeth next looks into a hive of Carniolans—"carnies" for short—a darker honeybee that originated in Slovenia. These are, according to Wikipedia, the second most popular honeybee for hobbyists, as they are non-aggressive, overwinter well, and will adjust the size of their colony to the available nectar supply. They too are making honeycomb, so much it's bulging beyond the frame's borders. We peer down into the hive's depths: no dead or confused bees here.

To fight the problems that plague local hives, Sullivan and other Island beekeepers have been trialing other kinds of honeybees. Often, these bees are descended from survivors of earlier mite- or disease-plagues: they've learned coping mechanisms like grooming mites off their bodies or swarming away from infested hives. Some bees literally kick mite-butt. For instance, after varroa was discovered in the USA, the USDA brought over a type of Russian bee that had been coping with mites for over 150 years. Surviving generations had developed what beekeepers call "varroa-sensitive hygiene (VSH)" and what a commoner might call "seek and destroy" behavior: when these bees sense mites lurking within pupae cells, they cut open the brood cell, drag out both mite and infected baby and toss both out of the broodnest. As you can imagine, they are more aggressive bees, and (as Margot Boyer found six weeks after she bought her first colony of Russians), they tend to swarm sooner than you'd expect.

Then there's the English "Buckfast" bees, developed at Buckfast Abbey in Devon—one of Steve's favorites. In the 1920s, after Britain's hives were devastated by acarine disease brought on by tracheal mites, the Abbey sent its beekeeper, Brother Adam, around the world in search of a better bee. 100,000 miles later, Brother Adam returned with selected bees and bred a creature that was gentle, resistant to mites and other maladies, could take the British climate (so like ours), produce good honey, and not abandon the hive. They aren't easy to get: Steve got his from the famous apiary Weaver family in Texas. "They are wonderful bees," he told me.

Sullivan has a lot of hope in the colony we inspected last. "Minnesota Hygienic" bees practice VSH: like the Russians, they too seek and destroy by uncapping brood cells and throwing out mites that crawled in before the cell was sealed. The bottomboard screens many beekeepers install in the bottom of their hives prevents mites from re-invading. Rubicz spritzes his bees with a drench of lemon grass and spearmint and sugar; "it causes them to stop and groom themselves and this gets rid of the mites." And Sullivan had strips of a natural miticide made from hops hanging on her frames.

After an hour's look-see, we stopped—the bees seemed a little testy at all this smoke and poking our noses in their hives. Sullivan seemed pleased with their health. And good thing: this hobby isn't cheap, care- or risk-free: the suit, smoker, hives, and the bees themselves will set you back over $300. Then there's the heartbreak of caring for critters that die or disappear. At some point, you have to wonder—for me, around the time I was struggling out of my bee-suit—is keeping bees worth the trouble and heartache?

"Well, without bees, we'd do without honey—and more importantly, without fruit. All our fruits—apples, pears, peaches, plums, cherries, apricots, berries—must be pollinated by bees," insisted Cheryl Grunbock, an Islanderer who has sold her honey at the farmers' market. "Bees are the most delightful, hardest-working, most useful pet that you can have. They're addictive: when I got my first hives, I would just sit there and watch them do their little dances on their porch, instead of getting my chores done."

Cheryl's a good witness as to the difference bees can make with fruit set. "I moved here in 1999. That first spring, I noticed bees were visiting my fruit trees. The next year, only a few bees, not much fruit, and in the third year, not one bee and a lousy harvest. (Yes, I had mason bees—the fruit club recommends them—but they came out too early that spring.) Wondering why the dismal harvest, I guessed it was a lack of bees. So that's the reason I decided to get honeybees. And after I got them, I started to notice much better fruit production."

"Then I got a property on Pinder Island in B.C. The next door neighbor had a fruit orchard that was struggling, but the sellers had told me they used to harvest lots of apples from those trees. Yet by the time I got there, not one fruit—and all the other neighbors are saying, 'We don't have fruit either.' So I'm thinking, maybe this is the same phenomenon of No bees. It wasn't easy, but I got some honeybees up there. Voila, that year, everybody had apples! It's two examples rather than one, so I don't think I'm crazy."

Convinced she's lost bees to pesticides, she's tried to persuade local stores to stop selling them. "A lot of folks use Round-up on dandelions, which are a source of nectar for bees. Get some exercise—PULL your weeds."

BeeGAP: Mason Bees to the Rescue!

I wasn't quite ready for the whole honeybee thing, but I did want to see our orchard bear more fruit. Local beekeepers kept mentioning mason bees, aka blue orchard bees. Elizabeth Vogt had said, "Mason bees are actually BETTER than honey-bees for fruit trees; they are less expensive, their numbers build up year after year, they take some maintenance but far less than honey-bees."

And when a friend told me she "rented" mason bees from a guy up in Woodinville, then invited me to his presentation at Vashon Allied Arts, I discovered a True Believer leading a circle of initiates in a long-term effort to save the world: BeeGAP, short for Bee Gardeners Adding Pollinators.

Dave Hunter, President of the Orchard Bee Society and founder of several bee businesses including his retail Crown Bees, was a skinny, energy-pumped 40-something who has never changed his barbershop order from "kid's crew-cut." Dancing nervously from foot to foot in front of 25± Islanders gathered at the Blue Heron, he said "The folks I'm working with at Cornell University believe the honeybee problem isn't fixable. Eventually—" and he popped up a slide showing two diverging lines—"there won't be enough honeybees to pollinate all orchards. We need to develop ways to use solitary bees to meet pollination demand."

Unlike honeybees, the mason bee is what's called a "solitary"—it lives alone in tunnels in snags, banks, or reeds, laying her eggs in the six weeks she's flying during spring. The eggs are laid end-to-end in the tunnel-like nest—females in the back, expendable males in the bird-peck zone up front—and there they incubate from late summer on until breaking out in spring and starting the cycle over. Because they need a chilling period for dormancy, mason bees can be refrigerated and easily mailed to customers in late winter. The bees require nesting cavities 6" in length and 5/8" wide in a roofed place in the sun, plus a source of mud that the bees will use to pad their nests. Dealer Dave sells bees, tubes, and bee-condos, and sends to his clients a monthly "bee-mail" with To-Do lists during mason bee season.

His BeeGAP volunteers get all this—plus mud—for free each spring. Everyone was here today to receive their tubes, each filled with 200 bee-eggs, a baggie of choice Duvall mud, nest blocks full of nesting tunnels, plus wooden boxes built by Jerry Gerhke, BeeGAP's local contact. Each volunteer sets her colony in a sunny place near orchard trees, timed so the bees will wake and be flying when the fruit trees are in bloom. By summer when the nesting cavities are (hopefully) full of bee cocoons, the nests are shipped back to Dave. He harvests the bees and stores them correctly, and so grows on an inventory of mason bees he can sell to commercial orchardists up and down the West Coast—and beyond. He has bee-raising projects for the Southwestern and Eastern states, and he's involved with an FDA advisory board exploring the use and management of native bees for almonds, apples, cherries, and blueberries. His ultimate goal: at that point when "we need something other than honeybees to pollinate the nation's crops," he wants to be ready with a million mason bees.

And he wants these Islanders to know he's pleased with their efforts: "Last year your return of bees was 150%. Two years ago, it was 300%." He explained how to increase bee reproduction by placing their house near pollen and in the morning sun where the bees can bask until their bodies are warm enough to fly. It's surprising how few mason bees you need for an orchard: for the dozen trees in our community orchard, he recommended just 20-25 bees. "They're lousy collectors, but excellent pollinators," he explain. "They land 'splat splat splat' on the flowers and these little explosions of pollen get all over their fuzzy bodies."

On the first sunny day after Dave Hunter's presentation, I grabbed bees, box, and a 3' post, and took my mason bee project to our community orchard. In the corner facing Mt. Rainier, I pounded the post into the ground and set the house on top, orienting it to the morning sun. At the base of the post, I set a little dish of Dave's Delta Mud on the ground. Then I carefully pried open the tiny box. Oh! there's some bees already hatched, struggling in the bottom of the box. I stuck the box in their new hotel, and they wobbled out groggily like drunks after a convention bender. When I returned later that afternoon to check on them, they were all out and gone—no sign of them.

But later that spring, I found a few tubes topped off with mud walls—those mason girls had been laying eggs. The dwarf apple trees that I had been spraying against diseases were loaded with tiny apples by the end of June. Apparently the little masons had been doing their job.

The following September, Dave Hunter's monthly "Bee-Mail" said it was time to harvest the cocoons my mason girls had laid over the summer. Why? Because the larvae need to go dormant in a cool, safe place. Leaving the cocoons in their tubes out all year leaves them vulnerable to pests, to wet weather causing mold, and worse, subject to an early wake-up during a warm winter thaw, WAY before there's any flowers to pollinate.

So, following orders, I got out a fine sieve, an exacto knife, a cutting block, and sat down at the table to harvest cocoons. It wasn't easy: the tubes were made of dense cardstock, and it's never easy to slice down the length of a round thing anyway—imagine trying to dissect a pencil without slicing your own fingers. But, when I sifted the dirty detritus that fell out each tube, out of the disappearing dust emerged tiny oval cocoons—my next-year generation of mason bees. I'd bought 25 bees, and here were 50—a return of 200%! Dave might not be proud, but I was, thinking of the 26 apples that our community's dwarf apple trees had produced that summer. Gee, would a 200% return of bees = a 200% return of apples? Enough for 3.71 apples per household?

Our community orchard would still need work—even after pruning away 30%, these trees were still too tall to harvest without very tall, very scary orchard ladders. They would need pruning another year, and perhaps a summer, too. To find out what to do, I took myself and my chainsaw to the Fruit Club's summer pruning workshop. And there, I embarrassed myself but good.

Spring's in full swing... ❧

Ever quicker the days lengthen. Ferry riders start to see daylight during their long commutes. As the air warms, bees take wing toward the first blush of blossom in the trees. First it's the white flowers of bird cherry, serviceberry, then elderberry and Pacific dogwood just as the daffodils fade. Fruit trees bloom: apple at least, apricot if weather's perfect. Buxom rhododendrons and bumps of azalea turn into blobs of color. Thundercloud plums, Kwanzan cherries, and magnolias gush in glorious clouds of pink and white. And then the petals fall, leaves push out and unfurl, and the scrim of new growth unites into a soft, plush canopy of green.

In the post office, odd beeps from the back announce the arrival of baby chicks to restock backyard flocks. Dave Hunter sends out his first bee-mail. Dr. Bob Norton of the Fruit Club is out in the orchard with his "puffer" making a personal delivery of pollen to each and every tree, pinching off all but "king" blossoms if the tree looks well pollinated.

At GreenDale Garden, Bill Green gets out the tractor to turn the soil, knowing I'll call May 1, plan in hand, ready to go. In the high school greenhouse, the garden club and the hort program start competing for space as 1"-cell seedlings are potted on into 4" pots. The VIGA manager starts to worry where she's going to put all the growers this year. Plum Forest Farm flogs its first eggs, spring kale flowers, and last year's jam. Langley Fine Gardens take their first truckload of transplants to Thriftway, then on to Seattle, Tacoma, even to Portland.

It's the season of the green tsunami. Can you keep up with the wave?

Move' em on out!

In the few weeks around Mother's Day, growers are moving young plants out to plant sales, the farmers market, and the food bank farm.

It's 10:00 Saturday morning, and at the VIGA Farmers Market in the Village Green, the market manager is clanging the opening bell. From around town, folks start drifting toward the VIGA stand, coffee cups in hand. The shed fills with chattering browsers, as farmers lean over displays to catch buyers' questions. A cork pops from under Vashon Winery's tent, as fiddlers in the musicians' tent out back wheedle away.

Holding down the market's SE corner are several tables of young plants from Pacific Potager: peas, greens, lettuce mixes, herbs and flowers, and 65 different varieties of tomato plants—just some of more than 3000 plants grown since January. From under her signature straw hat, owner Michelle Crawford fields questions from three buyers at once—

Yes, you can plant these tomatoes now: I'll be planting mine until mid-June.

No, you don't have to harden them off—everything I bring here has been outside at least a week, probably more.

Into your tomato hole, add a quarter-cup of all-purpose fertilizer, some bone meal to prevent blossom-end rot. Fish fertilizer helps with transplant shock.

I'll have ripe tomatoes here by mid-July. Will yours be ripe then? Depends...

A few vendors like Pacific Potager, Langley Fine Gardens, and Colleen James specialize in growing plant starts for spring sale. Farmers too sell a few starts if they have extra. Flats from Langleys and Bel-Red Greenhouse have adorned local storefronts since March, while the garden club, Vashon Island Pet Protectors, Montessori's Pacific Crest Farm, and the high school horticulture program will put on weekend plant sales May through June. Even the food bank has volunteers growing on flats of vegies for spring planting. In this period leading up to Mother's Day, young plants are coming out from under tender protection, from greenhouses to garden sales, headed into the wide world. Time to move 'em on out.

Pacific Potager

For Michelle Crawford, Saturdays during the market season begin early. "It's a gargantuan effort to get to the market! On Fridays I pre-pull starts, make pictures to go with the plants. I get up at 5am on Saturdays because it's still a farm day and the stand needs to look good, the hand-watering done, etc. Then we load the van, leave by 8am, are ready for market by 10."

Michelle's Pacific Potager farm is on the south end of Vashon, about three minutes from the Tahlequah ferry. Her white cottage with the white picket fence is surrounded by three hoophouses, with a big white sign announcing what's for sale in the stand. During spring, the stand is stuffed with hundreds of tomato starts—at least 65 different varieties—plus flats full of vegetables, herbs and at least 50 varieties of flowers—about 3000 plants altogether. "I want people to have a LOT of everything. The whole glory of gardening is, hopefully, in its exuberance. When you are cutting thyme for roasted vegetables or a roast chicken, you want a generous handful. So I grow WAY too many starts—though some make their way to the food bank."

After June, the nursery operation turns into a farm, when Michelle plants 800 unsold tomato plants in her hoophouses. By mid-July she has ripe tomatoes: the cool-weather varieties first, later heirlooms and paste tomatoes. She sells only through her farm stand and the market, but customers come to her from Bremerton, Bellevue, Seattle, Tacoma, and Bonney Lake.

She first sold tomato starts 20 years ago and started Pacific Potager five years later. "It is truly a family farm! My parents come in May to help with the girls, the watering. My dad turns 80 this year, and we love it when they are here. All the girls help some, and two like to help at the market. It's good and real for kids to see how their parent earns a living, and to be able to experience that in real time, see how it works. My girls are now planting flowers, so that makes me happy."

"It is not easy to grow tomatoes some years, but we are all in this together: I learn a lot from my customers and fellow tomato growers. My grown kids in Seattle, who frequent farmer's markets, say that our market has the most variety of goods and the best presentation."

Langley Fine Gardens

Off the SW corner of the market shed, a pavillion tent sheltered four tables stuffed to bursting with young plants. Two 20-something interns from Japan answer questions as well as their English allows. They're here thanks to an 18-month Japanese farm internship program that brings them to Big Bend College in Moses Lake, then to Langley's farm for 13 months of practical farm experience, and finally to UC Davis to learn organic methods of farming rice. With aging farmers, limited land, and a huge population, Japan is food-insecure, says Leda Langley, and her farm is helping that other island grow a new generation of farmers.

Matt and Leda Langley run what's currently the Island's largest wholesale nursery for plant starts. They started in Ballard 13 years ago in a 10x13' greenhouse in their backyard, growing flats of plants they'd wholesale to Swansons, Sky Nursery, City People's, and other retail outlets. "We were TINY. We'd take five flats of specialty starts to, say, Swansons, and they'd tell us 'We could sell 50 of these.' So when our Seattle customers told us to get some land, we didn't have any fear it wouldn't work." They found acreage in Dockton and set up their hoophouses, fields, and a farmstand, where payment is made by stuffing cash into a tennis ball and rolling it down a chute that runs right into the Langley house.

Most of Langleys' business—"nearly 100%"—comes from their off-Island accounts: eight garden outlets in Seattle, three in Tacoma, three on Bainbridge, and two in Portland, Oregon. They also sell their starts and (later) produce at farmers markets here and in West Seattle, where the interns get a chance to practice their English. Langley's once sold produce at the UW District Farmers Market, but no longer—"We got killed by the competition from Eastern Washington."

In February, they start 80-100 varieties of tomato starts and frost-hardy plants in 70' double-wall hoophouses. (They used to start in January, but eventually realized they were spending on heat without gaining any growth.) They begin deliveries in mid-March after plants have been hardening outside for at least a week. "We tell our retailers when they'll get our first delivery; most small growers do it that way. We don't want our lettuce to get frosted and turn to slime."

"Spring is our Christmas: we make most of our farm income in four weeks from mid-April to mid-May—10% just last week," she told me. Their season for baby plants ends by mid-June; after that, they turn to growing squash, potatoes, and other crops in their field and hoophouses off Hake Road. For gardeners who want to grow a fall-winter garden, "we do a very few plant starts to keep those gardeners happy."

"My advice to young growers is to start at a farmers market: you'll see if your stuff is pretty enough to sell at the price you need. And don't try to sell to EVERYBODY: you'll spread yourself too thin. We get calls from nurseries every week, but we just can't take more on. Somebody on the east side where land is cheap should grow the kind of specialty stuff we do."

Colleen James Perennials

At her table, pretty blonde Colleen James is chatting away as she hands a deer-proof salvia to a customer. "Here at the market, it's like we're a big family. I like to talk to people about their gardens, what works, what they want. I like the relationship part of gardening. I'm not interested in production."

But if you look at her crowded tables, and visit her place on Burton, you'd laugh to hear her make that last claim. The porch of her nouveau Victorian, her greenhouse, her front yard, even the guest bedroom over the garage, is stuffed with plants in flats and 4" pots. Seed stalks dry on tables, on kitchen counters, even on chair-backs in her living room, with bowls or papers underneath to catch the falling seeds. She's propagated thousands of plants for sale at her home, at the farmers market, and in 2011 at the Seattle Arboretum Plant Sale, where she surprised herself by making a couple grand.

Her specialities are shade perennials and deer-proof plants. "We don't have a deer fence, and after deer ate flats of starts, I decided to grow only things that deer don't like." She grows over 100 perennials and annuals, many of them choice or scarce: daturas, lavenders, agastaches, hostas, pinks, Siberian and Japanese iris, and at least 18 varieties of salvia. Abelia 'Confetti', Acanthus 'Gold Rush,' Acer 'Autumn Moon,' Aconitum, Agastaches 'Ava's Hummingbird Mint,' 'Golden Jubilee' and 'Orange Sprite,' Ajuga 'Black Scallop' and 'Toffee Chip,' and Angelica gigas—that's just her A list.

Since Colleen's family moved here from Gig Harbor in September, 2005, she's become a Master Gardener, a market vendor on Saturdays, and does some garden design consultant "to help people create something wonderful." She used to make jewelry as her creative outlet, but as a rare form of macular degeneration started to erode her eyesight, she turned to gardening and growing things. "Now my medium is flowers, and I have a bigger canvas for my creative side. That's why the garden is so healing and good for me."

Her market day starts around 8:30, when she packs her Volvo station wagon with 16 flats of plants, tables, chairs, umbrella and hat. Sales must wait until the 10am bell, but she can always field questions. "There will be moments when I'll have 4-5 people wanting information, while someone else will want to enthuse at length about their garden, and I have to say 'Hold that thought! I'll get right back to you!'"

A few other growers offer plant starts, but it's a minor part of their spring business. Richard Odell, known for his dahlias, offers some vegie starts "because I might as well, I'm growing them for myself." Jamie Froy and CZ Reims grow starts for the Country Store and occasionally sell at the farmers market. And while neither DIG nor Kathy's Corner participate in the farmers market, they do sell (and at Kathy's Corner, raise) vegie starts.

Nonprofits' Plant Sales

Jen Parker, who runs Pacific Crest Farm with husband Bob Keller on Maury Island for the **Seattle Montessori School**, grows seedlings for their spring fundraiser in Seattle. "We create a 'Vegie Garden Mix' or a "Edible Flowers Mix'—things like basil, calendula, nasturtiums, bachelor buttons. Then I grow plugs of everything else: lettuce, eggplants, peppers, etc." She sells any extras at the farmers market alongside her fresh produce.

Vashon Island Pet Protectors also does a plant sale in late May, as does the **Vashon High school Horticulture** program. While both sales are fundraisers for their primary mission, growing plants for the high school's sale is a big part of the curriculum through spring quarter. But the mother of all Island plant sales, ongoing for many years, has to be...

The Vashon-Maury Island Garden Club's Plant Sale

Early early November, some fool in the garden club is recruited to become the Master Coordinator for the coming year's garden sale. The year I joined, that fool was Kathy Bosler, fellow food bank volunteer and former project manager for US West. When she read through the 45-page manual the club had compiled on how to run the garden sale, she thought, "Holy cow, how am I going to wrangle all THIS? 57 truck deliveries? 2000 labels? 3200 square feet of sales space? Several hundred emails? Over 4000 plants?"

It's understood by club members that the sale is the Big Event: everybody's expected to participate in some way. Someone has to gather pots, someone writes publicity. Somebody takes charge of gathering items for the Boutique. Somebody scouts for a location (lately it's been at the old Napa Store at the shopping center by Vashon Post Office), negotiates the rental, and cleans up the space. The event needs sign painters, pot waterers, plant diggers and movers, etc, etc, plus garden gloves, tape, scissors, labels, markers. Luckily for Kathy, she had a veteran of the sale before, Lucy Harter, to help her coordinate the many moving parts.

Kathy thrust me, a gullible new member, into running their seedling operation in the high school greenhouse. The ladies gave me very clear orders. "Tomatoes in gallon pots, NW varieties—and no weird-colored ones! Lettuces, spinach, onions, cucumbers, beans, basil, herbs—and less cabbage, broccoli, and cauliflower! And yes, CORN!" (which I thought was crazy—but everything else, Right On!) It has been long tradition for Kay White's staff to grow tomato plants for the sale, but we figured you can never have enough tomatoes to sell—I planned to sow hundreds.

The club has a long-standing agreement with the school's horticulture program to share its big greenhouse and an order of supplies. In January, I met at the greenhouse with Mike Calder, the welding teacher who was subbing that year for Amy Bogaard, the usual hort teacher who was on leave. We agreed on a mutual purchase of potting soil, pots, flats, and fertilizer from McConkey's Supply near Puyallup, plus a little extra cash as a goodwill donation to the hort program from the club That, plus seeds from Territorial Seed Co, quickly used up our small budget of $300. McConkeys would deliver in mid-February, in time to start planting by Feb. 17.

Using an online garden planner, www.growveg.com, I filled virtual greenhouse tables with virtual flats of plants so I could foresee how much space we'd need. On the 17th, six of us met at the greenhouse to sow the first seeds—mostly tomatoes and onions, a very few broccoli and cauliflower. Heeding the call for tomatoes that work in our climate, I chose Stupice, Siletz, Manitoba, Siberia, Early Girl, Oregon Spring, and that ever-popular cherry, SunGold. No weird-colored tomatoes for us.

Every week that spring, we half-dozen nuns of the greenhouse met Fridays at 10am to sow, transplant, water, fertilize. It was a cold, gray spring, and we enjoyed the greenhouse's warmth and our mutual murmurations as we stuck seeds and labels into soil-filled cell-packs. Someone watered on Mondays; later we added Fridays. A month later, we potted tiny toms into 4" pots and had sown everything but the basil.

We weren't alone in the greenhouse. The club also subsidized Julia Lakey's seedlings for her food garden at Vashon Community Care, so she was sowing her own flats right beside us. Mad propagator Caroline Brinkley from Gold Beach soon ran out of grow space in her garden and asked if she could move some of her perennials to a table in the greenhouse. The high school students, led by Mike and assistant Vor Hostetler, showed up by March 20th and soon had their own flats filling the south end of the 60' germination table. And their younger plants soon outstripped ours—quite the head-scratcher until the sun showed up one March day and revealed the shade of a big cedar over our end of the greenhouse.

In mid-April when we potted toms into gallon pots, I counted more than 1076 plants—spinach, chards, herbs, marigolds, peas savory and sweet, lettuces, basils, beans, two kinds of cukes, and four kinds of onions. We had 17 tomato varieties, over 350 plants, most in gallons, many in flower. The hort program's flats had met ours in the greenhouse's middle, with Julia Lakey's starts squeezed in between. The greenhouse was stuffed with plants.

But no corn—we nuns could never agree on them. They'll be too early. They'll outgrow their flat. You need at least 45 plants in a four-foot block for good pollination. Were we creating a gardener's advantage or just something to sell? The greenhouse decided for us: it couldn't fit one more flat.

Meanwhile, another 800 plants— tomatoes, 100 fuchsia baskets, scented geraniums and pelargoniums—were growing at Kay White's greenhouses on Maury Island. Caroline Brinkley's perennials filled half a bench, plus members would bring plants. Posters showed up everywhere: in windows, on bulletin boards, on signs at 18 different intersections. The April meeting of the club ran five hours, with Bosler and her crew criss-crossing the room to put down names on last-minute To-Do lists. One month to go.

Set-up at the Old Napa store began two days before the sale. Six people, four trucks and two trips moved those 1076 plants, and I spent the afternoon organizing them. When I arrived to price plants the next day, I discovered that not only had Kay White's crew brought their truckload of tomatoes, a stranger had donated dozens more—mostly cherries, mostly weird-colored. I spent two hours sorting that well-meaning mess back into alphabetical order. (Later I learned they came from Lynda Rhodes and her 90-year-old dad, Bill Deaton.)

Though the sale always starts at 9am Saturday morning, a photo of us in funny flower hats had to be shot at 7:30am. Tables of perennials filled the back of the old Napa store; greenhouse tomatoes and vegies down the right; Kay White's on the left, with everything else plus the check-out crammed toward the front. By 8am, sellers were outside buying our baked goods; by 9am, the line stretched down to the grocery. When the doors opened, they SWARMED us: buyers to the left, buyers to the right, behind and beside me, practically in my shirt... Linda Rhodes showed up to help, and we juggled answers and tomato plants as fast as we could, while Julia Lakey leapt in to handle the vegetable sales. One customer asked me, "Do you have any more corn for sale?"

"MORE corn?" I dragged her to Julia, asked, "Did we HAVE corn?"

"We did. Jet brought in two flats of 6" corn starts at 8 this morning."

"Where'd they go?"

"Sold 'em ten minutes after we opened." There's that argument settled...

When the noon bell rang, I looked up and found we'd sold all but 75 tomato plants. Could have sold dozens more SunGolds and other cherries if we'd had them—and lots of weird-colored ones, too. All told, the sale pulled in over $9000, most of it slated for local beautification projects, scholarships, and support of the high school hort program.

Eeeeee-ha! We ladies really do know how to move 'em on out!

Harden off plants, then chose the right time to transplant

Plant starts = a head start in spring for your garden. Many an eager gardener has told me in March, even April, "I've plugged in my lettuce/peas/spinach seeds, but they're not growing at all." With long cool springs, low light-levels, trees shading gardens, and high water-tables keeping fields and plots waterlogged, many plants can't muster the energy to grow until May. If you wait until then to stick a tomato seed in the dirt, you'll be lucky if you have ripe tomatoes (or basil, cauliflower, onions, or any peppers at all) before October's killing frosts. Gaining a month or two by either buying transplants or starting your own not only allows them to bulk up quickly when the weather's good, it gives you instant gratification: you're planting a little something you can see, not seeds that disappear in the dirt.

But don't be QUITE so eager to drag that seedling into the Great Outdoors. Young starts grow inside are TENDER: they have soft tissues not accustomed to rain, wind, cold, or direct sun. Plant a tender young thing into a sun-blasted field, and tomorrow it will sport big pale splotches of weakened leaf-tissue called sun scald. It'll look like it's cowering, poor thing. Ahhhh, if only you had hardened it off for a week.

Hardening off is a 1-2 week process of exposing tender, indoor-grown plants to the outdoors for ever-longer periods. In late April on a gray but not freezing day, move your tomatoes (and other seedlings with a few pairs of true leaves) outdoors for a couple hours, then back inside. Next day, four hours. Day after, two or three more hours, and so on, increasing the length of time each day. By week's end, you leave the plants out all night (unless there's a late freeze coming, heaven forbid!). Your plants should start to look huskier, darker, even (if it's a tomato) a little hirsute on stems and leaves. If it's yellowing, showing roots out the bottom, or reaching its leaves up like it's assuming a yogic "Tree" pose, the plant wants to go into a larger pot.

Pacific Potager and Langleys don't put their plants on sale until they are hardened off. Greenhouse operations (including the Garden Club growing project) may not have the opportunity to harden off before it's time to Move' em On Out. If you are uncertain a plant's been hardened off, ask—and do it yourself if needs be. Your plant babies will thank you for it.

For a Vase of Flowers

Daffodils, sunflowers, and other vase-worthy flowers grace our roads and farm stands, while the ruins along Beall Road bear witness to a cut-flower industry that provided work for hundreds of Islanders.

Perhaps, if you drove down Wax Orchard Road up through 2011, you noticed the Daffodil Barn. Like a Georgia O'Keeffe painting, a huge daffodil spread its petals across a gray barn door. And in April, at the foot of the barn, hundreds of mixed daffodils bloom. Quite the sight.

These daffodils were planted in honor of the farm that was. In 1978, a San Francisco food photographer with thick glasses and long, graying hair took his young wife on a road trip. Bruce Harlow had founded California's first waterbed company, rode that to success, then he and his wife Jan (like many of this generation) decided they wanted to "get away from it all." His brother-in-law Matthew Mosteller recalled: "I think we all read Mother Earth News from cover to cover back then. Jan and Bruce came up here on a road trip and fell in love with the island, which was still very rural at that time, and purchased the farm." The Harlows bought an old farmhouse on 27 acres; Bruce, when he wasn't off on business, enjoyed being a gentleman farmer and do-it-yourself'er. He dressed up the "farmer-built" house ("axe-flattened logs on rocks," said Matthew) in Victorian gingerbread, added the barn, and with Matthew's help, built a cabin for their parents.

"Bruce had farming in his Iowa blood and thought daffodils were a good crop for this region, so he instigated the creation of a family corporation, Northern Lights Farm," said Mosteller. "We planted the whole field north of the driveway in daffs, with the intent of selling cut flowers and then bulbs as they reproduced. As it turned out, harvesting the flowers in late winter was cold, back-breaking labor. Although the first couple years produced nice flowers, they started growing smaller and suffered some disease. The blush fell from the bloom, so to speak. Later, when Bruce heard about 'Nashi' asian pears, we planted an orchard. I recall digging a lot of holes in typical Vashon, uncooperative, exceedingly stony, glacial till soil."

In May 1985, the gentleman farmer sold the farm to Margaret and Tom Hodnett. "To make up for the fading daffodils, he painted the big flower on the barn door," claims retired realtor Mary Jane Brown. The Hodnetts kept the barn, but sold the tarted-up house to Mary Jane's daughter for $1; they had plans to build a new, Asian-style house on the old foundation (easier than getting new building permits) and wanted the Victorian outta there. Robbins & Co. was hired to move the two-story house a half-mile south. They did so, in a snowstorm, and mid-transit the house got stuck between two telephone poles. Out came the chain-saws, off came the garden room (they nailed it back on when the house settled into place). The Victorian is still there, gingerbread pink and white, overlooking Tammy Dunakin's goat pasture on Wax Orchard just north of the Camp Sealth turn-off.

By the late 90s, the only daffodils left in the field were in low spots safe from a mower's blade. So Margaret hired a younger woman, Kari Dickerson, to help her plant more daffodils around the old barn. Kari remembers: "We planted 950 daffodils. There were still daffodils in the field from 20 years ago, and Margaret wanted to honor them."

With flowers, we remember, we share loveliness, we spread a little love.

Daffodils to brighten Island Roads

Many years ago, I took a drive to the Oregon Coast and was inspired by all the daffodils blooming along the rural highway. In gray coastal drizzle, they nodded yes yes yes in sunshine yellow, gone native along road verges and above drainage ditches where they probably had drooped over and dropped their seedheads downhill.

So in one of my first blogs in 2009, I proposed that Islanders plant more daffodils along the road. "Since many a Vashon garden is down a driveway, much of our spring bloom is a private, out of sight affair. What a gift it would be to all, to see those bright splashes of springtime along our rain-gray roads!" I pointed out that many Island roadsides are the grass-n-ditch variety, on banked-up verges where the bulbs will get good drainage. If you plant at least eight feet from the road, your daffs will probably be beyond King County mowers. Or you can shelter them at the foot of your mailbox or newspaper tube, where neither the County or you are likely to mow.

Daffodils are a great choice for an island planting. Our soil offers the pH range (slightly acidic) that daffs prefer, with plenty of spring water and little to none in summer. The plant contains a repellent alkaloid sap, so deer and rodents won't eat them (though not slugs, unfortunately). Those properties off the Vashon Till, such as the south end of Vashon, most of Maury, or along the outlying slopes, will have the well-draining, light soil that allow daffs to thrive and naturalize.

To my plea for more daffodils, did the Island respond!. I was collared in yoga, in stores, at meetings, by folks who wanted me to know they'd planted their bulbs—and where. And maybe it's because I was looking for them, but that spring, it seemed like more daffodils bloomed here, there, everywhere.

Those bulbs will brighten our roadways for years, if they perform anything like earlier plantings. There's a wonderful daffodil colony at least ten years old, planted with bluebells and birches on 87th heading down to Tramp Harbor. There's another just north of Burton, where fly-fishing guide Mark Rutherford planted daffodils around 1997 along his driveway. He said, "The first year we used bone or fish meal and all the bulbs got dug up by raccoons attracted to the smell. If we take care of them less, they survive better."

Daffodil bulbs are available in bulk bags at local groceries every fall. If you want a wider selection, visit Washington Bulb Company, the largest bulb grower in the nation and located just north in the Skagit Valley. These are the hosts of the annual Tulip Festival that draws hundreds of tourists and shutter-bugs every year. I bought my first shipment of bulbs from them back when they were "Roozengarten" and was very impressed at the large, multi-nose bulbs I received. What a bonanza of daffodils the following spring!

For a longer-lived bouquet, PURGE your daffodils

That toxic sap that makes daffs distasteful to moles and deer is also noxious to other flowers in a bouquet. To purge that sap, put cut daffs in a bucket of cold water for 15 minutes, then lift and see if the vicious sap runs out the ends. If yes, dunk into a second bucket of clean water, wait 10-15, lift and look, repeat until the stem no longer drools.

Daffodils & More: Cut flowers from Mary Ann Roberts

In April 2012, Mary Ann Roberts gave a talk on growing daffodils to the garden club. A south-end resident for over 30 years, she remembers the Daffodil Barn's flowery field in its heyday and invited me to come see her own cutting gardens where she grows flowers to sell.

In over 13 acres of second-growth forest, she and husband Jack nurture a woodland garden of rhododendrons, azaleas and specimen trees. In the sunnier spots—but still with hours of shade each day—Mary Ann manages to raise enough cutting flowers to sell "to keep us in plants and books." Several deer-fenced patches averaging 100 sf are dedicated to (mostly) a single type of flower: here a gladiola patch, there a stand of lilies, a corral full of alstromeria ligtu hybrids, and a combined patch of peonies, campanulas, and phlox.

Her season begins with daffodils, cut and brought to the nearby farmstand of Pacific Potager. Owner Michelle Crawford also sells their bouquets of daffodils at the farmers' market. This year, growing trees cast too much shade over the old patch, so Mary Ann had to find them a spot with at least 3/4s of the day in sun. She grows sweet williams over another patch of daffs, as they'll tolerate each other's soil and water requirements (though dianthus prefers slightly alkaline soil) the deer don't bother either plant, and the Sweet william foliage completely masks the yellowing foliage of the daffodils. And she can sell these sweet williams because "Islanders love deep rich pinks, like the pink in a 'Sarah Bernhardt' peony or the watermelon pink of an 'Alma Potschke' aster."

By June, she can harvest peonies, campanulas, and by month's end alstromerias and lilies—enough flowers to stock Pacific Potager, which operates on the honor system as many of the Island flower stands do. By Fourth of July, she has enough flowers to create 9-10 bouquets and sell them from the co-op booth at the farmers' market as well as the stand. Throughout the season, she also sells to Blooms & Things, the Island's only florist shop.

And as she drives toward Vashon to make her delivery, she'll pass the competition: two of the three "Calico Gardens' stands, colorful as carnivals and just as prone to empty your wallet with your sudden yen for flowers.

Calico Gardens: bouquets on the honor system

For over ten years, Calico Gardens' blue and yellow flower cart in Burton has offered garden-grown bouquets. There's a second stand at the old Roast-erie at Minglement. These stands are restocked Thursday through Sunday, eleven months of the year, the bouquets stuffed into plastic drink cups, pay-ments on the honor sytem. Who ARE these trusting folks?

"Calico Gardens" is Delinda McCann and Noni Morrison, both long-time south-end residents and friends of "a certain age." I caught up with them in Delinda's garden near Tahlequah in 2010.

They first met at WSU as students, then graduated, married, had kids. Years later in 1980, after Delinda moved to Vashon, she walked into the Methodist church and heard a familiar voice call out, "Hey I know YOU!" As the two women got re-acquainted, Delinda listened to Noni fantasize about a flower business. Finally Delinda blurted out, "Tomorrow we start! We'll put some bouquets in my daughter's coffee wagon and sell them to the south-end ferry commuters."

It went well enough—how could they fail at $1 per bouquet?— but with-in a couple weeks, the women got the OK to move to the Burton marina's parking lot at the intersection "as long as we didn't put up a permanent structure." Today, you'll find Delinda's cart there, across from the Burton coffee-stand; Noni fills the stand at Minglement and another at her home at 248th & Wax Orchard.

The two women start harvesting and arranging on Wednesday evening, fill their stands by 9am Thursday, then restock through Sunday. On a busy weekend, they might sell as many as 60 bouquets, but 25 is average. They get lots of business from men: with the cost of a bouquet under $8, it's a little something for the wife they can buy on the way home.

Selling on the honor system has its risks. When I asked about a best day sales record, Delinda blurted out "Minus EIGHT!"—she'd been ripped off one weekend. One of their favorite horror stories is of an older lady they've nicknamed "Flora" who cherry-picked the roses from each bouquet and then drove off without paying. "She handed them to her grandson—what an example!" So they check the stands several times a day, and Noni's hus-band brings the bouquets home every night.

Delinda showed me around color-themed beds that hold roses, glads, dahlias, snapdragons, feverfew daisies. "This section is yellows, snapdragons start the apricot, over there's pink, and the white corner keeps me going in spring. In back I grow blues: bachelor buttons, hydrangea. I almost always add a bit of blue because people buy it: they love the blue."

"So Islanders have color preferences?"

"Oh, yes, and it's different each year. This year, nothing pink sells."

Noni laughed "And this year, it's purple with orange! Anything BRIGHT to counter the gray!"

Like Delinda, Noni grows her flowers at home behind a tall deer fence. She stocks a smaller stand near the SE corner of 248th & Wax Orchard. "Let me show you my new greenhouse," as she led me into a new SunGlo. "We put amaryllis into our Christmas bouquets, so I'm experimenting with propagating them. We also force tulips in here."

By Valentine's Day, Calico Gardens has started its season with bouquets of daffodils, hyacinths, forced tulips and whatever else is pretty. Business is good through Mother's Day, then sales slow until the first of August, "when people are having parties and more guests. Bouquets make good hostess gifts." By Christmas, they're filling their plastic cup vases with amaryllis, winter-blooming honeysuckle, holly, camellia, and red-twig dogwood. The business then shuts down for January, "our only down month." They also supply a couple of churches and have some weekly subscribers.

"We LOVE to be called in for weddings," says Noni. "Our specialty is when Mother arrives on Wednesday and no one's arranged for the flowers! There are a lot of ex-hippie folk on the Island and they don't like formal stuff—they want 'fresh out of a meadow' bouquets. So we make our bouquets homey and informal, like what you might pick at Grandma's house."

We go up and down her rows, where each rose, lily, and dahlia is carefully labeled. Mingus Tony, Akita, Sandia Shomei, Sunny, Crazy Love, the fiery dinnerplate dahlia Gladiator—Noni loves the names. Last year she lost 100 of the 130 dahlia plants that she normally overwinters in her gravelly loam soil, so these plants are replacements from Swan Island Dahlias in Oregon.

"To keep a dahlia bouquet going, you condition by putting 1/4 teaspoon bleach and sugar into very hot tap water, add the flowers, then set the bouquet in a cool, dark place. It's best to pick in the morning when the flowers are freshest. This conditioning starts the cut flower drinking so that it stays hydrated and lasts longer."

"For a beautiful bouquet, you're looking for tall and thin, some foliage, something major like a big rose or dahlia, something frizzy or feathery like a few stems of white fever-few as a background for a yellow dahlia, some tall glads filled in with snapdragons..." Noni's bouquets are sumptuous eye-dazzlers, and she sends me home with a real beaut—purple dahlias tipped in white, pink pompoms with a golden center, green-bossed yellow susans set against the smouldering leaves of a purple smoke bush branch.

"Why do we empty nesters do this time-consuming work?" said Noni. "Our husbands wouldn't budget for all this landscaping we want to do. We started this business so we could grow what we wanted."

If on the block past Minglement Roasterie you turn right at 191st, you'll follow part of the route of the Island's 1937 Lily Festival. About ten years after the highway was paved end to end, motorists were invited to come to Vashon to view its many fields of Regale lilies.

In the mid-2000s, lilies bloomed here again, along with lupines, delphiniums, dahlias, sunflowers, and other gaudy blooms. **Boutique plant nursery DIG** developed a two-acre cutting garden off this very corner, starting in 2004. Like the Calico ladies, owner Sylvia Matlock recognized the appeal of "what grandma would have grown": the field was full of spring bulbs, peonies and roses, lilies and lupines, British delphiniums, cleome, cosmos, zinnias, asters, dahlias, sunflowers, and love-lies-bleeding. Matlock ran the field as a CSA subscription service and laid out the plantings in rows for quick harvest. Though she closed the field in 2009 "to focus on the nursery and helping our customers and landscape clients," there's still evidence of the old plantings: a lilac hedge, fat foxtail lilies and red-hot pokers still grow on the fenceline along 191st.

There's an old French corruption of a funeral epitaph, "The Rose, she lives the life that roses live," that perfectly expresses the short life of the cut flower. Perhaps it's tempting fate to build a business on such perishable objects. Yet around the corner and up Beall Road is a reminder that our desire for cut flowers is both ephemeral and ever-lasting: the ruins of a 100-year-long enterprise, the Beall Greenhouse Company.

Beall Greenhouses: growers of cut roses and orchids

"In the 1960s, airline pilots used to tell us that you knew when you were approaching Sea-Tac airport because you could see the lights from the Beall Greenhouses," Tom Beall Jr. told me.

Today as you can go along Beall Road, you might drive by the old greenhouses and not notice them. Wooden frames that once held the glass of 92 greenhouses now play pergola to a new forest growing in beds that once grew roses. Artists have cleared out a few greenhouses for studios, but that's all that's usable of what was one of the largest producers of cut roses and orchids in the world.

Every working day starting at 4am, 3000-4000 long-stemmed roses were shipped from the Beall greenhouses—2 million roses a year. What orders the company couldn't fill from Vashon, they supplied from their 50 rose houses in Palo Alto, California. All told, they had over 1.5 million sf of land under glass, over 100 employees in summer, and another 40 in Palo Alto. That's the same size as today's second-largest U.S. rose grower. Beall Greenhouse Company was Big Business.

The operation got started in the late 1880s, when a young greenhouse expert from New York, Hilen Harrington, saw opportunity in a region booming from Yukon gold strikes and the arrival of transcontinental railroads. By 1898, five years after the Northern Pacific Railroad reached Seattle, Hilen's nine greenhouses were pumping out tomatoes, cucumbers, and lettuce to feed regional demand. In a 1915 interview with the *Vashon Island News*, he talked about the Island's slighter warmer climate, good shipping facilities, "best soil in the state, best water on the continent, and no saloons..."

Hilen was so quickly successful that by 1892 he could hire Chinese labor to build a Queen Anne-style mansion just north of the greenhouses (it's still there). When gold was discovered up north, he expanded with more greenhouses, more produce, and added cut flowers (single girls were scarce in Seattle then, and a suitor probably gained an edge if he came calling with flowers in hand). Soon, Hilen gained a partner— a new arrival with money, sons, and horticultural know-how named Lewis Beall, Sr. Harrington and the Beall men incorporated in 1902; when Harrington retired ten years later, his partners changed the name to Beall Greenhouse Company. By then, the plant had 36 greenhouses heated by coal, employed 20 workers, and were shifting to roses, carnations, and orchids for the cut flower trade. (They briefly returned to vegetable growing during World War II.)

When Lewis died in 1926, Wallace Beall took over general management, with his sons Tom, Ferguson, and John heading divisions. Ferguson Beall, who everyone called "Fergie," developed a passion for orchids: he hunted for new varieties in the jungles of South American in 1938 and hybridized hundreds of new varieties in the Beall laboratory. During WWII, he brought over for safe-keeping 8000 British orchid plants that were being bombed by the Nazis (apparently the German pilots mistook the English greenhouses, with their large, sun-flashing roofs, for aircraft factories). By the war's end, Bealls had emerged as the largest grower of orchids on the Pacific Coast, with 42 greenhouses in orchids, and even more in roses for the long-stem trade. In 1947, they opened a new facility in Palo Alto, managed by John Beall, where California's famous sunlight gave roses beautiful color. By the 1950s, they owned two wholesale warehouses in Seattle and Tacoma.

Flowers have to be perfect to sell to florists, so the Beall crews coddled their plants. Each greenhouse had its own supervisor, with a night watchman to keep an eye on temperatures. Roses were kept at 62° at night, 68° during the day, while each orchid house provided a climate tailored for the variety grown there. Oil burners supplied steam heat rising from pipes 6" from each bed or bench, with fertilizers fed through the watering system.

Given such conditions, oh how the plants bloomed. "We'd cut thousands of flowers in a few hours," said Frank Shride, the former sales manager of the orchid division who started working at Bealls when he returned from WWII service. When he managed sales in the orchid division, his day began with orders from the East Coast—at 4:30am. "My day started a half hour before the orchid crew arrived," he told me. "I would walk through the orchid houses to check for problems, then check for flowers to hybridize, then to the office to check the mail." After a swing home for breakfast, "We'd start cutting orchids by 8- 8:30, Fergie going down one aisle, me the other," 10-12 people following in their wake to receive the stems. Once a workers' hands were full, he or (usually) she would proceed to the aisle's end, where a packer (usually male) would cover the cut ends with a little water vial, poke the vial into an 11x17" carrier, then carry those filled flats into the 38° cooler for a couple hours. "Cut, cool, pack—that was a process" Shride told me. "After cooling, the stems would be graded large/medium/small, the ends recut and retubed, then the stems laid in boxes full of shredded paper—we called it 'hay'—and the tubes taped in place so the blooms wouldn't touch and bruise each other. In the afternoon, they'd ship out with the last of the rose deliveries."

"Beall Greenhouse Co. pioneered shipping orchids by airfreight. For the Christmas and New Year markets, we would cut thousands of the Cymbidium variety, sometimes working 24 hours straight, eating whenever we had the chance. The Cattleya variety was a year-round product; white ones were especially needed for the June wedding trade," said Shride. "But I had so much fun working with the orchids, I never 'worked' a day in my life."

Barbara Steen, whose husband Max managed the rose division, liked working there because Bealls offered "mom hours" to women who wanted to work while kids were at school. When the women weren't packing blooms, they worked with Fergie and Frank on the orchid seedlings. The seeds from a single pod are tiny—thousands in a single pod—and were germinated under sterile conditions in flasks filled with agar jelly and about 25 seeds per flask. After 9-12 months when they popped little green leaves and got to a certain size, then the vials would be opened and the seedlings planted, 25-50 in a common pot." Good seedlings after two years would be potted on into 2", 3" and up to 6" single pots and join 25,000 other seedlings in their own greenhouse. After 5 years, a good plant could send out flowering stems with 2-4 blooms or more.

Barbara obviously thought the world of her employers. "They treated us very well, I think because it was family-oriented to begin with: Wallace & Mary Beall, their sons Fergie and Thomas heading orchids and roses, Johnny managing the Palo Alto plant. Bealls provided employment for so many people: Moms, high school kids, college kids." At its peak, the firm employed 112 on the Island during the summer, 60 in the winter, plus employees at the Palo Alto plant and the Seattle and Tacoma stores. Bealls even sponsored two local bowling teams: the women calling themselves "Beall's Best" and the men adopting the company slogan, "Island Grown."

For workers like her husband Max, manager of the rose division, the days could be long. "He'd start at 4am, even 2am. We had to move Christmas and Mother's Day because those times were such a zoo for my husband. But that was part of the life," said Barbara. "The men who worked with my husband still call on me to talk about those crazy times."

"Anyone from the south end trying to catch that first morning boat would have seen our lights on," said Tom Beall Jr., fourth-generation Beall and the last to work the greenhouses. Now a manager at Pacific Research, he worked at the greenhouses from teenhood until his 40s, and he has very fond memories of what the rose houses were like in the 1970s. "When we'd open the greenhouse doors about an hour after daybreak, we'd feel this puff of warm air carrying this fantastic rose aroma—back then, the smell wasn't bred out. The temperature was always 62° from the steam pipes, and you could hear robins chirping; because we opened vents in the late mornings, they found ways to get inside and build their nests in the greenhouses."

""Some of my favorite memories are of the summers when my father, Tom Sr, my three teenage kids and myself would start cutting roses early in the morning. We then had about 50 greenhouses in roses. Each house had eight raised beds about 3' across, a dirt aisle between, with the roses planted in soil every foot or so, 8000 plants in each house. We'd walk down the aisles, knife in hand, looking for flowers that were starting to 'whistle'—that is, the first few petals had begun to curl down, like your lower lip when you're about to blow. About 10-12 other rose cutters would be working in the neighboring greenhouses, all cutting at the same time to get the roses into the cooler as soon as possible. When our arms were full of stems, we'd go to the wrapping station at the end of the aisle, wrap the stems, then drop them into buckets of water that would be taken to the cooler. We'd start cutting at daylight, again at 11am, then 2pm, because there are always roses starting to whistle all during the day."

"We always had great topics to discuss during the cutting: the importance of family, the economy, what the future would hold, our favorite family dinners. It was truly a family affair. My brother and sisters might cut with us, or grade the roses for shipment, or drive the flowers to the airport. You worked until you got the job done. There is no such thing as turning off a greenhouse full of roses until the next day—the blooms would be too open for the market. We all took turns working the weekend—plants keep growing every day of the week!"

The cooler was about 40 feet long by sixteen and held at 38-42°. The bundles of stems were lowered into big tanks of cool water, bolt upright so the flowers wouldn't be bruised. Workers didn't strip off leaves or thorns because that would break the cambium layer, preventing water from rising further up the stem. After 8-24 hours, the roses would be pulled from the cooler, graded for length of bud & stem, then each grade would be bundled into 25s and wrapped in newspaper. Men would pack the bundles into heavy insulated boxes, 400 roses to a box with a handful of ice thrown around the stems, then load the boxes into the vans in time to catch the first morning ferries and deliver to their wholesale stores in Seattle and Tacoma. Another truck left by 3pm to catch the airlines (Bealls was once Continental's biggest customer). In a typical day, we'd pack and ship 10-15 boxes, sending out 3000-6000 rose stems a day."

In the 1960s, the corsage trade was in decline, as out of fashion as the girdle and the beehive hairdo. Shride said, "Around 1960, Fergie and I took a trip around the Coast to visit other orchid concerns. Afterwards, I went into the office and said 'We're going to have to sell orchid plants, because the cut stem business was going downhill.'" They were already expert hybridizers, had the inventory, and as the plants don't require soil, they could shipped bare-root. By the mid-70s, Bealls was putting out an orchid catalog several times a year, selling whole plants in 2-3-and 4" pots for $6-35 each, some for more. "The most expensive plant I ever sold was the clone 'Golden Anniversary' for $15,000 to a client in Taiwan," Shride said.

Shride said, "It might take all afternoon to make one hybrid cross." The orchid department kept their own stud books, plus researched those of the Royal Orchid Society that tracks the world's named orchid hybrids. "Our numbered crosses were written in our master stud book and in small books of records we carried from lab to greenhouse. These books allowed me to ascertain the quantity of plants on hand, from the sterile laboratory to the sales from each house."

By 1976 Bealls closed the cut orchid division and went strictly with whole plants. That was the easy change: throughout the 1970s, Bealls was under pressure to adapt to forces global in scale and beyond their control. State-subsidized competition came from Canada, which had natural gas reserves that could heat greenhouses at half the cost of Beall's oil-heated facility (those same greenhouses still put out winter tomatoes with the "B.C. Hothouse" label). The Arab Oil Embargo of 1973 drove Beall's heating costs out the glass roof. The Palo Alto plant run by John Beall, now surrounded by houses, became burdened by rising property taxes and fuel costs.

And then there was the growing competition from South America. In her revealing book *Flower Confidential,* Amy Stewart describes how a 1960s grad student report on the best places to grow flowers in the world started a stampede of the world's flower industry toward the equatorial mountain regions, particularly in Kenya, Singapore, Colombia, and Ecuador. "If you wanted to open a flower farm," she writes, "you'd follow this line around the globe with your finger, looking for a place that had enough rainwater, a cheap labor force, a decent airport, and roads that could handle big refrigerated trucks. That's where you'd build."

Dutch, American, and Colombian growers set up a joint venture, Floramerica, in Colombia in 1969. Within six months, their new farms were shipping flowers to the United States. Suddenly our old Island business had to compete with employers who paid workers $150 a month to grew roses under plastic, on land that was sun-soaked and dirt-cheap.

The Bealls saw the change coming and got on board—at least for a few years. The company sold the Palo Alto facility to a condo developer in 1972, then sent Tom Jr. and his Uncle John of the Palo Alto plant to Bogota, Colombia. They were invited to become part of Floramerica, but after a year, in 1974, they split off from Floramerica and used the Palo Alto proceeds to set up a rose farm under the Beall name. In an article written by John's daughter Johna, she describes the Beall/Bogota rose farm. "They had an elevated plateau in the Andes at 8,500 feet above sea level, four degrees north latitude, with twelve hours of sunlight each day, and rich volcanic soil. No need to heat the greenhouses, less costly labor, and a good exchange rate from Colombian pesos to dollars."

Said Tom Jr., "When we went down there, there was no rose exporting. Once we started our operation, we expanded very rapidly and became the largest rose-exporting company into the U.S. in South America."

But, he admitted it was a scary time to be in Colombia. Drug cartels and paramilitary groups were using kidnappings for political and financial exploitation. Tom Jr. told me, "Every once in awhile, a child was kidnapped from the French, English or American schools. You had to send your kids to school with a bodyguard. It was not the way I wanted to bring my family up." So he returned to Vashon in 1976 to help his father manage the greenhouses. That year the company split into two: Tom Sr. and Jr. took over the Island operation, while John Beall kept the Colombian farm.

The market's shift in favor of foreign-grown flowers marched on: in 1971, only 4% of cut flowers sold in the U.S. were imported, but over the next 20 years, imports grew to 73% of the market. By the early 80s, Tom Jr., now plant manager, realized he had to begin downsizing. Shride and a partner bought the orchid business and moved it to the Kent Valley, but he was near retirement age, and the young partner proved unable to keep it going. Downsizing continued; when the firm was down to four employees and ten greenhouses, Tom Jr. closed the business and took a job at Pacific Research.

John Beall continued to grow roses in Colombia—at its peak, the farm exported 8 million roses a year to the United States. But In 1991, hoping South American farmers would grow something besides coca for the drug trade, the U.S. Congress granted Colombia and Ecuador duty-free status; by 1994, those countries had grabbed 55% of the U.S. rose market. Though Beall roses were considered premium, selling retail for 85¢/stem, they competed with South American roses selling for 38¢ and sometimes dumped for as little as 4¢. The difference hurt all domestic roses growers: Stewart's book claims that there are now only 59 rose growers left in the U.S., producing "less than 10% of the roses sold in the United States."

After John Beall died in 1994, his youngest daughter Johna ran the farm, commuting between Bogota and Vashon for years. But that same year, under pressure from U.S.-based growers concerned about South American farms dumping their roses on the market, the U.S. imposed a 34¢ per stem tariff on all roses from Colombia. Johna went to Washington D.C. to plead for an exemption for Beall Roses as a 105-year-old, U.S-owned enterprise. They didn't get it, though larger growers with more influence did. The last of the Beall Rose enterprises closed in June 1995.

Johna writes, "Ours was not the largest farm, but our roses were thought by many to be the best quality. In those last several years, I traveled 4,111 miles monthly between Vashon and Bogotá to supervise farm operations and North American sales. I'd done my best to keep it going."

In 1989, 101 years after the founding of Beall Greenhouse Company, the 28-acre site was sold to Charles and Nancy Hooper; five years later it was given King County landmark status. By the 1990s, several artists cleared out space and built studios under some of the more intact glass roofs. Ironically, one of them, Catherine Michaelis of Mayday Press, depicted in her screen-prints and handmade books the processes and strange transports of seeds, perhaps inspired by the growth enwrapping the old greenhouses.

Blooms & Things

Along the way to the ferry, the Beall vans would deliver some of their rose stems to the florist shop on Vashon's main intersection. Islanders wanted roses then, and they still want them today. "My four top-selling flowers are roses, lilies, gerberas and alstromeria, in that order," says Carol Ahlfors, who bought the shop in June 2010 and changed its name to Blooms & Things. When she took over, she was told Islanders didn't buy roses. "That's anything but true. I sell an average of 150 rose stems a week. I get interesting rose colors such as bicolor, green, and black-reds such as 'Heart' roses, because Islanders like the unusual."

Carol is a slim brunette with a high ponytail, bangs, and dimples that rise right up to her eyes. She's got years of floral training and expertise behind her and was once the West Coast sales rep for Oasis, the company that makes floral foam. But if you look past the coolers, buckets, and vases, the ribbons and foam of the traditional florist shop, you might see Carol and her assistant at her work table hand-tying bouquets of Island-grown flowers. During the growing season, at least a third of her stock comes out of Island gardens, including her own. Carol herself got started with this shop when she sold her own flowers to the former owners.

During the growing season, Carol puts on the sidewalk a display of small $5 bouquets from her garden. "I sell 6-10 of these Island bouquets a week, and they've been instrumental in developing the community of folks that make up our customer base. I have regulars like elderly on fixed income, folks out of work, children/teens on limited incomes....all ask for them and are quite disappointed when they sell out."

When I got a tour of the Ahlfors cutting garden near Lande's Corner early one misty July morning, I expected to see more flowers. But then, the point of a cutting garden isn't for a blowsy display, petals dripping on paths under open skies. No, in a cutting garden, you CUT, when blooms are just opening, then tuck them into buckets of water in a cool dark place to condition for several hours—as she did with last night's cuttings, resting overnight in her garage. And you plan your garden to have just enough flowers all season long. "If the bloom came all at once, it wouldn't do me any good," she said.

The cutting garden sits in the larger lawn like a box made of deer fencing—and good thing, too, as a two-point buck was shopping around the yard for a snack. Her husband Chuck does much of the weeding and maintenance, giving his wife "time for the pretty stuff." Here they grow 20 David Austen and hybrid tea roses, 30 square feet of sweet peas grown in a trench of horse manure ("it's the British way"), and 40 dahlias she's kept going for eleven years by pulling them before winter. Asiatic and Oriental lilies tower next to a bed of catmint and herbs. Yellow yarrow, coreopsis, daisies, peonies, and penstemon hug the deer-fence. Scabiosa and tretelleia cover spring's french tulips. Carnations and sweet williams cover other bulbs. "There's a lot here planted in a small space." And that's just one area: outside the deer fence are 600 naturalized daffs, 200 hyacinths, euphorbias, mini callas and sea thistles (eyrngiums) that the deer have no taste for.

While her own flowers keep the cost of her "Island Bouquets" down, she also buys wholesale from several Island growers. When she gets a delivery, Carol recuts the stems into a warm water solution infused with sugar, pH balancer, and very small amount of bactericide. "Part of what you get with a professional florist is money spent on flower food, hydrating treatments, artful use of color and style and of course, great design! We're competing against Costco, Ikea, Trader Joes, so a florist MUST offer great customer service, long lasting product, good value for the price. All my arrangements come with a care tag, and I get complements all the time that my bouquets LAST. Music to my ears"

To that florist's goal—that her flowers flourish in the vase as long as possible—Ahlfors brings quite the set of credentials, starting with a degree in microbiology. After a career stint fighting infectious diseases, she turned to floriculture in the late 70s, studying at Cal-Poly, then in Holland. In 1986 she was inducted into the American Institute of Floral Designers and won the World Flower Council Award. She taught, repped for Oasis (inventors of floral foam), was published in trade magazines, and by 1994 when she left the industry, "was one of the top ten floral designers in the United States," she said. Along the way, she got a certificate in Ikebana Sogetsu school. She started selling her flowers to Blooms and worked part-time for them for 2-3 years until buying the shop in June 2010.

"Men buy for special occasions and want long-lasting arrangements. Women are more interested in color, style, making an impression; they buy for themselves or for hostess gifts. Blooms has many weekly contracts (restaurants or offices) and what we call "good husband" contracts where they pay in advance for a yearly subscription. That said, you also have to increase hang-time in your shop, so we have added gifts, housewares, some furniture and antiques, and work by local artists. A modern professional florist cannot depend only on holidays and occasions to sustain their business."

Other Island Growers

It's tough to make a living growing flowers. Competition from foreign growers, low prices set at Dutch auctions where prices descend until a buyer bites, and the Great Recession's hit on discretionary spending means that flower farming on Vashon is now a sideline, not a mortgage-lifter.

Carolina Nurik may be familiar to Islanders as co-founder of the Vashon Fruit Club. She also has a "huge cutting garden" at her Tahoma Farm near Raecoma on Maury Island. She grows things like larkspur, hydrangea, monarda, liatris, bells of Ireland. She'll dry yarrow or the pods of nigella or poppy, make Christmas wreaths with the colored stems of dogwood, kinky kiwi, or hazelnut. She used to sell to Seattle wholesalers, but found they don't pay enough to even cover transportation costs. "So this is more of a passion. I sell to people I LIKE, like Carol and others."

Dan Carlson of Kareli Farm on upper Maury also sells his sunflowers to Blooms & Things, as well as to the local Thriftway and to Metropolitan Market in Seattle. Like Carolina, he farms not for the income but because he's passionate about it—a former King County planner, he worked on the county's campaigns to pass bond issues to buy and preserve farmlands. "It is a hobby farm, and my income comes from other work (he teaches at University of Washington's Evans School of Public Affairs). So I had to think of a farm product that would not lose money and had efficiencies."

"How I got started in sunflowers is a funny story. I bought this land that was part of Kenny Larson's 150-acre red currant farm (people say it was once the largest red currant farm west of the Mississippi.) I started growing raspberries here in 1980 and made a confiture that I sold at specialty markets in and around Seattle. But this property is a little dry for raspberry production (it's a very dry, hilltop sandy loam), and it was hard to get labor, so the raspberries were waning. Then I took a booth at Seattle Tilth's 'Taste of Organic Seattle' festival, and I brought my jam and some sunflowers for booth decoration that had volunteered in my garden. And all these people made a beeline for my booth, not to buy my jam, but to look at my sunflowers. They'd say 'Oh, so beautiful…I grew up with…my grandmother grew…' The lightbulb in my head went click!—why struggle with something difficult to grow when I can grow something that WANTS to grow here? So a little bit at a time, I replaced the raspberries with sunflowers."

He found a partner in his daughter SonJa, who was 10 when he started planting sunflowers and liked to help, had a good eye for bouquets, and wanted spending money. They started growing 10-20 different varieties and colors of sunflower, from very pale yellow through reds and dark mahogany. Typically, harvest starts the 3rd week of July and goes into September, when he and whoever helps (SonJa'S now grown and gone) make up bouquets of 5-7 stems; he delivers them twice a week before work. He also sells at the VIGA Market, switching to sales of his chestnuts in the Christmas season. .

A pair of **Lavender Sisters** harvest fragrant wands from their separate properties. Merilee Runyan and her sister Katy Jo Steward, who has a lavender field and shared garden on the north end of Westside Highway, pick and deliver fresh-cut lavender twice weekly to the Metropolitan Markets in Seattle, Tacoma, and Kirkland. They make a family affair out of the harvests, inticing friends and family with a communal breakfast or a potluck dinner after the work is done. For several years they were among the lavender farms (plus Lavender Hill Farm, Fox Farm, and a couple other sites) that hosted a Vashon Lavender Farm Tour in mid-summer. One of them, **Lavender Hill Farm** in Burton, is open for u-picking lavender from bloom to July 31st; they sell oil, soaps, sachets, and other products made from their lavender.

In the Lisabuela area, **Mary Robinson** has grown flowers for just one discerning florist for 20 years. To this Madison Park shop she takes all kinds of things that have "that wild garden look"—forced branches of forsythia, plum, and apple, pussy willow, red current, and salmonberry. Blooming stems of fothergilla, crabapple, azalea, enkianthis, weigela, viburnum. Flowers of columbine, foxglove, baptisia, rue, sage, wild rose, umbels of parsley, and angelica, leaves of hosta, kiwi and mint. (When she got to the annuals, I couldn't bear to hear more). "It's completely organic. If I stick to what grows well here, I don't have pest or disease problems." She credits Tilth Producers' conferences for teaching her how to farm.

She considers herself a flower farmer, but she also teaches as a substitute at the local school. It's hard, she says, to live on the income from farming alone. She has used King County's tax exemption programs "because a couple thousand dollars off your expenses makes a HUGE difference, and I am benefitting the environment by providing food for birds and bees."

Zilla Copper of Calypso Gardens, who grows flowers on 115th off Bank Road, agrees. "It's not what most people would call a living—I could not pay a mortgage on what I make now. When I did flowers in Seattle and had a part-time summer job, no problem." She began by selling bouquets at the Village Green, then shifted to the Queen Anne Thriftway stores (now Metropolitan Markets) and Ballard Market before selling exclusively to the local Thriftway. When the economy went south, so did Thriftway's flower sales, so Zilla returned to the VIGA market with $5 and $10 dollar mixed bouquets, plus vegetables. She finds flowers much easier than growing vegetables, but vegetables sell better; thanks to her greenhouse, she can harvest 'French Breakfast' radishes and early greens for the first spring markets, then grow heat-loving vegetables all summer. "You make more money on flowers: you just weed and harvest. With veg, it's a way tougher deal. But I'm selling more: the economy's improving."

It's somewhat sad to drive by the ruins of the Beall greenhouses and see how forces beyond Islanders' control swamped such a big enterprise. But flowers keep blooming, and we keep buying them. Though flowers themselves may be short-lived, our love of them, our *need* for them, seems everlasting. That's what keeps Island flower farmers in business.

Is it Summer yet ... ?

Rain and chill breezes still dog the Island, but the occasional day of 60° winks at approaching summer. Pacific dogwoods bloom for the Spring Art Tour. Aubrieta, candytuft, lithodora spill in pastel pools over rock walls. Rhodie flowers and the last of the spring tulips fade, but soon the first rugosa roses open to release their cinnamon scent. In sunny abandoned spots, colonies of foxglove arise in graceful bloom.

In garden beds, the early spring plantings of peas and mustard are going to seed. The old is hoed under to make way for the summer garden: beans, tomatoes, basil, squashes and, for the truly hopeful, corn. Spinach and lettuce leaves thicken into lushness, making good hiding places for prowling slugs. Driplines are laid, lines and garden hoses tested for leaks. The grass needs a mow every day after tomorrow.

Those gardeners selected for the Vashon Allied Arts Garden Tour are growing compulsive, forever pulling that "last" weed or buying a last minute plant at DIG or Kathy's Corner before the June show. The garden centers, staffed up for the season, unload delivery trucks full of plants that hog space in the parking lots. Designer tomato cages in vivid colors are stacked for impulse purchase beside the check-out counters. The shelves stink of fertilizer and chemicals, as the gardener returns for another can of Sluggo.

Around the exceptional warm days, gray skies and rain malinger. Apples still need spraying against scab until the rains quit. Folks take umbrellas to the Fourth of July fireworks and perhaps to the Strawberry Festival a week later, where the namesake fruit is trucked in.

But by mid-July, a high pressure system settles in. Lavender bushes smoulder into blues and royal purples. The leaves of trees once soft with new growth darken, thicken. Gardeners, hot for the first time this season, seek cooling relief in the shade newly born.

Hoeing the rows together

Shared gardens teach, give sun and good soil to those that don't have it, and spread the bounty when there's more than one family can eat.

One April day, as I was gazing at the truckload of alpaca poo that friend Bill Green had just dumped into the back of my pick-up, I said to him, "My aunt says that in my next life, I'm going to be a farmer."

"Why wait?" said Bill, who at 78 is on his third farm and always happy for help. "Nathan wants me to expand the fencing around our vegetable patch from this weird L-shape into a rectangle that's easier to get his tractor into. We don't need the extra food, but if you want to put in a little time..."

And that's how I came to share the full-sun, alpaca-manured, twice-tilled vegie patch that I call GreenDale Garden. It's at Vashon Island Alpacas, just north of Sunrise Ridge, land that was the birthplace of Vashon's once-famous Olympic Berry. Today half the land is back in forest that Bill logs sustainably; the other half is given to pasturage for his herd of alpacas and to houses for himself and wife Lee, and his two sons Nathan and Harlan. From the top of his upper pasture on a clear day, you can see the entirety of that berry's namesake, the Olympic mountain range.

We agreed that he and Nathan would prep the soil, I would prepare the plants. After piling maple leaves and corn stalks on last summer's garden, he and crew would pile the alpaca poop on top, all winter long. Sometime in spring after the water table dropped, they'd swing one deer-fenced wall aside so Nathan could get the tractor in to till everything under. We would probably be planting by mid-April, first of May at the latest.

Meanwhile his wife Lee and I grew transplants, me for inside the fence, Lee for outside the fence where her squashes, cucumbers, and zucchini would be left alone by deer. Over Christmas, I ordered seed packets, worked up paper plans at GrowVeg.com, and read everything I could find about raised bed gardening. In February, I sowed flats of tomatoes, green onions, cabbage, lettuce, spinach, kale. As the plants grew in number, I started to wonder: how would we divide one 30' x 100' plot into areas his and mine?

Finally, in late April, Bill called. "There's rain scheduled for the next couple days, then high pressure and warmth coming for the rest of the month. When can you start?"

I came right after lunch, seedling flats in hand. And to my surprise, I found we were going to plant in rows. When I joined him inside the gate, he handed me one of two 4' stakes joined by a very long string. He had me plunge one stake into the ground, then he unwound the string as he walked across the plot, pulled the string taut, and shoved his stake into the dirt.

"So—we're not doing raised beds?" I lobbed into the cool air.

He shrugged, reaching for a bow rake leaning against the fence behind him. "I've done raised beds. They're a lot of work: lots of bending over and hand-weeding. This way, we can run a hoe up and down the rows, and it doesn't take any time at all."

He dragged the rake across the soil under the string, then to my utter amazement, Bill stepped right on the string and the soil beneath, walking up the line like a tightrope walker. I think I might have gasped, indoctrinated all winter by garden writers that you never, EVER walk on garden beds. I think he must have heard me, because he quickly said, "I once noticed that weeds sprouted fastest in footprints I'd left in the soil, so I figured, why not plant the seeds I want there?"

Turns out, since water moves upward via capillary action, Bill was just increasing groundwater's climb-ability. The reason water makes soil and other objects wet is that H_2O molecules love to glom onto other objects (what scientists call adhesion). As it grabs, it pulls along other H_2O molecules through surface tension, which expresses water's bonding nature to hold itself together at all costs. These forces of physics can send water climbing up narrow spaces, defying the force of gravity. But when the space between objects is too wide, water can't bridge the gap, gravity breaks its surface tension, and water collapses. This works whether the soil is clay or sand, as demonstrated by the rising wet in your footprints on a slightly wet beach.

Having tight-roped to the end, Bill flipped the rake and, as he walked back up the row, scribed a furrow where we would drop our seeds. I ripped open a sack of pea seeds, poked them into the furrow every two inches, then rubbed a handful of soil between my palms to cover the seeds loosely. As I stuck my finger to make a seed hole, I could feel the moisture in the darker soil underneath. We would not, it turned out, have to water much until mid-summer; the soil had enough water in it to make seeds swell, sprout, and rise up into the light. We planted rows every three or four feet, depending on the eventual size of the plants—over 25 rows in all.

As the weeks passed and our rows bristled with sprouting green, I came to love one of Bill's hoes, a Corona dagged hoe that could skim just under the surface of the earth. Using it felt like housework, like vacuuming a carpet: push push, walk walk, push push. Bill would follow, raking the uprooted weeds to the row's end, leaving behind a footprint-free dust mulch that would discourage new weed-seeds from germinating. At some point the alpacas would come gallumping down from the upper field and line up at the fence, eager to eat any weeds we'd toss over, their high-pitched mews and groans a sign of camelid delight.

This system worked great: in our 90-minute work sessions every Friday, we could weed between all the rows and have time left over for other tasks: putting in tomato cages, tying up vines, thinning out rows or planting a new row. By late May, we were harvesting radishes and early greens. But by mid-summer, we had a harvest bigger than we Dales and the Green clan could eat. In a spirit equal parts generosity and desperation, we agreed to start giving produce to the food bank. So every Tuesday morning during my volunteer stint, I would swing by the farm and pick up the extra chard, kale, lettuce, spinach, beans, even tomatoes and corn that we couldn't handle ourselves. By season's end, we had given half the plot's harvest to the Food Bank—nearly 500 pounds worth, and a win-win for all.

The Lutheran Church Garden

When I reach the food bank's back door loaded up with produce from GreenDale Garden, I'll often find James Dam there, weighing in his sacks of vegetables from the Lutheran Church garden.

In spring 2004, members of the Lutheran Church, envisioning a garden full of vegetables to help the food bank, asked director K. C. Pilon what she might like to receive. Her reply: "anything but zucchini—we get plenty of that from Island gardeners."

The set-up of this earliest garden to support the food bank became a real community effort, as a *Beachcomber* article by Nancy Brenner reported: "The Food Bank passed along a big bag of Ed Hume seeds. Blue Moon Farm [run by Margaret Hoeffel, Martin Koenig, and Jean Bosch] provided a rare purple bean. Kathleen Odekirk started plants in her greenhouse. True Value donated deer fencing and four bags of lime. Island Tofu donated okara, the nutrient-rich waste from tofu production. Jim Biel provided wood chips for paths between the 32" x 25' beds."

The school's hort program coordinator, Mary Robinson, suggested that the Lutheran's garden grow summer crops, as the high schoolers were already raising seedlings for spring crops. Maintenance of the garden quickly settled into Tuesday morning work parties of 3-5 people. They grow beans, chard, lettuce, cole crops, peas, corn, raspberries, and garlic on a clay loam soil. Eight years later, though their backs are older and the need isn't as great, the Lutherans are still growing and giving produce to the food bank.

The Food Bank Farm & Garden

Island gardeners have long given their zucchini and other excess home-grown to the food bank. Washington-grown fruit and vegetables also come from Northwest Harvest. But for the other ten months of the year, the food bank didn't have much fresh food to offer.

Yvonne Pitrof took over the food bank in September 2004 and quickly "started to fantasize about our food bank being surrounded by gardens," she told me. It's easy to visualize: the location on Sunrise Ridge enjoys full sun, good soil, water, and easy access for deliveries of soil amendments, lumber, or power equipment. And as the Great Recession worsened after the winter of 2007-08, so did the need for fresh food: Vashon's clientele increased 25%, going from an average of 150 households per week to a high of 210.

Hard times have often brought back the popularity of vegetable gardens, and by 2008, the idea of growing your own seemed in the air, everywhere. Seed catalogs reported record sales. The locavore and farmers' market movements went into high gear. The summer of 2008, Vashon College ran a 6-part lecture series called "The Sustainability Series: The care and feeding of Vashon," which started with a talk on "Feeding Ourselves." That November,

George Page's Sea Breeze Farm opened a retail market and restaurant serving its own farm-grown meats and produce. In January, over 60 people showed up for VIGA's class on "Raising Your Own Vegetables," prompting instructors Nancy Lewis-Williams and Cathy Fulton to schedule another class a month later. By March 2009, as First Lady Michelle Obama planted a vegetable garden at the White House, Islanders were phoning Kathy's Corner for work crews to help them install their own raised-bed vegetable gardens.

Bitten by the same planting bug, Pitrof took a proposal to Vashon Rotary Club in Spring 2009, asking for help to start a food-producing garden at Sunrise Ridge. Rotary agreed to donate monies for lumber and deer fencing; volunteers from the club set up the fence. Neil Jungemann recruited friends to help him build a wooden tool shed. Folks with tractors came and tilled up the thick sod. Volunteers, many of them food bank customers, dug a dozen raised beds on either side of a central path. Farmers donated transplants. The first seeds and seedlings were planted that May.

Thinking that more is better, another volunteer encouraged Pitrof to meet with David Kirkland, whose Happy Garden Farm on Maury Island had fallow land. Kirkland was slowly persuaded to let the food bank use a quarter-acre for a pilot project. King County United Way gave $10,000 for supplies and a coordinator, with the understanding that excess produce would be sent to White Center's Food Bank, which had a garden not nearly large enough for a clientele of 5000 families. Jenn Coe, a long-time food bank volunteer and seasoned Island gardener, was hired as coordinator. The beets, greens, and garlic at Happy Garden did well enough, but not the host: David Kirkland died that December, and the project had to find a new home. On Wax Orchard Road at 240th, homeowners Amy Greenberg and Chris Robison offered use of a half-acre they weren't using, and United Way kicked in another $25,000 in general funds, "in large part because of what we were doing and continuing to do on the farm," Pitrof said.

This fenced, sun-soaked field held a row-crop and hoophouse operation growing popular, high-nutrient veggies such as spinach, chard and kale, peas and carrots, broccoli and cabbage, beets, beans, and winter squash, with two hoophouses growing tomatoes and basil. Jenn Coe got seedlings from many sources: for instance, the garden club donates their unsold tomatoes after their big spring sale. In early spring, she runs her "Foster Seedling" program, lending a flat and pack of seed to any volunteer who'll raise seedlings at home until Jenn's ready to plant in the field. "Most folks do a single flat," she said. "The farmers tend to do more." Langley Fine Gardens and Pacific Potager donated plants, as did Island Meadow, Pacific Crest, Alli-Lanphear farms and the high school horticulture program after their sales.

But after the donations, the field still has to be tilled, planted, weeded, and harvested. That's dozens of long rows of crops, more than Jenn and her part-time intern can handle alone. So every Monday, Jenn sends out email calls for anyone who can come help during the 3-hour work parties. And people come—one, two, a group at a time. One or two high school students getting in their required hours of community service before graduation. Moms and their preschool children. Youth from AmeriCorps. Teams from businesses, churches, nonprofits, or clubs like Kiwanis or the Rotary often come get their hands dirty. The farm field was plowed by Phil Bomber, Dave Church, Cliff Lindgren, John Burggraff, and Jennifer Williams, while Herbie Beck tilled the plot near the food bank. And of course, food bank clientele can come help at the farm, or garden whatever they wish to grow at the Sunrise Ridge garden.

The farm, with its short list of sure-fire crops, produces food nearly all year: Coe has led harvesting parties at the farm as late as December 27, and leeks, greens, and cole crops overwinter well. And each April, as foster seedling flats bristle with green and the water-table starts to sink, the "tractor-angels" fill their tanks and inquire when the field might be dry enough to plow. With all that community help, in its first full season the food bank grew and gave away over 6000 lbs of produce—more than enough to distribute here and across the water. And that's been the goal: to use our plentiful land-base to produce more than enough food to share.

It's a great thing to open the refrigerator at the food bank and see it stuffed with crates and grocery bags loaded with fresh food. Out in the distribution area, shelves of crates filled with potatoes, tomatoes, and cucumbers are tipped toward the clientele, frilled by the greenery of curly kale and carrots, spinach and basil. Whether it comes from hobby gardens, from subsidized farms or from Northwest Harvest, it's all fresh, good, locally-grown food. By Wednesday night, it's all gone—being eaten at tables around the Island or heading in the Food Bank's truck to hungry folks across the water.

The Garden at Vashon Community Care

In 2006, garden club member and former teacher Julia Lakey created a small vegetable garden at the Island's nursing home. Her mother lived at VCC for years, and Julia thought a vegetable garden would be tasty for the residents as well as remind them of family gardens in their past.

Designed in a circle, the garden was planted in snap peas, cole crops, lettuce, potatoes, squash, and beans. But watering was always a problem: it was expensive, and volunteers weren't available to run a hose over the parking lot and keep traffic off it. And while she could give her crops to staff and volunteers, food safety regulations forbade serving them to the elderly, who are considered vulnerable to food-borne bacteria.

In 2012, inspired by a dry garden created by Paul Gautschi in Sequim (with half the rainfall of Vashon), Julia decided to try his "Back to Eden" method—watering seeds only until they germinate, then give beds a deep mulch to retain rainwater. Over the winter she piled on a 12-16" deep mulch of wood chips mixed with food-grade okara, the residue from tofu-making at Island Spring Tofu factory. Though winter compressed the mulch to 4", Julia tucked in transplants in late March and, though rain dwindled after April, gave the widely-spaced plants no extra water. By August, unwatered for two months, her cabbage, broccoli, chard and kale were sturdy and the corn shoulder high. She plans to add more chips and amendments this winter for larger harvests and fewer weeds next season.

In 2013, Julia undertook training for Food Safety Certification. Two members of VIGA who grow for the school district mentored her plan. Her efforts were rewarded when the kitchen manager started to incorporate her vegetables into residents' meals.

Sharing the Sun

On the upper Westside is a vegie patch big enough to feed a restaurant. On the grounds of the lavender farm he was caretaking back in the 1990s, Fred Johnson dreamed of planting the "homegrown" he'd need for a new diner he'd call Fred's Homegrown. He tilled under a quarter-acre of field for the project, opened the Vashon restaurant sometime around the century's turn, then found—no surprise—that the restaurant took up all his time.

But instead of leaving homeowners Katy Jo Steward and Steve Pasquall to care for "more rows than any two people need," as Katy Jo put it, he paired them up with a series of couples who needed garden space in the sun. One of those couples, gardening here for over ten years now, is John and Vicki Browne. Down in the alders of Paradise Valley, they run Judd Creek Nursery, propagating and selling native plants like nootka rose, wild hazelnut, native crabapple, currants, and huckleberries, camas root, trilliums, and three species of native strawberry. The site's too shady to grow anything eatable besides peas, berries, and leafy green stuff, so a couple times a week, the Brownes drive up north into the light of the lavender farm.

Because there's plenty of room within this fenced garden, each couple can garden as they please. To the east are the older tilled beds, and there in the 40' x 80' space, the Brownes grow a glorious sprawl of food: bean teepees, brussel sprouts, squash vines entangling the ankles of corn. To the west past the lovely garden house are plantings in a formal circle. Here Katy Jo and Steve have planted 42 heirloom roses, edged with boxwood, the paths covered with wood chips. In the center run three 14"-high raised beds, each nearly 30' long. Red-stemmed chard guards a tangle of everbearing strawberries. A short trellis holds cherry tomatoes. Clouds of curly parsley front cabbage. Tidy checkerboards of food.

Katy Jo said of the timbered beds, "It's sooo much easier to weed now." John, still a little stiff after a horrible winter accident (in the aftermath of a snowstorm, he was chainsawing a road-blocking tree when a car slid into him) also appreciates the raised beds. "You can sit on the edge to weed and harvest, rather than grub around on your hands-n-knees." When I mentioned the pests I saw nestled into cabbages during my first visit, years before, John laughed and said, "Yes, we used to use plasti-mulch on the paths, but they are a slug-haven, so we replaced the cloth with wood-chips."

Katy Jo loves their mutual arrangement. ""It's very pleasant to be out in your garden and be with somebody you like. One of the wonderful things (besides that we love them) is that they are expert gardeners: they understand the process and the soil and they know plants, and they don't have sun where they live. The soil here is crappy clay—it's like farming cement—but we have just kept working it, adding lime, compost by the truckload, cover-crop every winter, tilling it in. Mostly we take care of our own spaces, but we share on amendments, buy cover-crop together."

John offered this advice: "Perodically discuss your philosophies about gardening. You want to know what people consider a weed. We've had people who liked lamb's quarter, chickweed, goosefoot. Earl and Angie planted a tea-bed of camomile ten years ago: there's still a little of it here. When we were all several households doing this together, out of common courtesy we'd take all the common weeds out, save seeds, then re-introduce them. You wouldn't want some calendula by chance, would you?"

"I really recommend garden-sharing," said Katy Jo. "It's wonderful. And it's good to share the sun whenever you can."

Vashon Cohousing

West of town on Bank Road and down a short gravel lane, you'll find the Vashon Island Cohousing Community. As of 2012, 32 adults and their kids live here in 18 cottages clustered on four acres within twelve of wetlands and woods. The funky, wood-shingled cottages, swaddled in by perennial beds and orchard trees, have a cozy proximity to each other, embodying the cohousing philosophy of Living in Community.

The complex sits on land that once grew strawberries for Masa Mukai, one of the Japanese-American berry farmers that were so successful here in the first half of the 20th century. On the grounds are some elderly fruit trees from an old orchard, including a variety called "Duchess of Oldenburg." But most of the trees were planted after the houses were built, according to Mark Musick, one of the members who envisioned and helped found Vashon Cohousing back in December 1989. "The opportunity for individuals to have garden space, the intention to plant berries and fruit trees throughout the landscape, were in our goals from the very beginning," Mark told me. "However, we didn't start planting fruit trees and berries until after we completed our construction phase, which was a little over a decade ago. First we transplanted a few apple trees from Pete Svinth's orchards on Maury Island (now Pacific Crest Farm), and then we began planting apples, pears and plums. More recently we planted a couple beds of blueberries, and we're talking about planting raspberries on our south border."

When you buy into cohousing, not only here but elsewhere, you buy into the idea that You're All In This Together. This includes putting in several hours a month on maintaining the shared spaces: roads, paths, lawns, a large dining lodge and meeting space called the Commons House, playgrounds, perennial beds, orchard trees—anything owned in common that needs work. But these tasks don't just magically happen: it takes somebody pushing from behind to set dates, appoint tasks, round up tools and materials. In 2012, that person (at least for the gardening) was Rick Edwards.

With a be-spectacled, goatee'd face and thin build, Rick looks like he belongs under a pith helmet—until you hear his sweet Tennessee accent. He was a registered nurse at Virginia Mason; six years ago he moved into cohousing and a year later took WSU's Master Gardener program, all day every Tuesday for six weeks ("What a hassle commute for Island folks THAT is," he confided). Once on cohousing's site committee, he became the garden's shepherd. "We ID projects that need work, focusing on the gardens twice a year. For instance, when the fruit is ripe, we have a work party to pick the fruit. It's counted, divided across the households, and then I send out an email. '35 apples per family, now in the Commons—come get 'em!'"

It was Rick who enlisted Dr. Bob's advice on how to prune and restore the community's fruit trees. During the Fruit Club's summer pruning workshop, we descended on the complex to see the winter pruning he and other cohousers had done that winter. Growing amid the steep-roofed houses, the orchard trees provide shade and privacy screening as much as fruit. Apples, black cherries, peach and plum, pears asian, bartlett, and seckel, even figs spread their limbs over perennials and shrubs; more remnant apple trees line the entrance drive. Knowing that fruit trees often need spraying, I asked Rick how he fits this task around the presence of children. His answer bespoke the cohousing ideals of cooperation and communication. "If I just start blasting away, people might say 'We don't know what you're doing, so talk to us … what's your plan, what products are you using, are they organic and safe?' So I always use organic products with a sticking agent, I wear a mask, and I warn people that I'm going to be spraying the trees but I'll be done in an hour. If the kids must come out, then I'll stop."

Gardening as a community, he's noticed, pulls in the little ones. "The youngest kids are the most helpful in the garden. They get out there with

Mom or Dad, use their play shovel, learn how to identify weeds and how to pull them. It's a 'learning about nature' thing. Once they get to be ten or eleven, they could care less."

Along cohousing's southern fence lie the pea-patch beds, one for every household that wants one. They're 4' wide by 15-30' long, in companionable rows side-by-side, with black agri-cloth holding down weeds between them. Not all households take one (some farm in the coop next door), but most do because it's a fenced sunny site with the best soil on the property. If you want to raise vegetables in cohousing, here's your spot.

The soil is challenging—clayey and cobbley and over glacial till—but it's got a fine crumb from years of amending. The garden committee takes soil samples after harvest, tucks in a cover crop for the winter, then amends in late winter before assigning beds. When I visited in late June, two beds still held cover crops of buckwheat and red clover. "This is pretty good soil," said Rick. "The reports from UMass lab said it has plenty of organic matter, but it's low on minerals so we should be cover-cropping in deep-rooted things that will pull minerals to the surface. The areas longest used are low on phosphorus and calcium, so we've been actively amending those areas."

With some of cohousing's budget set aside for garden improvements, Rick and his "hard-core group" installed driplines with manual turn-offs at each bed. And what a difference water makes. When I first visited after an August drought, the gardens looked dry, weed-scragged, worn out. When I visited again just after the next year's June solstice, the beds were full of ready-to-eat produce, a testament to good tending, a week's worth of rain, and the cresting light of the solstice. Poppies blared their trumpets next to blue-green cauliflower. Snap peas ran up their strings. Looseleaf frilled beside fat cabbages, next to red beets color-rhyming with 'Russian Red' kale. Standing hoops testified to plants wintered over, anticipations of new seedlings to be sown for fall. Everything looked fresh and appealing. "None of this makes it to the Food Bank," said Rick. "We trade amongst ourselves."

Two areas are communal plots for sprawling crops like squash or potatoes. When they're ripe, the gardening crew harvests everything, then divides the bounty into bags for every household. Then Rick sends out another email to all: "The potatoes (or apples or pears) are available in the Commons House. Come help yourself."

Thinking back to those dog-days of August, I suspect that cohousing's gardening has room for both moods of *homo communitas:* our need for individual expression and for communal effort. Here, a group pushes the whole garden to its optimum condition, then gives up control to individuals pumped for spring. As seasonal energies peak for gardens and gardeners, the tired gardener is probably happy to return her bed to the group's control for their garden-nerdy rituals of Test and Amend.

Is it easier to step up to the task when you know you'll be working together, shoulder to shoulder? The answer's a resounding YES! at the next property south, just beyond cohousing's back gate.

Shoulder-to-Shoulder Farm

Just the other side of Cohousing's south fence, through a gate holding up the word "Farm" in iron curlicues, you come to a much larger joint venture in gardening. Long beds hold kales, cabbages, carrots, or are buried under scratchy tangles of turban squash and long-pie pumpkin. If it's a Monday morning, you'll find a dozen or so workers, mostly women and younger men, bent over the rows to scratch out weeds or harvest what's ripe. This is Shoulder-to-Shoulder Farm, a collective of (in 2012) eleven families, u-pickers and gleaners that has farmed this acre together for over six years.

S2S Farm is not part of Vashon Cohousing, but its founding mother, Margaret Hoeffel, has been a cohousing resident since 1994 and started (with Jean Bosch) "Blue Moon Farm" in 2000. For years they ran a winter CSA, cultivating 37 raised beds and three hoophouses on a fertile acre, serving two dozen CSA subscribers, plus the farmers' market and Minglement. But in Pamela Woodroffe's book on island agriculture, *"Tales of the Tilth,"* Margaret admitted that working one acre wasn't economically viable. She was farming seven days a week, while raising three children with partner Martin Koenig. After Jean Bosch left to do realty, she and intern Renee pressed on, but eventually, she admitted to me, "My body gave out."

An alternative way to use the land came knocking from next door: Dana Schuerholz, who was running Homestead Wilderness School on neighboring acreage, asked Margaret if her school's families could use the Blue Moon land to grow crops for themselves. Her group had the hands, Margaret the land, tools, driplines, expertise—so why not work together? Perhaps hoping that many hands might make light work, Margaret agreed.

"The idea was, we'd work out a budget for seed, water, lease, insurance, all these expenses, divide that by the number of people who agreed to work, and they paid up front," Margaret told me. "Dana and I were managers: she led February through June 21, and then I would take over for the fall-winter crop. The goal was for everybody to be learning, so someday we wouldn't need a manager." Everybody was to work six hours a week.

The plan started with ten families, each paying around $325 for the full season. Usually Moms with kids in tow would arrive every Monday morning and work as much of their six-hour shift as possible. But by year three, it was plain to Margaret that that the six-hour requirement wasn't working: too many catch-up hours at the end of the season, too many members splitting their memberships with inexperienced newcomers and creating a big, unwieldy group. So at the next winter planning retreat, she suggested "a four-hour work session, no half-shares, everybody's equal, and we do a monthly three-hour work party to blast through the projects we fall behind on." And everyone responded "Four hours? That sounds nice!"

Six years on, the four-hour system is going strong. Margaret described a group that had grown in expertise and commitment, with enough energy left over to spearhead projects like a new greenhouse for winter crops, funded by a no-interest loan from one of the member families. "Within the four hour system, everybody is learning, taking responsibility. And now I don't have to do so much—I too work only four hours a week" (instead of the 30 hours of her Blue Moon days).

But Margaret is still a leader: when I visited, she was at the head of a hand-n-knees weeding gang working down a long row of broccoli underplanted with clover. She gestured another young mom over: Hedy Anderson, in an Outback hat and black yoga skimpies, a candymaker whose King Caramels are a VIGA Market hit. When I asked Hedy why she was a member, she replied, "Because it's just the greatest thing—why WOULDN'T you want to garden with your friends and grow all this beautiful produce in so few hours? I think more people should try gardening this way!"

With a little basket of coriander seeds on her elbow, Hedy hopped and strode about the long raised beds, pointing out the chubby turban-head squashes, the garlic hanging like shrunken heads in the storage shed, walking me into the greenhouse with flats of spinach and parsley scheduled for planting that day. When I asked her how they divvy up food, she pointed to a clipboard on a worktable. "That lists how many of each crop we can take each week. Or, I look over a row, figure I can take a tenth of what's ripe. Or, (gesturing to harvest boxes in the shade) I take a tenth of these beans."

Next stop: the first of two tomato houses, trellised with Stupice, Momotaro, Carmello, and Black: "My super favorite ever: it's early, acidic, maroon-red inside, delicious." In the other hoophouse grew the weird-colored ones like Valencia, Lillian's Yellow, Green Zebra, SunGold cherries just for popping in your mouth. "We definitely get enough tomatoes to sauce here."

She led me past the walls of beans, where we discovered Criss Fournier picking bush beans. Hedy told me, "She's trying out for a substitute position: if one of us can't make it, we call in a substitute who works for a day's share." The group has other flex-plans. Three U-picker shares are sold in January for $250 each; when there's a big crop of something, the U-pickers are invited to, say, come and pick X-pounds of tomatoes. The U-picker weighs her day's haul and deducts its value from $250, picking enough by season's end to zero-out her investment. There's a gleaner's share for $120 owned by Mark Musick: when a row needs to be cleared out, he's given a deadline to pick it clean before the row is tilled under.

Looking over the long rows with names like "Moon Bed," "Grandmother Bed," "Sunrise Field 1 and 2," at all the sun-tanned shoulders and hatted heads bent to the farming work, it looked to me that Shoulder-to-Shoulder Farm was wildly successful: the farm is the embodiment of abundance. And the members are up for more. Near the entrance, the frames of two big hoophouses were up, waiting for their poly covers. Hedy said, "A couple of winters ago, we lost all our winter crops to that big freeze. This new member, Mike Yates, who has an engineering background, at the annual winter retreat proposed, 'Let's get a big greenhouse so we can have more winter crops.' He found, online, a Poulsbo farm wanting to sell their two hoophouses for $5000. We didn't know how we'd come up with the money, but then member Renee said, 'My husband and I will loan the group the $5000 and you can pay us back, zero interest, over five years.' So now each of us pays $100 extra a year as our part of the greenhouse loan. Some of us went to Poulsbo; Mike had it all figured how to take them apart. Took a couple days to move them here, but then, we have more time than money."

Margaret seemed a little wry at the notion that her old farm might regain some of its winter emphasis. "With two more greenhouses to grow winter crops in, we will have to ask ourselves whether we do without the winter break, whether we have the energy to farm all year round."

Energy, on this sunny morning, seemed far from running low. When I asked about fruit plants, Hedy talked about planting dwarf fruit trees. The U-pickers were out picking. The weeders were still scratching through the broccoli row. Member Karen Bower was peeling garlic in the shade of a big maple. The only person not completely into it was Hedy's son Finnbar, flexing his playstation muscles on the stoop of the kid's playhouse.

Hedy dropped her basket of coriander seeds on the worktable next to Karen, picked up a clove. "So today we're holding our first-ever pickle party. The garden is pretty squared away at this point, so we have the time. We're going to make three kinds of pickles: some garlic dills, some with these coriander seeds, and some bread-n-butter pickles—they're sitting on ice in the Commons House right now."

I ask Karen why she comes all this way to garden. She said, "I love working out there with everyone. My place doesn't really have a good spot for a vegetable garden: it's in the shade, deer are all over the place, and it's just me, so creating a space would be a lot of work. Then I happened upon this…"

She indicated, with a toss of a shoulder, the many raised beds, the grow-houses, the border of beneficial flowers, the playhouse under the shade of the big maple, even a Maypole.

I put the same questions to member Tracy Barrett. "I like to learn, and I can't plant everything at my place—don't have enough room for all the kale I want. And farming with friends is so much better."

I couldn't agree more. When you hoe the rows together, your garden yields more than healthful food or weed-free rows. You sow the seeds of friendship and harvest sweet memories—and those are crops beyond price.

2012 full members of Shoulder-to-Shoulder Farm: Margaret Hoeffel, Hedy Anderson, Amy Wolfe, Elizabeth Randall, Lynann Politte, Renee Marceau, Risa Stahl, Mike Yates, Tracy Barrett, Lauryth Johns, Karen Bowers, and Annika Fae.

Growing an Island Tomato

Yes, we can grow flavorful tomatoes here on Vashon. You just have to apply a few tricks picked up from Island growers.

2000 miles north of its native home, the tomato has a tough time growing well around Puget Sound. Instead of the constant sun and 70° temperature of its native Andean mountains, an Island tomato may endure drought, gray skies, chilly nights, and August rains that bring on late blight just when the fruit's turning red. It may never ripen at all.

If you're growing tomatoes in your garden, you may look at your pale green fruit and wonder if they're ever going to be better than deep-fried hockey pucks. Then you head to the farmers market and see (with great envy) LOTS of big, ripe tomatoes for sale. The tables of farms like Hogsback, Pacific Crest, or GreenMan are laden with tomatoes red, green, yellow, and striped, round, pointed or multi-lobed, small as a nickel or big as a baby's head. Now these folks know how to grow a Puget Sound tomato.

But you can too if you borrow some of their techniques. For one of my first articles for the *Beachcomber*, I asked local growers how they managed to grow such beautiful tomatoes. Let's revisit them as they grow on toward the VIGA Market's "Tomato Taste-off" at the end of August.

How our farmers grow those ripe tomatoes

By mid-February, Michelle Crawford is sowing tomato seeds in plug flats on her kitchen counter. Her farmstand on the south end, Pacific Potager, is famous for the dozens of tomato varieties she's trialed in our climate. By mid-April, she's selling her plants at the farmers' market; each in its 4" pot is about a foot high, some with a flower or two. She'll sell plants into May, then by mid-July switch to selling ripe tomatoes at her farmstand. "A home grower can only grow so many plants, but in high summer they can come here to my farmstand and try many more varieties. Each variety has a slightly different taste," she said. I can easily see buying a whole tomato sampler.

Inside her plastic hoophouses are long, slightly raised beds, each covered with black agri-cloth punctured every couple feet with an 8" hole. "My parents come in May to help plant all the tomato plants. Someone digs a hole, someone else throws in a quarter-cup of Down-to-Earth organic fertilizer (4-6-2) and a couple tablespoons of bone meal to prevent blossom-end rot (adds calcium). Then we bury the plants to just below their their top leaves, as roots will develop along the underground stem. Once the plants are in, we water with a little fish fertilizer to help with transplanting shock."

Michelle's method is typical of the Island's small farmers: using seedlings they've grown themselves, they plant under cover to control conditions and get the earliest ripening. Because the farmers want to sell fruit over a long season, many grow both early bush plants to have fruit by July, then see out the season with indeterminate viners that ripen in mid-season (August) and keep ripening fruit as long as the plant is still growing. A covered situation like a greenhouse or tunnel intensifies the heat and thus speeds ripening, so these growers can get a 90- or 100-day tomato like 'Brandywine' to market while it still feels like summer (well, maybe Indian Summer). This method is an investment—plastic and pipe for a tunnel or hoophouse, irrigation lines, plug-flats, probably grolites for the seedlings—but it works.

Up at Timken Farm above Colvos Passage, Mark Timken sows his to-mato seeds indoors into 72-cell flats. The flats are set on heating coils, then when the plants extend their cotyledon leaves, they're moved to an unheated greenhouse in full sun. "I don't see how you can grow good tomatoes without some kind of covered system," Mark Timken told me. "I've tried it and it doesn't work: our climate is too cold and wet." Mark keeps a weather-eye out: temperatures dipping into the 40s can stunt a young tomato seedling, so he keeps some reemay cloth ready to throw over the tableful of seedlings to give them about 5° more warmth. When it gets too hot (over 90°), he'll roll up the plastic sides of the hoophouse to let cool air in.

Once the seedlings get their first true leaves, they're transplanted into 4x6" pots with an enriched soil mix. "Our ratio is three parts potting soil, one part worm castings, 1/3 cup of fertilizer per pot. The plant's going to live in that pot, planted pretty deep, until tranplanted into the soil under the hoophouse. When they get to the point where they're 12-18" tall, getting thick, roots filling out the pot, then we put them into the ground."

Every farmer stressed enriching soil with good compost or amendments. Rob Peterson of Plum Forest Farm puts a lot of effort into making high-quality compost (see the compost chapter). "Test your soil to see if liming is necessary," he mentioned; the calcium found in ag-lime, bone meal, or wood ash helps prevent blossom-end rot, those brown blemishes on first fruits caused by a plant's inability to draw calcium from the cooler soils of spring. Other farmers advised loosening garden beds with a broadfork, avoiding nitrogen-heavy fertilizers (grow fruit, not so many leaves), and avoiding soil that has grown tomatoes, potatoes, or peppers in recent years.

By early May, most farmers' tomatoes are in hoophouse ground. Shorter bush types may be growing into tomato cages; the taller indeterminates will each have its own stake, or perhaps a stout wire or jute-line hanging from overhead horizontals. In Paradise Valley, Karen Biondo grows 'Stupice', 'Oregon Spring', and 'Early Girl' in her hoophouse, among many that she uses in her pizza wagon at the farmers market. Her tomato beds run down either side of a central path, each plant a single stalk wrapped around a string stretched to a horizontal wire above her head. She removes the extra leaders, excess branches, suckers rising from branch crotches. Summer growth pumps out more foliage than the plant needs to build sugars in the fruit, so that too gets pruned to improve the plant's air circulation. "I am a ruthless sucker pruner on our indeterminate varieties. The plants will get 8' tall and loaded with fruit. Be ruthless! Your tomatoes will thank you for it!"

When flowers start to show, it's time to open up the hoophouse to pollinators. If it's too cool for bumblesbees to do their thing, then you can be the pollinator. Biondo explained that when a tomato flower is shaken, the pollen grains on each flower will loosen and vibrate down into the flower's ovary. Usually this happens when a visiting bumblebee does her "shimmy-dance" on the flower—but if she's not around, you can do the shaking. Pollen gets tacky and won't fall into place when temperatures climb above 90°, so to keep fruit pollinating, open doors or turn on fans to let the heat out.

By mid-July, the first tomatoes are ripening, but as Biondo warned me when I visited, their taste might disappoint. She handed me a Stupice tomato, an extra-early variety then ripening for two weeks. It was plenty sweet—and then she handed me a later variety, a fruit off an Early Girl. It was red, alright, but mealy in taste and texture. And that was her point. "They are not really ripe, they're just red. I think we spend too much angst and energy trying to get the earliest tomato, which is not necessarily the best. The most delicious tomato is sweetened by the warm summer sun. How can we taste that before we have a good run of heat?"

Looped around each plant in her hoophouse was a coil of weep-hose. By depending on irrigation instead of rain, the grower gains some useful controls. Ripening can be encouraged by treating the plant to a little drought, which tells the plant "It's your last chance to reproduce, so get on with making those seed-carrying fruits!" As fruit ripens, its skin becomes less flexible; if the fruit absorbs a storm's worth of water, the skin may crack a little on the shoulders (not a problem), then a lot, opening the fruit to mold.

August often brings heavy rain and another reason growers are glad to be growing undercover: they don't want late blight. Once this fungus is in the soil, rain or overhead irrigation splash spores from infected soil up on the plants. Within days, long dark splotches grow up the trunk, the branches, then the fruit, which turn tan and taste like pencil erasers. Copper spray is a good preventative, but it's a better strategy to have a roof over the plants. Once late blight hits your plants, uproot them ASAP and get rid of the plants—and NOT in the compost bin.

By August, mid-season tomatoes grown in full sun should be ripening. If it's a good tomato year, even the 100-day heirlooms like Brandywine or Beefsteak stand a chance. At Hogsback Farm down in Dilworth, the soil just inches from their drip-lines was dry as dust in the hoophouse. But their heirloom tomatoes—Red Zebra, Green Zebra, Pink Brandywine, Ruby Gold, Japanese Black Trifele—were pruned and trained, easy to pick, market ready. The farm manager Bryan Lowry showed me how to tell when a non-red tomato is ripe: press on the bottom blossom end and if it gives a little, it's probably ripe.

How a hobby gardener can grow good tomatoes

After taking these tours to see how the "pros" grow their tomatoes, I felt I had half a chance of tomato success. Plus, I grow tomatoes not only in my "hole in the woods" garden, but at the alpaca farm where tractor tilling, alpaca poo, and full sun gives advantages my place doesn't have.

Each year in early March, into the kitchen I drag a closet-sized contraption I call "The Start Cart"—a four-shelf, plastic-wrapped greenhouse on wheels from True Value. Under three grolites hanging side-by-side, I park two flats sown with seeds—tomatoes and onions usually, but anything that's better started indoors. A heat-mat warms the air inside the cart to 60°; when the grolites are on, the temperature rises past 80°. Clear domes keep the flats from drying out; when I see the first shoots emerge, the domes come off.

In my Start Cart, the young tomatoes grow in their 1" cells until they have true leaves. This first soil has no fertilizer: I learned the hard way that seedlings are very sensitive to over-feeding. For instance, though your compost pile might happily sprout with tomato plants, tomato babies do not respond well to being planted in straight compost. Nor can they take much fertilizer. One year I got impatient with seedlings stuck in cotyledon stage for three weeks and tried to nudge them along with what I thought was a weak solution of a tablespoon of fish fertilizer in a gallon of water. Turns out, that was nearly full strength; within an hour of their forced feeding, my tomato babies were bent over like they were trying to hurl. Panicked, I spritzed them with pure water, then purged the soil by dunking the whole flat in the bathrub. No luck. By 4pm, I was giving each plant its own sponge bath, each leaf draped over one finger while I dabbed it tenderly with a warm sponge. By evening—whew!—they'd perked up, and by the next day were indeed putting out first true leaves. Still,10-15% of my seedings didn't survive. My rule of thumb now is, if the plants are at 10% of their plant-out size, use a 10% dilution of the full-strength feed, and so on proportionally.

Slowed growth can also be a sign that they want to be potted on. When the first pair of true leaves unfurl, I pot the tomatoes into 4" pots, 15 to a flat. Then, day by day I chase the sun, moving the flats from east morning windows to south kitchen light by lunch. Indoors they'll grow to several inches high as I start feeding them more often. When roots show, growth stalls, leaves droop or turn yellow, I pot them on into gallon pots.

When nights warm near the 50s, I move the plants outside into a little 5x5' greenhouse. On sunny spring days, the temperatures inside climb past 80°—just what a young tomato plant needs. Middays, I'll move the plants outdoors for a couple hours to start the hardening-off process, covering them with an arch of wire fencing to protect against deer.

When nighttime temperatures settle over 50°—usually by mid-May—it's safe to plant tomatoes into the ground. Some folks like Joe & Tony of Monument Farm plant their tomatoes earlier because they've got a protected, warm site. You can risk cooler nights if you have such a situation or if you cover your plants with reemay or plastic film—just check the long-range weather forecast for the occasional late April storm.

Here's how I fill an 8x3' raised bed with bush tomatoes. I first roll out some black permeable plastic-mulch cloth over the bed, cut it to length, then cut X-slits every 24-30 inches. Marking those spots with sticks, I lift the cloth away and switch to digging gallon-sized holes for the tomatoes. I'll throw in a shovelful of compost, maybe a tablespoon or so of all-purpose fertilizer, some bonemeal. Then in goes the plant, right up to its top cluster of leaves; the stem will grow new roots all along its length. If the plant has flowers, I pinch them off: I want the plant to spend energy putting down roots this first month, not making bland, premature fruit. I carefully re-lay the black cloth over the bed, helping each tomato plant through its X-slit. Then I poke the legs of 4-tier tomato cages around (not through!) the buried plants until its lowest circle is sitting on the black cloth (takes some hammering with a rock, which can buckle the legs of the whimpier 3-tier cages—yet another reason I prefer the stouter cages). Finally, I roof the whole affair with clear plastic. Some years, it's one big tent made with poles and plastic over all the whole bed. Some years I use dry-cleaning bags pulled around each tomato cage, with a big hole on top to keep the bag's roof from turning into a rain-hammock. Both these roofs are easily raised so sunlight and pollinating bees can reach the plants when conditions are good.

The sunny alpaca farm where I garden-share with Bill Green has better conditions than my home garden—full sun, moisture-holding soil, nature's own fertilizer. Here, we take a chance on mid- and late-season tomatoes with more vine-like growth: Stupice and SunGolds, Early Girls, even 100-day Brandywines. Given perfect conditions, the plants grow like crazy: we constantly prune to keep the plants open to light and air. But we're still looking for that perfect support system. Teepees, stakes, training on strings to a high-wire—all let plants droop like saggy socks. The best system so far: train the plants up a panel of chicken-wire fence stretched between two stakes; all those wire intersections keep tied vines from sliding earth-ward when the fruit-load gets heavy. If the fruit does touch the ground, a carpet of black plasti-mulch helps keep the fruit clean, as well as prevent late blight spores from splashing up off the soil when the August rains inevitably arrive.

Surprisingly, given my hole-in-the-woods situation, my swaddled raised bed has been known to ripen early tomatoes like Siletz before the alpaca farm can. Go figure. In a good year, that mean tomatoes in late July, dining *al fresco* with tomato-basil-mozzarella salad, bruschetta on toast, BLT sandwiches with lettuce-leaf basil. Enough tomatoes for sauce-making and salsa, for the food bank, for drying or popping whole and unpeeled into freezer bags to peel later under hot running tap-water. This exuberance of tomatoes makes all the prep and pruning so very worth it!

But what about those green tomatoes?

But in a bad tomato year, homegrown tomatoes may still be green in early October. What to do? Leave them on the vine in the October rain? Bring them indoors to ripen—and how does THAT work? And is there a recipe for green tomatoes that's actually good?

Leaving them on the vine: This depends on whether your garden still has some warmth in early fall, whether your garden has ever had late blight, whether you have the ability to withhold water.

To ripen, tomatoes need temperatures at 55° or greater—unusual for October. It helps if your tomatoes are growing in a greenhouse or against a masonry wall; the warmth will keep fruit ripening.

You can bring on ripening by treating the plant to drought: this signals the plant that it's running out of time. Shutting off the spigot helps in other ways. Red tomato skins lose flexibility; since its skin can't stretch to absorb, say, the water of an autumn rain, it'll crack instead. Then there's those last gasps of late blight coming from soil-splash. Unless you can cover your plants through the fall, their fruit might be more reliably ripened indoors.

Ripening indoors: Tomatoes ripen from the inside out—cut a white tomato open and you may find a first blush of red in its core. If you pick a tomato that's starting to turn pink or pale orange, it will turn fully red in

7-10 days. If you have apples in your larder, take advantage of the ripening ethylene gas that apples pump out—put a couple in a bag with your green tomatoes and that gas will help ripen the toms. Do not put tomatoes of any color in the refrigerator: it kills their taste and stops the ripening process.

Once November cools temps into the lower 50s, the ripening will pause unless you bring the tomatoes indoors. You can hang whole vines upside-down, fruit still attached, to encourage ripening. I did this once, hooking the vines over the up-turned frame of our guest bed (I think guests had to use the couch, which shows you where my priorities are!) and quickly learned to put a tarp underneath or pick tomato plops out of my carpet. Another recommended method is to layer tomatoes between newspaper sheets, then check everyday for the ripe ones. Personally, I'd do this within a room I visited daily, not in the "Out of Sight, Out of Mind" regions where a few day's forgetfulness could lead to a moldy, fruit-fly-infested surprise.

For recipes for green tomatoes, see the chapter on freezing and canning.

Truly Green Tomatoes and Tomatillos

Truly Greens are varieties, such as Aunt Ruby's German Green or Green Zebra that stay green as they ripen. The way you tell they're ready to eat is to (pardon the expression) feel their bottom. If the blossom-end gives a little, if it's softer than the sides, it's ripe. Aunt Ruby's German Green makes a superb BLT, and any green tomato adds color contrast to a red tomato salsa, and freshness to a salsa verde.

But for an authentic, Mexican-style salsa verde, you need tomatillos. They, and their relatives the groundcherry and the decorative perennial called chinese lanterns, are nightshades like tomatoes but on the branch *Physalis*. Tomatillos grow as sprawling annuals that put out a round 1" fruit covered with papery husks at every joint and node; you harvest when the fruit fills the husk or it yellows. You've certainly been presented with a little bowl of green salsa verde at any Mexican restaurant that serves salsa with chips. Start them indoors two weeks after you start tomatoes, or outdoors when first frost danger is past. If you let a tomatillo plant go to seed (or leave a few ripe fruit on the ground), you'll probably have seedlings next year!

The Tomato Taste-off: a rainbow of flavor

If you want to test-drive tomato flavors, go to the Tomato Taste-off at the end of good tomato years at the VIGA farmers market.

On August 26, 2009, I found VIGA Secretary Lindsay Hart surrounded by color: red, orange, golden tomatoes, even ones that were supposed to be green. "The whole point of the Tomato Taste-off," said Hart, "is to educate people that there are tomato varieties other than Early Girl or Big Boy." Each sample plate was labeled by variety and category: best slicer, cherry tomato, biggest, weirdest, and heirloom.

It had been a great tomato year, and there were loads of varieties here to sample in the blind tasting. Even I was competing, with a Siletz from my backyard. At 11:00, a crowd of tasters, toothpicks poised, pounced on the samples: Ramapo, Paul Robeson, Jaune Flamme. Such suggestive names: Egg Yolk, Amber, Brandywine. I scribbled notes: "Oregon Spring: short taste, good meatiness, more tang than sweet—a 3. Black Sea: a briny note, meaty texture, juicy flavor—a 4." Aunt Ruby's German Green: oh, this is good... big fruit, clean, citrusy flavor, well-defined seed cavity—a 5."

When I tried a piece of my own tomato, my face fell: good ol' Siletz just didn't the flavor of these farm-grown tomatoes. Oh well.... I elbowed past a young teen hovering near his (I suspect) tiny Sungolds. I speared, barked "oh WOW!" and marked my ballot: Best Cherry.

The largest category was the weirdly shaped, colorful heirlooms. Evergreen had a light citrusy flavor. Japanese Black Trifele was pear-shaped. Jaune Flamme, the color of tangerines. Mortgage Lifter, just plain HUGE. I speared a chunk of the famous, rose-red Brandywine and bit. The flavor, meaty and sweet, filled my mouth with an alcohol zing. I thought, "THIS is that taste I want—and it's in an heirloom tomato."

Voting stopped at 1:00 with 134 ballots in. Local growers circled, waiting. When Hart called out "Best Slicer: OREGON SPRING!" Jasper Forrester of GreenMan Farm yelped, danced in place, then bowed to receive "The Bronze Tomato" pendant that Hart designed and husband Jeff White cast. Local woodworker Ralph Moore presented a plaque he'd made in honor of his grandma who "back in Lawrence, Kansas, used to grow these wonderful slicers that she'd peel for us grandkids."

Pacific Crest Farm's seven-inch Ruby Gold earned "Biggest" while Island Meadow Farm took "Weirdest." Hogsback Farm won "Best Heirloom" for its Brandywine, while 12-year-old Dylan Grace-Wells of Stop Sign Farm won "Best Cherry" for those delicious Sungolds.

What makes them so sweet?

Days later at Hogsback Farm, I asked farm manager Brian Lowry what makes heirlooms special. "They are older varieties whose seeds have been saved by gardeners from year to year. The seed 'comes true'—you'll get the same fruit from that seed as the mother plant produced. They're not genetically modified."

Heirlooms have been treasured by gardeners for their taste, but slice open a ripe one and you'll see why they've lost favor with industrial growers. Inside is a gelatinous seed chamber—taste this and you'll discover where a tomato's acid tang comes from. Now bite into the outer wall: this is where sweetness concentrates as the flesh converts from starch to sugars. These qualities—a jelly center surrounded by starches breaking down into sugars—makes an heirloom too fragile for shipping. Commercial tomatoes are picked green, then ripened with ethylene gas from the outside in, instead of the natural ripening that occurs from the inside, out.

"For a really ripe tomato," said Lowry, "look for uniform color and a bottom that's a little soft." He handed me a Brandywine. "This one will be good today, and perfect tomorrow."

And perfect it was.

Winning, Favorite Tomatoes

Earliest: Siberia, Stupice, Northern Delight, Siletz, Glacier
Slicers: Stupice, Oregon Spring, Golden Girl, Early Girl
Cherry: Sungold, Cherry Grape, Sweet Chelsea, SunSugar
Sauce: Genovese Roma, Milano, Speckled Roman
Heirloom: Brandywine, Jaune Flame, Azoychka

Other favorites: Black, Green Grape, Gold Medal, Caspian Pink, Goldie Yellow, Aunt Ruby's German Green

Growing a Garden Tour

Island gardeners have cultivated and grown the Vashon Allied Arts Garden Tour into a multi-day fundraiser for the arts.

It started with a bored shopgirl. Penny Grist, a 1970s transplant with a mushroom cap of hair and upturned nose, was working as Gallery Curator for Vashon Allied Arts, the Island's art center, in early 1990. Midweek she worked at the Heron's Nest, VAA's arts and crafts gallery then in the old Odd Fellows building. But midweek was slow: not much to do except answer the phone and daydream about her new interest, gardening.

Her home near Portage had a beautiful view overlooking inner Quartermaster Harbor. A few seagull flaps across Portage lived Ilse Reimnitz, who painted with Penny in a watercolor group they'd started in Sharon Munger's barn on Cove Road. Penny loved to visit Ilse's garden, with its poppies and irises, dogwoods and roses, grapevines growing over a barrel-roofed pergola. Though she'd never been on a garden tour, it occurred to Penny that people might pay to see places like Ilse's garden. Why not organize a garden tour to make money for VAA? She picked up the phone and started calling friends.

"Ilse agreed, and then I called Art Hansen (internationally famous artist known for rain-soaked landscapes and giant poppy prints). He said, 'No way, but my friend Clifford Kemp has a great garden.' I kept calling and found five gardeners who were willing. We picked a Saturday in June, and I organized a show called "Art in the Garden" to run at the same time."

Enthusiasm grows for gardening around Puget Sound

Americans have always loved gardening, but during the post-war period the gardens of the maritime NW seemed limited to an accepted palette: rhododendrens, azaleas, and candy-pink Kwanzan cherry trees, arborvitae and junipers, hybrid tea roses and baskets o' fuchsias. I think it was boredom that inspired a post-70s psychedelic generation to seek out, with great enthusiasm, a wilder, looser, and certainly more colorful plant palette.

Americans' interest in gardening surged in the mid-1980s, especially in the Pacific Northwest with its temperate climate that canw nurture a wide range of plants. Seedsman Ed Hume had been going since 1977 with his syndicated TV program and local seed racks. But in 1987, the *Seattle Weekly* published its first column by Seattleite Ann Lovejoy; she would soon move to Bainbridge Island and expand not only her garden but her writing activities to a total of 18 books and countless magazine articles for the *Seattle P-I* and national magazines *Horticulture* and *Fine Gardening,* a bimonthly color mag started in May 1988 by Taunton Press. Heronswood Nursery run by Robert Jones and plant explorer Dan Hinkley opened in 1987; its catalog featured plants that Hinkley introduced to the U.S., while their garden in Kingston, Washington became a name-drop destination in the gardening world. In February 1989, the Seattle Flower & Garden Show opened to overflow crowds at the Seattle Convention Center. The Seattle Arboretum's Plant Sale was in full roar in the late 1980s; I'll never forget waiting in a long line, my heavy box of plants joining a chorus of hundreds scraping across the asphalt as we plant lovers nudged our boxes ever closer to the cashier.

But on Vashon, choice had yet to bloom. In 1990, Kathy Wheaton created a small garden center at her Ace Hardware franchise. There were a couple of nurseries, including Peter Ray's wholesale nursery Puget Garden Resources with its emphasis on unusually colored plants like corydalis 'Blue Panda' with its gun-metal blue foliage and pale blue flowers. But, said Grist, "the gardening scene wasn't very big: still lots of rhodies, not a lot of choice."

So Penny's little garden tour started on a shoe-string: a few phone calls, a poster, a story for the VAA's monthly newsletter *Island View*, a show in the gallery on floral art. She got friends to bake cookies and help her make hundreds of tuna & watercress sandwiches for an English Tea. In their garden, hosts **Beth & Ed Holmes** "worked our buns off" to get their five acres in Lisabuela ready. Ed worked up their ravine into a woodland retreat with a bench overlooking a stream. Beth kept busy in the vegetable and perennial garden with its poppies and peonies, geraniums and bachelor buttons. Said Beth, "We both worked hard to make our place as weed-free as possible, anticipating Who Knows What... We didn't have help, and it was the same year we adopted a child. By that Saturday, I do remember the sense that 'Oh GOOD! The work is over!"

Host **Steve Abel** recalled, "Our primping for the garden tour were just minor blips in a trajectory from alder forest in 1974 to now. We did put out more bark and mulch, did more clean up and weeding than usual, and I mowed more carefully than usual. However, we (with Marie Stanislaw) never put out a bunch of petunias for instant color." Steve had grown up near the Seattle Arboretum; on his acres above Tramp Harbor, he wanted "to create something like an arboretum, with mature trees and shrubs, long views, lots of open space. From our garden, visitors could get a sense for what they could do on their own property: by using a lot of native plants and near-natives, by placing a few colorful trees like acer palmatums, they could create a comfortable property without the fussiness of perennial gardens."

From the beginning, the Vashon Garden Tour featured both small gardens tended by working folk like Ilse & Hartmut Reimnitz and ambitious gardens powered by money, obsession, and hired help. The most ambitious were often the home gardens of landscape professionals, such as the garden of **Clifford Kemp**, a well-known landscaper for clients in Medina and Hunt's Point. His widow **Mary Robinson** recalled, "For his Vashon garden he thought big, in the style of the gorgeous large gardens that he remodelled and put in for his wealthy clients. He knew he was HIV positive, and as then it meant only a few years of life, he put all the money and energy of his last five years into the garden." Kemp's garden sounds wonderful: a five-acre arboretum with an acre of orchard including 75 different varieties of apples, grape & apple espaliers, vegie and berry plots, dense mixed plantings around the house, lawn, and pond, flowers all year round. "It really was an amazing garden," said Mary, who still works the cut-flower business he started. "Large, densely planted gardens were not common on Vashon, but he liked to share his with folks to encourage them to think and plant big and to use a diverse palette of plant materials. He welcomed the VIGA folks and was very proud to be included on that first garden tour."

That first tour, probably on the first Saturday of June, was only open a few hours. Beth White said "A lot of people came through. It was a time to beam and be proud and be happy that the work was over!" Also open were the cottage gardens of **Paul & Mary Macapia** and of artist **Joe Petta & Joan White**, and master gardeners **Dorothy & Chris Anderson**. The tour made a few hundred dollars and above all, said Grist, "It was fun!"

The next tour was organized in 1992, and again **Clifford Kemp's** garden was open, though he had died in December, 1991. Mary said, "In 1990 Clifford had his crew, but in 1992 it was myself, Ariel Holtz, a few friends and family. The number of people who came was overwhelming, but I was so proud of Clifford's work and the beauty he created that it was worth it."

For $7 on that July 18, you could see **Kay White's** ten-acre estate garden in Raecoma; **Russ & Peggy Casson's** rocky, sun-soaked, heather and pine garden in Gold Beach; **Jan & Courtleigh Guerci's** gardens of lilacs, rockeries, and shrub borders; and **Peter Serko's** woodland garden around his log home. Also on the tour (the first of three times) was the garden of **Beth de Groen** on the north tip of Whispering Firs Bog. She said, "I worked 3-7 hours a day in the garden back then. As you get closer to the tour date, you start feeling that there are Things Undone, so you start obsessing. Every other host I've talked to, they run to the local garden store during that last three weeks to buy plants." This tour was the first—and last—tour scheduled in July, a season not great for flowers but warm enough to make a girl want to peel off all her clothes. Beth, stepping from her outdoor shower that morning with nary a fig leaf on her, found herself giving an early-bird visitor rather more of a garden peek than she'd planned to.

Perhaps reacting to the heat, the following year Grist scheduled the tour for May 8th, the earliest it's ever been held. **Beth de Groen**, again asked to open her garden, said, "The one time it was done in May, it rained a lot and was moist and cool and all the rhodies were in bloom, it was a much better than in July." Also on the tour in 1993 were the **Judith Lawrence**'s farm, once home to Betty MacDonald, author of *The Egg & I*; the Gold Beach garden of **Pat & Bob Morgan**; **Ilse Reimnitz's** garden again, **Bea & Don Ostlie's** 4-year-old garden on Maury Island, and the home garden of **Lisa de Rango**, landscape contractor and master gardener.

In 1994, the tour returned to June, with only five gardens: **Pam Sturgeon & Ken Sandell**'s north-end, high-bluff garden; **Jack Tolerico & Bill Wayburn**'s Lisabuela garden on a stream flowing into Colvos Passage; **Amy & Alan Huggins**' garden high on the Shinglemill Creek watershed; architect **Ibsen Nelsen**'s garden in Upper Burton; and the one I wish I'd seen, the pink-stuccoed house owned by **Mary Rothermel & Tom Northington** that was inspired by Monet's home and garden in Giverny.

A New Nursery and New Energy

Puget Sound's economy boomed in the late 1990s. The Clinton years brought peace and a budget surplus, the Internet mushroomed, and the Dow topped 10,000 as a market mad for any website with a shopping cart inflated the valuations of Internet stocks. The wealth effect showed, here on Vashon. As well-off Islanders spent on leisure, culture, and art, the income raised by VAA's fall Art Auction sailed, for the first time, past six figures.

Gardeners have always joked about their hobby's way of throwing money into the ground. But with wealth in the air, gardening catalogs started advertising not just their plants, but tools, clothing, gadgetry, furnishings. Writers like Lovejoy wrote about planting in layers to mimic the forest understory—a strategy that, for nurseries, could mean more dollars spent per square foot. The display gardens at the Seattle Flower & Garden Show were kitted out in fancy hardscaping: flagstone pavers, ironwork, patterned tilework, mountain boulders from Marenakos stone yard. It didn't seem enough to have a well-planted garden: it also must be well dressed.

In 1995, a new nursery made a colorful splash along Vashon Highway. Sylvia Matlock, graduate of the Art Institute of Chicago, and her partner Ross Johnson opened DIG Floral & Garden, filling chartreuse & cobalt racks with almost-as colorful plants. A year later, they moved DIG to the field behind a four-square house next to Vashon Athletic Club on 191st. Even the big cottonwoods couldn't hide Sylvia's carnival palette of color: lime & cobalt, violet, chocolate and China red painted on sheds, shelves, even a writhing circular pergola. Her plants, many of them from Puget Garden Resources, were as exotically colorful: along the highway, a thick border of jumbo plants frothed forth in hot & cools: euphorbias, rudbeckias, sunflowers, and a hard-pruned golden catalpa against burgundy smoke plant, cooled by blue gums and steel-blue cerinthe spilling its bracts of midnight blue toward the road. Sylvia specialized in shade plants, sedums, grasses, and plants that deer don't love, but she also tricked out her nursery like an upscale boutique: glass bubbles floated in giant pots, mosaic work by Clare Dohna enwrapped giant urns, towering gabion cages filled with gray rocks guarded each entrance. For Sylvia, DIG was art, and it was all eye-candy.

And they were good at drawing in customers: spring mailings, workshops organized by employee Cathie Crouse, a chalkboard sign out front that once screamed "U-NEED-A EUPHORBIA!" Matlock quickly involved DIG with VAA and its garden tour. Said Jensen, "Sylvia designed and installed that front garden at the Blue Heron with some of her signature plants: heavenly bamboo 'Plum Passion,' euphorbia, sedums, mahonia 'Charity' and sent Crystal over to maintain that garden. Sylvia was always fabulous about knowing who were avid gardeners and had fabulous gardens."

In 1995, the garden of **Peter Ray,** owner of Puget Garden Resources, and his partner **Jean Emmons**, renown botanical illustrator, were included in that year's tour on June 18th. Also on the itiniary were **Bob & Bonnie Gregson's Island Meadow Farm**, the first CSA farm on the Island; a repeat of the Anderson garden now owned by **Sam Lanier & Andrew Peet**; tree feller **Jim Biel & Lisa deFaccio's** 5-year-old garden on a high bank on Maury Island, and **Rod & Joanne Fosmark's** mature garden they'd been working on since 1959. The $10 ticket ($8 to VAA members) included five gardens and the Traditional English Tea at the Blue Heron. And there was art in the gardens for the first time: Penny Grist, who had taken up in sculpting, had recruited the Northwest Stone Sculptor's Association to show their work in the gardens.

Taking the tour for the first time in 1996, I remember joining a squeeze of visitors inside a tiny vegie plot in the (if I remember correctly) **Bill Hewgley & Stephen Bogan** garden with its mixed borders and brick paths. Our garden tour was proving popular: its single Saturday was packed, perhaps thanks in part to Sylvia Matlock's handing out tour brochures from DIG's vendor stall at the Seattle Flower & Garden Show earlier in February. DIG sponsored another ancillary to the tour: the first **DIG Birdbath Show** with works by mosaic artists Clare Douha, Elaine Summers, and other Island artists to draw tour visitors into DIG that day. Again, the tour featured gardens old—the 2nd-generation garden of **Nancy & John VanDeVanter,** who spent his childhood summers on the Burton peninsula picking Olympic berries for his grandmother around her white Victorian cottage—and new, in the 4-year-old garden of **Sheryl Tomkinsen** with its 120 roses, mixed border, and greenhouse. **Joe Petta/Joan White**'s garden full of roses and herbs was again on tour, as was the native habitat garden of **Helen & Joe Meeker.**

Growth, and Growing Pains

By the late 90s, Grist's interest was shifting to gardening, making jewelry, and building tall wooden sculptures. To help with the tour, she recruited board member Sherene Zolno, who gardens a steep hillside on Indian Point (see chapter 3). At first Sherene just lent Penny a hand—she contributed desktop publishing skills and organizational drive—but by the year 2000, Sherene had taken the lead. Between 1995 and 2000, Grist, Zolno, and a growing band of volunteers turned this little tea, flowers and $4K affair into VAA's second largest fundraiser, bringing in over $25,000.

Zolno told me, ""My first year, I only added a few sponsorships, replaced the single-page flyer with a tri-fold brochure, and got DIG to hand out my flyers at the Flower and Garden Show." Grist focused on finding gardens (always tough), publicity and, in 1997, opening her own garden for tour. She said, "Tour always used to depress me: I've come home to my property, blackberries from lot-line to lot-line. But I cleared land, built rock walls, put in borders, and worked at it consistently. By the time I was on the tour, my place didn't depress me anymore." It couldn't—when I toured the **Penny Grist** garden that year, I remember large beds cut into lush lawn, huge orange poppies crashing over Shasta daisies and lupines. Her sculptures, resembling towering Kanji symbols, stood regally over each bed and wall.

My garden journal from 1997 enthused over the Tuscan-inspired Maury garden of **Gar LaSalle & Nina Ferrari** with its fenced rose and vegetable gardens, tree walk down the middle of the wide lawn, and white rambling roses arching over the garage doors. I also remember the charm of **Marcus (McNabb) Berg's** garden on Cedarhurst: a young importer of Asian statues, he had studded his garden with Buddha figures and bent young cedars into natural archways. Also open for the tour were the gardens of **Shirley Burton** and of **Joan Kirschner**, who regularly put on a Celebration Dinner for all the garden hosts to thank them for their hard work. The tour was open the full weekend for the first time, so the gardens were less congested. If you needed a break, you could enjoy the free English Tea at VAA.

"In the next three years, I really went to work," Sherene told me. "I found sponsors, arranged for nurseries to give special discounts, sold advertising, created publicity, and not only created the full-color brochure, but printed out 1000 from my home printer." Penny still helped find the gardens, and her byline appears under the articles that so colorfully describe each garden, but Sherene was growing the tour beyond its Open-Garden basics.

That expansion started in 1998 with a single workshop. Tour cost $15, but if you wanted to start in the morning, for an additional $12 you could take a class at **Peter Ray**'s nursery. In the afternoon, tour opened with five gardens: the Burton hill garden of **Ania & Larry Veldman**, **Mary Robinson**'s garden, **Susan McKeever's** cottage garden on the Burton Loop, and the garden maintained by gardener/caretaker **Rod Ciceri** around **Jack McCann**'s Mediterranean villa, with its wisteria-covered porch, box-edged paths, fountain over a koi pond, and "Vashon's most spectacular views of Quartermaster Harbor, Puget Sound, and Mt. Rainier." Also on the tour (and not for the last time) was the garden of **Cindy & Steve Stockett,** with its rose-covered pergola, water runnel, perennial borders, boxwood-edged terrace, and giant New Zealand flaxes looming over gate and pond.

McKeever described her garden as the "More accessible, smaller budget-garden. I had a toddler on my hip that year, so when he was napping, I'd run out and work in the garden. I took some plants to DIG to identify, then made a map and a guide so visitors could identify the plants. My style was 'Order in the Chaos'—very feminine, fluffy, with order with pathways and pots. I'd been to Heronswood, went to the Seattle Flower & Garden Show which then was really stretching, doing neat things. But what visitors to my garden REALLY wanted to know is, what WERE those copper things around the base of my bean plants? And I replied "They're slug zappers with a natural electrical charge: my secret pleasure is give the slugs a little pain!"

In 1999, Zolno expanded the tour to four workshops, plus the gallery's garden-themed show, garden art at Sharon Munger's Barnworks on Cove, and in DIG's Bird Bath show. She got Windermere Real Estate to be the first corporate sponsor, and she asked local bed-n-breakfasts to offer free tour tickets for 2-night stays. Even the English Tea upscaled: when the Island's largest landowner, millionaire **Tom Stewart**, asked Zolno if his garden could be on the tour, Sherene persuaded him and Jim English to host the English Tea in his huge barn. For many Islanders including myself, it was our first chance to get a peek inside Stewart's Misty Isle Farm, home of Black Angus cattle and the annual Western Washington Republicans' BBQ (to which most left-leaning Islanders were not invited). His 525-acre estate was landscaped rather like a golf course, with rolling lawns and pasture, rhodies and flowering trees against a backdrop of dark firs, and a pond stocked with trout fattened on a diet of dog food. Stewart's four-color brochure distributed at the English Tea was quite the contrast to the humble handwrit screed on Nature and Zen philosophy handed out in his own garden by **Marcus (McNabb) Berg**. (Berg's garden wasn't officially part of tour, but piggy-backing had become common during Garden or Art Studio tour. Many an Islander selling something—artist, farmer, real estate agent, yard sale host—puts a sign on the highway to snag tourists during big events.)

Also up in 1999 were **Don Cadman'**s narrow lot above Quartermaster Yacht Club with its hammock glade and flower-pots lining his terrace walls. **Ilse Reimnitz**'s garden was open again. The kitschiest garden ever was **Joyce & Ron Frombach**'s nautical garden, with its rowboat planter out front, the tugboat-shaped greenhouse behind, and narrow walkways down the high-bluff shore paved with beach glass and railed with boat oars. By far the most glamorous was the hideaway of **Jack Telerico & Bill Wayburn**; bus shuttles carried visitors down a Judd Creek ravine to a delta fanning into Colvos Passage, where a garden designed by Bill Hewgley featured mixed borders, brick paths, two ponds, and a grape arbor around the beautiful house, a bridge across a creek to a beach boardwalk, and a viewing gazebo tricked out with brand spankin' new copper gutters.

By Zolno's last year as coordinator, she and her volunteers were organizing nearly the year round. The search for next year's gardens always begins right after tour, when gardens are still in their prime. In January or February at the latest, all the gardens are found and photos obtained for early publicity—usually the 6000 flyers for the Seattle Flower & Garden Show. Magazines like *Sunset* and the *Seattle Times Pacific Northwest* must be pitched months ahead. Sponsors in by March pass along their logos for printed pieces and publicity in VAA's newsletter, the *Beachcomber*, and other media. By April, volunteers are found, and postcards, posters, and program brochures were proofed, printed, and mailed. May is all about last-minute prep and fulfillment: signs are readied, ticket packets mailed out, and private tours set up for the media, whose stories (such as my blog previews) appear in the weeks and days before the big weekend. A week before the tour, the Preview

Caravan gives hosts and volunteers a chance to look at all the gardens. Last minute checks with the hosts identify any problems. Chairs and tents go up at workshop and art market sites, and the Artists in the Gardens set up. Finally, there's one last thing to do: pray for sunshine.

By 2000, organizing the tour had become a very big job. By February, they had nailed down only one garden. Meanwhile Zolno, with the help of a core group of volunteers, organized TWELVE workshops, an art show and tea at the Country Store, and the first Artist in the Garden (Penny Grist's sculptures). Publicity was first-rate: Ed Hume mentioned the tour on his TV show, and *Seattle Times* columnist Valerie Easton did an article in *Pacific NW magazine* on the Gawith/Weiss home, which was also featured in *Metropolitan Home*. DIG offered 20% off to hosts and a free consultation— just one of 16 sponsors involved, including lead sponsor Windermere Real Estate. 29 volunteers were needed on tour days to cover the five gardens, introduce workshop speakers, sell tickets, and work the tea. There was the Preview Caravan, the Gallery Show, the Celebratory Dinner afterwards, the artists in the gardens, a printer that wasn't getting that year's artwork quite right.... and suddenly, it was All Too Much: Zolno took a reluctant bow and stepped aside a week before tour.

VAA's board scrambled, but pulled it off. Open gardens that year included the woodland terrace gardens of **Michael Cameron**; the seaside garden of **Ben & Merrill Jannison**, the Italian-inspired garden of **Linda Weiss & Ron Gawith**, a repeat of the **Fosmark's** garden, and a fountain-pond-terraced garden by **Susan Garlick & Jim Dorsey**.

After 2000, the gardening scene slowed all over the region. Attendance at the 2000 Seattle Flower & Garden show had fallen way down; founder Duane Kelly speculated that baby-boomers had finished their gardens. Garden publishers and nurseries noticed fading interest as well, worsened by the bursting of the dot-com bubble in late 2000. For 2001, VAA's Garden Tour was scaled back. Three gardens were repeats: **Beth de Groen**, **Sam Lanier**, and **Lisa DeFaccio**, plus those of **Darsie Beck**, **Sheryl Allen**, and **Shirley Bonney,** with featured artist David Erue. There were only six sponsors and four workshops, a book sale, a take-out lunch instead of a tea, and for the first time, a paid coordinator, Barbara Codd.

Under Barbara Codd's management, the experience of being at the garden was refined: manning them, handling traffic, making it a happy experience for the hosts. Susan McKeever, the first to work up an Excel spreadsheet for the tour, came on board as Volunteer Coordinator. In an attempt to catch the rhodies, the 2002 tour was held in late April, showing the gardens of **Kay White** and **Steve Abel & Marie Stanislaw**, **Joe & Suzy Green**'s "neat-nik" garden in Ellisport ("there wasn't a weed in SIGHT!"), **LynAnne & Gary Raven**'s farm on a 1920s homestead on the Westside, and the native habitat, hillside garden of **Edna & James Dam** (he of the Lutheran Church garden). Their garden hung on a much-terraced hillside overlooking a ravine of Baldwin Creek; I remember descending that hillside to their sun-soaked vegetable garden in the meadow, then taking the loop trail into their forest protected under King County's Open Space program.

Host Joe Green said, "Getting ready for tour was a little extra work, but we're both nit-pickers, we keep it tidy all the time. The weather was gorgeous, but the rhodies were just about gone. Big crowds, but they didn't do any damage: they kept out of the flower beds, real respectful, we didn't have to do any tidying up afterwards at all."

Susan McKeever remembers that "We weren't very organized, but the tour is so beautiful, it sells itself." A come-hither photo of orange Asiatic lilies, purple sweet williams, and white feverfew by Mary Liz Austin graced all publicity, including the invitation to the new Preview Dinner hosted by Back Bay Inn. With sponsor JL Scott's shuttles looping from ferries to gardens to events, the 2003 tour promised beauty and convenience. Open were the gardens of **Amy & Alan Huggins** and of **Steve & Cindy Stockett** ("a marriage of English formality and NW Zen simplicity"), plus gardens of **Janet Lynch**, **Don & Mary Lou Harlander's** on the Westside, and the Burton garden of **Gary & Theo Christman**, with its lavender field, Victorian greenhouse, and row of blowsy white 'Sally Holmes' roses. Unfortunately, 2003 was the year of an island-wide tent caterpillar infestation. Caterpillars crawling everywhere stripped the trees that summer; cars couldn't drive up Ferry Dock Hill without skidding on caterpillar roadkill. I remember, in the Huggins' ravine, taking my ease on a woodland bench and wondering "Could that gentle hiss actually be rain?"—then dashing outta there when I realized it was the dropping(s?) of thousands of caterpillars.

By 2004, the adjunct events of dinner, workshops, artists, and raffle settled into regular features of the tour. Back Bay again hosted a salmon dinner on Friday, June 4th, while JL Scott's shuttles took diners and weekend tourists to the gardens of **Beth De Groen** and **Pat & Bob Morgan**, **Linda & Raymond Martinez,** and **Christel & Hans Stierle.** At the Blue Heron, you could take a breather with a take-out lunch offered by Zoomies or sit listening to a seminar by the Lavender Sisters, Darsie Beck or *Soul Gardening* author Terry Hershey. The real showplace was the Maury Island home and garden created by **John Busch & Osman Person** in just three years. The spectacular orange Spanish Revival villa around a fountain court and ten-acre garden was primped up to *Architectural Digest* standards: off the courtyard fountain, wide-open french doors invited you to peer into the garden room with its *objets d'art* and floor-puddled curtains, striped silk couch with button-end bolsters set before a comforting fire. Sometimes being on the tour is a marketing ploy: this place was soon Casa Vista B & B.

In 2005, one could mingle at the "Taste of the Gardens" dinner on Friday, take the morning shuttle to your docent-led tours through art-enhanced gardens, eat lunch from Zoomies as you took in a seminar, buy a raffle ticket for a stone bench, then enjoy a cello concert at the Blue Heron that Saturday evening, June 4th. What wasn't on the program was the bad weather. A freak hailstorm blew havoc through the gardens just two weeks before tour, shedding debris across the gardens and dropping an 80' alder across the garden and deck of host **Cathie Crouse**, former workshop coordinator for DIG. Though her shade-loving hostas, lilies, heucheras, and alliums were untouched, she did have to rebuilt her deck and recreate the deck's colorfully planted pots. What will be, will be," Cathie told me. "Mother Nature throws so much at you. I let go and just enjoyed being on the tour."

Other open gardens that year were those of **Bobbi Arnold & sculptor David Erue**; **Cindy Johnson's Fox Farm** with all its lavender and roadside rose pergolas; **Saphire Blue & Gordon Smith**, and **Sheila & Bryan Park**'s Lisabuela property overlooking Colvo Passage. For Sheila, the tour was literally a life-saver: months prior, she was in an ICU with pneumonia after two years of treatment for esophageal cancer. Her doctors told her she was doing to die. But her male nurse, enthusing about going to the Bainbridge Island Garden Tour with his daughter, made her resolve to accept an earlier invitation to be on the 2005 VAA tour. "Lots of things help you survive, and the tour was it, for me. I was determined I was going to be on that tour! I couldn't walk very well, but I had this wonderful gardener who would work while I was in the hospital. Then after the storm hit, Michelle Ramsden organized some work crews, and one women put in three 7-hour days. By the time of tour, I could hang out by the lower pond and listen to people talk about the garden, not knowing I was the gardener. It was really great." Sheila's now healthy, gardening, back to doing the things she loves—like swinging her 16" chain-saw.

Though new coordinator and Heron's Nest manager Priscilla Schleigh didn't change the program much for 2006, she did add the Garden Angels—an inspiration suggested by friend and garden expert Debra Prinzing. Each garden is assigned an Angel, who then recruits more volunteers to handle that garden's logistics, traffic, and ticket-taking. leaving the owners—**Sam & Sarah Van Fleet, Lyn Solander & Nick Turchyn, Sari & Gene Lipitz,** and **Judith Henderson & Steve Foley**—free to play host and enjoy their big moment. But no number of Angels prevented Friday Night's Big Fiasco: down at **Sally Ann William**'s garden below Pt. Vashon, the VIP tour bus got parked in and had to inch up that steep hill backwards, setting the evening back an hour. The last hosts had to show off their garden by flashlight. It was a SNAFU no one wanted to see happen again.

After 2006, an overhaul for Garden Tour

By 2007, Garden Tour was overdue for an evaluation and overhaul. VAA also was in desperate need of more revenue. Board members Carol Eggen, who took over as Board Co-Chairs of the tour with Sylvia Soholt, observed that "Tour was too much work for the $16-18k it made. VAA's finances were precarious: they lived on fall's Art Auction funds and, by summer if not earlier, would be putting off bills until auction time. Tour has 100 volunteers, 5-6 homeowners, all these speakers—we felt there should be a better result. So we surveyed ticket-buyers, volunteers, hosts to get feedback, then with the Working Group (VAA staff and a paid Garden Coordinator) found the gardens and offered new ideas and strategies. For example, the Friday event didn't make sense: it was just a whistle-stop to the same gardens. But then, as we tried to recruit Whit & Mary Carhart, they said 'We're in the middle of construction on our pond garden, so we can't take 1000 visitors—but we COULD do a Friday party.' So that's how the Gala became an event in a separate garden, with the build-in benefit of a ticket to the weekend tour. And it's a really nice way to thank the hosts and volunteers." (who still got their preview tour a week earlier of the gardens of **Anita Halstead & Kelly Robinson**, **Dorothy & Jeff Dunnicliff**, **Leslie McIntosh**, **Mary Lynn Buss & Ronald Simons**, and **Sylvia Matlock & Ross Johnson**.) "In addition, we sold a private preview tour on Friday afternoon: two groups of twenty get a private showing of two gardens for an additional $45. We raised the ticket price to $25, moved the Garden Market to one of the open gardens, added a Silent Auction of artist-embellished objects (English watering cans this year, new director Molly Reed's idea), and we added more sponsors (13). After these changes, the tour's net was $40k vs. $18 the year before. It really helped VAA's finances at that time of year."

The five gardens open in late June, the Sunset Gala, Friday preview, silent auction, garden market, perhaps a plant sale, and artists in the gardens are still part of tour (as of 2013), coordinated by two board members, a paid coordinator, VAA staff, and a core committee backed by each garden's Angel and their volunteer crews for tour weekend. Looking at our tour's success, you'd never know a new recession was kicking the nursery trade in the teeth. On June 20, 2008, tour opened with a "Garden Connoisseurs" showing of **Terry Hershey**'s garden, followed by the Sunset Gala in the garden of sculptor **Julie Speidel & Joe Henke** overlooking Colvos Passsage (buffet by The Hardware Store Restaurant, wines by Palouse Winery), where diners could place their bids on the artist-decorated birdhouses of the silent auction. Open gardens included those of **Shirley Bonney & Doug Shaw** with the lifesize Chinese Warrior statue and wine-bottle labyrinth; knotgarden of **Mia McEldowney & Bill Mitchell**; **Janet & Tracy Bishop**'s garden across the street from the Burton post office; as well as the father-daughter garden of **Lynda Rhodes & Bill Deaton** on the Burton Peninsula (where the plant sale, full of Deaton's homegrown tomatoes etc, made over $1000). In the garden of **Steve Abel & Marie Stanislaw** (their third open), my own *plein aire* painters set up easels around his pond and painted reflections of his red Japanese maples on the water.

In 2009, the Sunset Gala was scheduled for the home of Daniel Klein and landscape architect David Pfeiffer. *Seattle Times* columnist Val Easton, a fan and friend of David, wrote about the tour with photos of the Driscoll garden in the newspaper's sunday supplement. That, plus unusual gardens and the superb weather forecast for June 26-28, super-charged ticket sales (for the first time offered through brownpapertickets.com). Who wouldn't want to check out a stumpery, created in the ravine of **Pat & Walt Riehl**, with its 100 stumps, 11 tree ferns, 120 epimediums, and over 1000 ferns? The steep hillside garden of **Bea McKelvey & Mike Johnson** defied gravity; the upper Dockton gardens of **David & Gigi Jack** and the French chateau of **Dick & Pam Driscoll** allowed you to bask in something-like-Mediterranean sunshine, then cool down in the forest sanctuaries of **Carol & Bob Ellis** and of **Diana Garrett & Nicholas Anderson**. Plantswoman Anita Halstead of Dockton partnered with new Islander Anna Martinson to coordinate tour, with the help of paid coordinator Nancy Foster-Moss. Anna told me, "What a treasure trove we have in this tour. We always try to have a showplace garden, a garden that's easy to care for, gardens that show off flowers or shade plants because we have so many microclimates. The weather was perfect, and we broke traffic records."

In 2010, I started writing previews of the VAA open gardens for my blog "Garden On, Vashon!" for the *Beachcomber*, starting with the garden of **Jonathan Morse** in Cedarhurst, whose color sense in plants and his huge, compulsively inventive gates and walls made his the "WOW!" garden of the year. Nancy Miracle and Leslie McIntosh coordinated that year, starting with the Friday's Connoisseurs' Tour in the gardens of **Sylvia Matlock & Ross Johnson of DIG** and of **Saphire Blue & Gordon Smith**. The Sunset Gala that night was at the Driscoll garden, showing off the artist-embellished planter boxes sponsored by LS Cedar (one of seven sponsors). Over a gray weekend of June 26-27, visitors toured the Morse garden, the simpler, gracious yard of **Greg Elliott**, plantswoman **Colleen James**'s garden and plant sale on the Burton Peninsula (with her usual perennial sale spilling from the porch of her yellow Victorian), the estate garden of **Kay White**, and the hillside perch of **Rick Skillman & Sherene Zolno**. Yes, THAT Sherene—the coordinator that went away.

It had been a tough year for Sherene and Rick: he'd had three back surgeries that year, and she had been laid off her job. "I told VAA that if you want my garden on tour, this is the year. And then, the slide happened." (see chapter 3). Sherene and helper Norm spent much of the early spring replanting that slope. "I was feeling very low about things in general, and that translated into a lack of confidence about the garden—it won't be good enough, pretty enough, we won't be ready. Then, two weeks before tour, we hosts got our preview tour of the other hosts' gardens, and Jonathan Morse's was up first. I had spent the afternoon drilling holes into my slope and jamming in a few ligularias, and then I get to Jonathan's and he's got a swath of ligularias at least 25 feet long. When I saw how beautiful they looked compared to mine, I just burst into tears. Rick had to stand in front of me to hide my gush of emotion."

Doubtless some of the past was purged in those cathartic tears. "After that, everything got better. Norm and I worked harder on the garden, then you came by. Your blog write-up was so complementary, it really started the healing. Then, the day of the tour, everybody was SOOO enthusiastic, thought the garden looked so beautiful, it really put me back together."

The garden tour, in many ways, shows off what the Island nurtures best: high ambition and hard work, to live in harmony with nature, to honor our history, to mark our places in eccentric and artistic ways. 2011's tour organized by Nancy Miracle and Chanda Carlson did all of that: the Cedarhurst garden of **Mary Bruno & Kate Thompson** was designed for their shady, wet site. **Cynthia Johnson's Fox Farm** basked in its lavenders while the garden of **Kathleen & Richard Farner** showed off Richard's love for modern roses. **Hal & Molly Green's Triplebrook Farm** honored Island history in its century-old orchard, barn, and chicken coop turned B&B. At the arboretum and garden of **Sally Fox & Steve Brown**, one got not just a garden but reflections ON gardening written by Sally in her woodland writer's cabin. And on the garden huts and artwork at **Richard & Karen Person**'s garden on Pohl Road, Karen had painted the bold colors beloved in their Norwegian homeland (even though their ancestors had immigrated from there to that property generations ago). All of them brought to their gardens the kind of passion reflected in that year's tour book-signing, *Monet's Passion* written by Elizabeth Murray, who spoke and showed her sumptuous slides from Giverny that Saturday night, June 25th.

If you long to have your garden on the tour, know that coordinators (like 2012's organizers Chanda Carlson & Karen Person) would LOVE to hear from you just as soon as tour is over and they can catch a breath. They'll come looking not only for an attractive garden to photograph, but parking, access, how the garden might fit with gardens already chosen (will this be the Showcase or the DIY garden?) Hosting on the tour IS work, but you decide how much prep you'll do—as did 2012 hosts **Todd & Mary Margaret Pearson**, who did their usual "low maintenance"—power-washing flagstones, power-pruning the boxwood hedges, and power-mowing a path through their lupine & meadowgrass pasture. Partners **Bruce Fillinger & Barry Foster** simply tidied, laid fresh woodchips over paths, and dusted off the chicken tchotchkes in their Chicken Museum, while **Sylvia Soholt** (who'd volunteered to be on the tour after calling, in her years as recruiter, "20 people for every one person who agreed to be on the tour") got friends to help her prep ("offer them chili"). At the westside garden of **Daniel Klein, partner David Pheiffer** actually gave a talk on simplifying a garden through design, pointing out how few weeds were able to grow through their kitchen garden's groundcover of Italian musk strawberries. Or, you can turn your moment in the garden tour into an item on your Bucket List, as surely **Mary & Whit Carhart** did with the completion of the hillside pond garden started right after the 2007 Garden Tour Gala and described in the next chapter. If you want to play a small role—say, be a Garden Angel one day of tour—contact VAA by April. You may know a lot about gardening or a little, but any kind of participation in this, VAA's 2nd largest fundraiser, helps cultivate a vital arts program for our Island.

Coming home from the garden tour used to depress me, too. Like Sherene or Penny, I'd arrive home and think, "My garden's not good enough." But I've learned to prep my own garden, just as the hosts do, in the weeks leading up to tour. Then, after I park the car one last time on tour day, the last garden I proudly, if wearily, wander through will be my own.

(Anne O'Leary & Anna Martinson coordinated the 2013 tour of **Cindy Ward**'s Humble Bumble Farm, **Steve & Cindy Stockett**'s Froggsong Farm, and the Maury gardens of **Ron Gawith & Linda Weiss**, **Chuck & Nancy Roehm**, and **Miles Small & Kerri Goodman Small**.)

What Works, Where

Let's drive around to visit gardens in various microclimates and soil conditions, from Vashon's north bluff to the southern foot of Maury.

When the local newspaper editor asked me to write a story about no-fail plants, I thought she was kidding—and so did the gardeners to whom I put that question. For one thing, there's no such thing as a "no-fail plant." Neglect, an early freeze or long drought, or the husband watering the deck-pots with his trouser hose can doom the toughest plants.

On the other hand, the Island enjoys a temperate climate and some frost protection, thanks to that great heat-sink, the waters of Puget Sound. And the Island has so many microclimates and micro-conditions that gardening successfully is—to lift the title from one of my favorite gardening books—a matter of *Right Plant, Right Place.* A sunny garden on Dockton Road can support windmill palms, while two blocks downhill, maidenhair ferns and hostas grow happily in a shaded garden on clay soil. And as rainy climates and steep slopes do not a settled soil make, your property may have both pockets of clay AND drifts of sandy soil.

And plants can surprise you. I've seen shade-loving hydrangeas and hostas thrive in full sun if they can pull enough water from the soil. I met a guy on Shawnee Beach who grew tomatoes in pots on his covered porch because its white paint reflected enough morning sunlight to ripen his tomatoes. Sometimes the micro-climate only has to be just big enough—like the 5x5' greenhouse I've parked in my one constant spot of sun.

So let's drive around to see what's working where for Island gardeners.

North end shoreline— sand and clay, shade and sun

Whenever you descend to the north-end ferry dock, you're driving above the garden of **Bonnie McCallister & Dean Haugen.** Their place is right down on the shoreline, with a wonderful view north up the shipping channel. But this sea-level view also brings their garden salt-laden air and lots of shade. Bonnie describes their soil as "dirt over clay—plus we're not the best waterers, so that adds stress to our plants.

Nonetheless, they have tucked a charming shade garden into the slope backing their Indonesian joglo hut. Here, accented by asian lanterns, grow Japanese maples over japanese forest grass, hydrangeas and ajugas, rhodies with daylilies, spiky phormiums and tufts of sedge. These plants get only morning light during the summer, with deep shade in the winter months.

On the other side of the dock at the base of the bluff, you'll find evidence of Lawton Clay, a layer of fine clay with so little oxygen in it, it's nearly blue. Perhaps this is why Bonnie and Dean's plants get by with limited watering: their soil sits on a dense clay layer that keeps water always within reach of the roots of their plants.

Less than a mile away on the northwest foot of the Island, **Sallie Ann Williams** also gardens on the shoreline, but she's got "sandy fill" just a few feet above the beach, without any clay beneath to keep the soil moist. Her house and its garden is often sprayed by winter waves. Despite the salt spray, a hedge of rosa rugosa thrives along her northern property line, and a 5' artichoke "that seems to love the salt" has been growing and fruiting for at least seven years.

"I have a 190° view here: I can see all the way down Colvos Passage, north to Mt. Baker, plus Southworth and Blake Island. But consequently I get winds from both directions and shade only at midday in summer." She grows phormium, crocosmia 'Lucifer', hardy geraniums, grasses, two kinds of corokias "that seem to love it here whether in pots or in the ground, and a red climbing rose, "Stairway to Heaven" that's happy in the salty winds. And though it's a small property, she's put in a garden house next to the street, where a hydrangea "blooms its head off in this wonderful raspberry pink—must be something in the soil."

Cedarhurst: shade, clay loam, and water runoff

The western shoreline bumps out west in the Cedarhurst area, creating another low-bank terrace of north-facing gardens. Behind the houses is a steep hillside containing a pocket of advance outwash, that sand & gravel deposit that holds our water supply. Because this particular spot isn't capped with Vashon Till, water perks out and down this hillside particularly fast, giving the gardens at its foot a constant supply—perhaps oversupply—of groundwater, about 4' on average a year. As you'd expect, the native plants are all water-lovers, like salmonberry, horsetail, tall buttercup, and the namesake Western Red Cedar, as well as your typical Doug fir, alder, and big-leaf maple that cast their shade over the gardens. The soil is a reddish-brown clay loam that crumbles well in the hand, supporting native huckle-berries, salal, and sword ferns.

Kate Thompson & Mary Bruno, whose garden here was in the 2011 Garden Tour, have learned to live with shade and excess groundwater. Af-ter tiring of shoes muddying their front entry, they raised the ground by pouring gravel over the mud, then added new soil and planted in that. This gravel-based "rain garden" is planted with woodland plants: ferns and bleeding hearts, the grasses hakonechloa and ribbon grass, with an entrance passage of bamboo, oxalis, woodland poppies, and a beautiful variegated Cornus controversa tree. The water perking through their yard from the slopes behind can trickle through the gravel without drowning these plants. And into the gravel paths, the women have set millstones, flagstones, and steel grid panels to make footing secure.

Behind their house is a tiny garden crammed with astilbe and ligular-ia, maidenhair and deer tongue ferns, bleeding heart and May apple—all plants that love the moisture and overhung shade here. It's so dim and small a place, you feel like you're in a cave glittering with glowworms, but it's just bits of cloudy sky bouncing off rain-licked leaves.

The back lawn stretches beyond the shade, and there the women have big viburnums (leather-leaf and snowflake), old rhodies, giant alliums, toothed saxifrages, with nootka roses and blueberries along the top of the shoreline bluff. They've also squeezed in a small vegetable garden wrapped in deer fencing; it's lifted off the wet ground by a low rock wall topped with chives and golden marjoram.

Like Bruno and Thompson, the garden of **Jonathan Morse** is over-shadowed by towering firs, hemlocks, maples, and cedars. This narrow ra-vine has the same weeds, the same understory plants, the same drainage problems—the water here becoming a seasonal stream gurgling through the salmonberries. And like the two women, Jonathan and his father Bill raised the grade of their garden with terracing: two 4'-high walls of riprap rock have improved drainage enough to give a home to lavenders, santolina, walking onions, dahlias. At the top where it's sunny, Jonathan created an alpine garden in pulverized granite, in which grows lowbush blueberries, hens & chicks, dwarf alpine firs, and a weeping Alaskan Cedar.

But since most of the Morse garden is in moist half-shade, Jonathan has chosen plants for foliage, color, and texture, rather than for flowers: for instance, in the entrance space, a bronzy Oregon grape, Mahonia x media 'Charity', towers over a purple persicaria and golden wood millet. A golden hop vine climbs into a purple plum. Carex grass fluffs its strands next to the broad leaves of ornamental rhubarb, epimediums, or hellebore hybrids. Because the light is low, variegated hollies and brunneras are lush, without a spot of sun-scald (though Jonathan admits that the apricot heuchera does get crisped). He's planted many conifers and broadleaf evergreens, but he's finding they're borderline hardy—they pump out new growth after autumn rains return, only to be nailed by early winter freezes.

When I asked him about his workhorse plants, he told me, "Geranium macrorrhizum is a great ground cover for just about any condition; it blocks out weeds, tolerates sun or shade, drought or wet. Hellebore hybrids are pretty much bulletproof; I have them in sand with sun AND in heavy clay with shade. Berberis 'Royal Cloak', 'Helmond Pillar', darwinii, and x stenophylla 'Corallina Compacta' all tolerate a wide range of soils and drought in my garden. I am particularly fond of Cryptomeria japonica varieties: I've had great success with them in varying conditions. And my favorite genus, epimedium, has performed well."

"I have such a diverse range of soils—native clay loam, sand on the upslopes, complexes that have developed from mudslides and years of human use." He's spent twelve years building this garden, which was bought by his engineering grandfather in the 1950s (steel I-beams dumped here by granddad, Jonathan used in one of his walls). With a self-designed degree in "Organic Plant Cultivation" from Fairhaven College at Western Washington University, and a former job at Island Lumber's gardening center, he has all the Right Stuff to get the best garden from his Cedarhurst situation. (In 2013, Morse left his position at Island Lumber to start his own garden design & installation firm.)

Gardens of the Till Zone

Gardens on top of hardpan till can be marshy wet, at least during the rainy season, because water backfills the soil for most of the year. In the garden of **Brian Fisher & Peter Criss**, their topsoil was mined off by a prior owner, leaving only a gray, compacted subsoil around their house. The two men solved this problem by, again, raising the grade by creating planting raised beds out of large rocks, paving the "floor" with fractured gravel. The beds now hold Siberian and German irises, peonies, liriope, daylilies, sweet woodruff, and Globemaster alliums leaning their purple heads out from under Japanese maples. Lilies and climbing roses rise into a big white wooden pergola that extends its arms from the house. In a sunnier area, heathers and heaths, blue oat grass and low sedums soak up the sun. Lamium and periwinkle provide groundcover in shadier areas, while under a half-ring grove of alders, Solomon's Seal, sword ferns and hostas edge the lawn in quiet green. Except for around the lawn, Fisher told me, none of this garden could grow here without the rock raised beds and imported soil they hold.

Across the top central plateau of the Island stretches the hardpan, holding winter's water in the soil, keeping plants in the soup. Just off the hilltop of Cemetery Road is the garden of **Sylvia Soholt,** garden host in 2012 and formerly an organizer for VAA Garden Tour. When she moved in, she quickly discovered that runoff ran down her driveway to the foot of her door. With the help of garden designer and writer Terry Hershey, she too "raised the ground" with a 2'-high stone terrace, then added a french drain between the drive and house. "The plants here have to like a wet, rocky soil, so I've got daylilies, ninebark, irises, potentilla, hydrangea, montbretia. What doesn't like wet, I put in pots that I sit right in amongst the others."

She too has a seasonal stream, which makes a boundary between civilized garden and wild woodland. Snowflake viburnum, a white laceleaf elderberry, a pittosporum, and an evergreen magnolia 'Elizabeth' she bought in memory of her mother add bulk to the garden, while oriental poppies and lupines splash their bright colors in late spring.

Her neighbor **Greg Elliott** played host to the VAA Garden Tour in 2010, and he too elevated his ground with rock walls built 12 years prior, with a french tile drainage system to divert water. Perhaps because this neighborhood was once farmed, the native trees look younger, shorter, dominated by pioneer species like alder, hazels, willow, and maples that crave the damp that hangs in this Alderwood soil until early summer. In this shorter-scale treescape, ornamental trees fit right in. Greg has planted an elderberry (his a purple 'nigra'), birches, kousa dogwood, three katsuras, a boxleaf azara near the front entrance where its vanilla scent can be appreciated, a paper-bark maple next to his garage. A willow once fell on his snowbell tree, which grew back wider than tall at the top of one of his rockwall terraces. Hardy geraniums spread in its light shade, while under the trees in moist areas, Arum italicum has naturalized alongside yellow buttercups.

If you want to see the mature size of many shrubs and trees growing on till, head south on the highway to the **Country Store.** Over the years owner **Vy Biel** and her staff have amassed quite the collection in her ten acres. Here you'll find the state's largest European hazel tree, near the NE corner of the store. Big specimens of parrotia, corylopsis spicata, and fothergilla grow in the swale just west of the parking lot, while across the footbridge is a collection of viburnums and mountain ash trees. During summer you can u-pick blueberries where, in winter, ducks paddle to and fro, there's that much standing water. Country Store also hosts **Colvos Creek Nursery,** which had a satellite nursery here by 2005 and then moved everything here when the December 2008 snows destroyed their three Maury Island greenhouses. Owner **Mike Lee**, a landscape architect by training, propagates Northwest and West Coast natives and drought-tolerant plants, mostly shrubs and trees,, including broadleaf evergreens from Australia and New Zealand. If you've got a daisy bush, unusual maple or pine, or a eucalyptus, it probably came from Colvos Creek Nursery.

East to the shore at Ellisport, geologist **Kevin & Nancy Freeman** have two side-by-side properties on KVI Bluff, on top of that hardpan bluff explored in Chapter 1. "And that's why we're growing most things in raised beds," he admitted. "You have to supplement with compost, which you can work a little bit into the looser top of the hardpan. The soil on the Island is not that rich, but there are areas of the native soil, places where there's been a forest duff layer developed over time, that has an organic-rich layer." Where erosion has chipped into the cliff's edge, he's planted Oregon grape for its deep, earth-holding roots.

Low-lying Clay

From KVI bluff, Freeman can gaze over Tramp Harbor to Maury island, where the north-facing cliffs are so dense with clay, the Reimnitz son Erik once carved a troll's face into the cliff that lasted for years. (Later it became the mascot image for his rock band, Troll's Cottage.) His parents **Ilse & Hartmut Reimnitz** now live on the Kingsbury Loop, where local rumor says the topsoil here was mined and sold, perhaps used to make the dikes in nearby Raab's Lagoon. "People say 'oh, that's some dead soil.' But it isn't—clay has a lot of nutrition in it—we can grow anything here," she told me proudly. By feeding their sandy clay plenty of compost, these two painters have created a sunny border full of rugosa roses and rosemary, phlox and artichokes, fronds of russian sage and red montbretia, yellow verbascum, yarrow, and coreopsis, shrubs like smoke bush, ninebark, butterfly bush. Clematis climbs up the studio wall between mason bee hives. A corner of the house is covered by sunflowers. They have a vegetable garden and an small orchard, both deer-fenced in their wide-open lawn, where Hartmut grows pears, several kinds of apples, a 'Frost Peach' "with 50 peaches on it this year!" plus cherries, black currants for Ilse's jam, and plums including a "Pt. Townsend Schoolhouse Plum, a big yellow plum, very good eating."

Centuries of settling water and summertime evaporation have given the low places of Maury Island plenty of clay. A crow's flight away from Kingsbury is the garden of **Roy Haase & Drew Balogh** on 75th. Water stands long in this neighborhood: skunk cabbage thrives in low areas near ponds that never dry out, even in droughty summers. To help drain the winter wet from his large lawn, Roy has dug small trenches by hand around his perimeter to pull water toward the woodland. And he trucks in compost to give his clay-rich soil more tilth. It works: his broccoli is half Roy's size.

Like many of us with acres to fill, he's planted a lot of big and bigger trees: larch, pin oak, Oregon ash, sequoia, California redwood. Many of them are water-lovers: cedars, dogwood, the maples Japanese, swamp, and featherleaf. He's also got a small orchard of pears and apples individually fenced against deer, two big hedges he power-prunes from a ladder, and a holly overrun by a white rambling rose. To the athletic club where he works Roy brings bouquets from his garden: delphiniums and peonies, roses and snapdragons, single giant blooms from his evergreen magnolia. Hosta, hakonechloa, astilbe, cotoneaster, and lily of the valley also grow huskily in his heavy soil, and silver lamium covers the ground of his woodland ("What a disaster," he shook his head as we walked through it to see his pond. "Can you believe all this came from one flat of starts?")

In Dockton along its western shore, you'll come to the garden of **Anita Halstead**, 2007 Garden Tour coordinator whose garden took second place in the 2008 Pacific NW Gardens Competition. The beach is just across the road, but there's not much sand in Anita's yard. It's mostly clay, heavily amended with the 2-year, 3-bin compost her husband **Kelly Robinson** makes. The mound garden within her driveway loop is mostly clay piled there by the builders; on it grows lamb's ears, variegated loosestrife, a Japanese maple, blue oat grass, sweet williams, montbretia 'Lucifer' and an undulating 'dragon' in boxwood topiary.

Between two big balls of boxwood you enter a thick border of hydrangeas, hollyhocks, and gold flame spireas, pink echinacia facing yellow loosestrife and red montbretia across the gravel path. It wends past daisies and alstromerias, past a small vegetable garden and toward a shaded garage, where another clay bank hosts lamium and maidenhair fern. Along the tree-shaded south of her house grow callas, columbine, azaleas, hostas, and many kinds of fern along the banks of a dry creek bed. You exit the shade where a coral cape fuchsia leans into sun, joining pink lavatera, more callas, and raspberry-red hydrangeas along a tiny lawn. It's a small garden stuffed with workhorse plants: shrubs phygelius 'Moonraker,' hydrangea 'Nikko Blue,' lavatera 'Barnsley,' cranberry viburnum and clipped box, with daylilies, knautia, alchemilla, and the self-seeding linaria, valerian, nigella, and rabbits' ears growing between the shrubs. All this might feel a little TOO billowy but for the clipped boxwoods, the pergola and tile pavings, the sharp edge to the lawn that all work together to contain this exuberant garden.

Anita is part of a beachcombing group, and let's join them now as they head south past Manzanita and the cottage garden of **Patty (Custer) Van den Broek.** Her's is one of those classic Funky Beach Cottages: a white & blue-trimmed two-story adorned with buoys, driftwood, and other found "treasures" like the dinghy resting on the barnacled boat-ramp, with flowers spilling over the bulkhead. The soil is such stiff clay that Patty has schlepped new topsoil, bag by heavy bagful, down her steep access stairs. Her list of workhorse plants is short because of the SW, salt-laden winter winds that tear across Dalco Passage; the rugosa rose on top of the bulkhead, she says, is what grows best. But shasta daisies, montbretia, nasturiums, euphorbias, and a wind-dwarfed lavatera grow sheltered behind the rugosa, and at the foot of the house grow climbing and hybrid tea roses. One's named for a past Tacoma garden club member, 'Ruth Alexander', the lady of what would become Lakewold Garden; you can easily imagine, in the days when Patty's mother and aunt owned this place, that this rosebush was bought at a garden club fundraiser, then boated over from Tacoma.

Up the Hill: the sand & gravel zones

Back in the car, you can drive out of Dockton and reach the sandy zone within a hundred feet of the water. On a high bluff overlooking Dockton Park, retired radiologist **Whit Carhart** has created a hillside woodland garden amidst towering firs (you might have seen it during the 2007 VAA Sunset Gala or on the 2012 VAA Garden Tour—it was definitely the standout garden that year) Though the soil is mostly sand, with the help of driplines every 12" and annual mulchings of compost he can grow a wealth of perennials, shrubs, and trees in full sun to half-shade.

He's sought out plenty of inspiration: he's a member of NW Horticultural Society, the Hardy Plant Society, and the NW Perennial Alliance, has taken horticultural classes in Seattle, volunteers twice a month at the Miller Botanical Garden in Shoreline from where he's taken many of his planting ideas. In his shadiest woodland, Japanese maples, rhodies, and snowflake viburnums stretch sheltering limbs over groundcover collections of candelabra primroses and unusual ferns, while in a moist patch grow rodgersias and saxifrage, may apple, meconopsis, big shrubs of mountain laurel. The sunny border opposite seems planned for color and shape: flings of golden forest grass front yellow yarrow and steely sea holly, red astrantia and coral cape fuchsia, while above them all bob wands of stipa grass, foxglove, and the purple balloons of globemaster alliums.

When I asked him about his favorite no-fail plants, he wrote back, "My favorite tree is Acer japonicum 'Aconitofolium' (Full Moon Maple) with a beautiful structure, deeply lobed leaves, and spectacular crimson fall color. For a shrub, I like Daphne odora 'Aureomarginatum'. Not only is the evergreen variegation interesting, its early spring bloom so highly fragrant is welcome after a long winter. If sited well (part shade, out of the wind, well-nourished soil), it is mostly "no fail" but does require some summer water. In perennials, I very much like helleborus. If the leaves are cut to ground before the blossoms come up, spectacular spring flowers lasting several months can be seen, then the foliage comes out anew."

As you drive up 248th toward the top of Maury, past the scenic overlook and around the corner, the land opens into a savannah of grass and bamboo. Here was once the largest red currant farm west of the Mississippi, today replaced by far smaller properties. Where once farmer Kenny Larson wrangled 150 acres of currants, now a retired fruit scientist, an urban planner, and a landscape architect turned nurseryman farm their 5s and 10s for their own pleasure. Seems that many of Vashon's post-70s immigrants—educated, older, often academics or from scientific or professional careers—come here looking to get dirt under their fingernails.

Turn east on 244th and you might spot Kareli Sunflower Farm owned by **Dan Carlson,** professor at UW's Evans School of Public Affairs. You feel like you're in California here with the madrones, the sunflowers, the golden meadows—and there's reason for that deserty feel. This road down 244th runs across two of Maury's four strips of recessional outwash, giving the soil extreme drainage. And this side of Maury Island gets 25% less rain than Vashon's north end. It's dry up here, as Dan realized when trying to farm raspberries. But while the raspberries did so-so, the sunflowers seeded themselves—and practically sold themselves, too, at farmers markets. Dan also has a few chestnut trees from Pete Svinth, who once ran an experimental fruit tree farm where Pacific Crest Farm is now; Dan sells the nuts as a Christmas treat at farmers markets.

On the western end of 244th is the orchard of **Dr. Bob Norton,** also on part of the Kenny Larson currant farm but on different soil: an Alderwood soil that he waters by dripline. Although at age 83 he's retired from his work as fruit scientist for WSU Extension, he's still trialing fruit to find the best performers in our Island climate. In 2012 he got an apricot tree to ripen fruit "which is pretty rare for around here," he boasted to me.

If you turn the corner at 99th Ave SW and Pt. Robinson Road, you will climb east up to the Raecoma neighborhood and the garden of **Sally Fox,** past president of the Garden Club. The hilltop soil here is an Alderwood sand and gravel loam that gets only about 38" of rain a year, so in summer to hold moisture, Sally covers her beds with newspaper or cardboard mulch augmented with horse manure. She depends on drought-tolerant plants, many of which came from Colvos Creek Nursery that used to be down the road. "Water is at a premium here, so I use a lot of natives and drought tolerant plants. Trees planted beyond four years ago aren't getting any extra water: they include deodar cedar (regular and dwarf), silver Korean fir, catalpa, golden pine, parrotia, katsuras, red gums, stewartias, thujas, juniper, cornus kousa. The Japanese maples are doing remarkably well without extra water."

"Here's the shrubs that work well for me: manzanitas, escallonias, elderberry, smoke bush, ninebark, viburnum tinus, snowberries native and cultivated; the native mock orange, the low cotoneasters, red twig dogwoods. Small shrubby perennials like hebes, parahebes, sedum, euphorbias have done well. Certain tall plants like verbascum, inula magnifica (that really tall daisy plant with the tobacco leaves), clumping bamboo. In the woodland round-about I have sword ferns (my hero plant), Oregon grape, luzula sylvatica marginata (requires nothing, it's my favorite woodlands edging plant). Tiger's Eye sumac, ceanothus; rock roses, thujas. Lots of grasses: my favorites are calamagrostis acutiflora 'over am,' molinia caerulean arundinacea 'sky racer,' and panicum virgatum 'squaw.'"

You drive from rainforest to savannah as you drive from Vashon to Maury, and along the way you'll find gardeners that have found what works in their particular place. We have vineyards, tree nurseries, bonsai growers, and lavender farms, have in the past had orchid, lily, dahlia, even marijuana farms (and probably will again: Washington voted in legal marijuana in 2012). And in 2013, I finally found that most un-rain-forest of plants: somebody living on Raecoma's hot gravel soil was, yes, growing cactus.

Heritage Berries

A few Islanders harbor the last of our heritage berries. And if you'll pick fruit for Dr. Bob, he'll let you pick for yourself in a day or two.

My knees were dirty, my back was already sore, and I suspected the back of my neck was turning as red as these berries. Half a dozen of us were crawling in the Maury dust down the rows of Dr. Bob Norton's strawberry patch, plucking varieties that I'd never heard of. It was a brilliant blue day, the first Friday after a typically drizzly Fourth of July, and Dr. Bob needed berries to sell at the farmers' market tomorrow. But first, he had to get them picked, and being a little old-of-back for the job, he had devised a friendly bribe: come pick for me today, you can come pick for yourself tomorrow.

My own strawberries had been delicious, but I only got a few. A chipmunk—and then his three brothers—wiggled through my bird-net hoops and raided my patch day after day. They'd line up together, nibbling, then drop their half-eaten berries and scram whenever I came charging out of the kitchen, arms in full flap. No matter how many rocks and pipes I laid on the net's edges, they always found a way through. The next year, it was a raccoon. Netting works against birds—not critters with paws.

So I was glad to take Dr. Bob's bribe. Despite the Island's past reputation as producing 100,000 crates a year of "the largest and best-flavored strawberry in the world (as that 1909 booster's pamphlet by John Reid declared), today the Island's vast fields are long gone. The last commercial fields were turned into U-picks in the 1970s when farmers could no longer attract enough paid labor; the U-picks lasted only a year or two before the farmer turned the field under for hay. My gardening pal Bill Green ran a U-pick strawberry field in the 70s down near Portland; his son Nathan talked about weekenders who'd cherry-pick through the rows leaving half the fruit behind. "They didn't clean-pick," he complained. "It just wasn't worth it."

Dr. Bob didn't let us off so easily. When I showed up, he was handing out not only flats for the good berries, but plastic containers for the others. "See how red this one is? That's what I want for tomorrow's market. See how this isn't as brilliant red? Leave it: we'll get it next week. I don't want any with even a spot of brown: taste one and you'll see why. Put those in this old take-out tray. All the browns and moldies go in here, too. I want the rows picked pretty clean: just leave the unripe ones for next week."

Allstar, Stolo, Honeoye, each in its own row. Puget Crimson, Seascape, Jewel. Elongated or squat, sweet or tart. I recognized Albion, an everbearer I'd planted on Kathy Wheaton's recommendation; Dr. Bob said it was his best day-neutral. All of the berries in these rows were still on probation. As we brought our filled containers to Bob, he asked, "What did we think of their taste?" (Our comments can be found at the end of this chapter.)

I didn't think much of these probation berries, but at the end of the afternoon, Emily Macrae sent me to the patch of Tillamooks for a quick ten-minute pick. Now THESE were more like what I remembered from childhood: big, fat fellows that filled the mouth with ripe berry sweetness.

I asked Dr. Bob if he grew any Marshalls, that strawberry that had given Vashon its early reputation for great berry farming. "Too soft for the fresh fruit market," he said. "Flavor is good, but not better than some of the newer varieties like Shuksan or Honeoye."

Yesteryear's Big Berry Business

When you page through newspaper clippings about Vashon agriculture before WWII, you can't miss the superlatives. Island farmers weren't afraid to claim their farms, their yields, their 'Marshall' strawberries as the biggest and best. The land where I'm picking Dr. Bob's berries was once said to be the largest currant farm west of the Mississippi. Down the hill, the rising slopes of Dockton were carpeted by Theo Berry's strawberry fields that, all together, were said to make up the largest field on the Island. West of Vashon-town, the Mukai family raised strawberries on a 40-acre farm said to be "the largest strawberry field in the world."

From Vashon Heights to Morgan Hill through the first half of the 20th century, Vashon Island was a solid grid of 5-10 acre farms growing fruit, berries, and laying hens. Someone in the bell tower of the Methodist Church might have, say in the mid-30s, looked west and seen strawberry fields covering the acres from the post office to the big Mukai fields and cannery on 107th. North of town were Tokio "Tok" Otsuka's fields across from Ober Park and downslope to what's now Hogsback Farm. East, where Island Lumber is now, were Fred Ernisee's fields of currants and berries. Turn south, and fields of currants and berries would have stretched from the south edge of town all the way to the Matsuda fields behind K2 and Mingle-ment Roasterie. A block south of that was the famous Olympic Berry Farm, and on the other side of Sunrise Ridge was Mr. Morgan's peach orchard, where Kathy Wheaton of Kathy's Corner picked as a kid.

The plateaus and valley bottoms of Maury Island were just as covered in fruit. Dockton resident Gordy Nelson, in a letter to the Heritage Museum, wrote, "When I was growing up, most of the now open fields were planted with currants, gooseberries, loganberries, cherry trees and some strawber-ries." Trucks from Smuckers or Sunny Jim Preserves in Tacoma sent out buyers and, later in the season, trucks to pick up loganberries and currants from Dockton fields. Wives often ran the fields while their men were off fishing, paying local housewives, kids, B.C. Indians who came down to pick, and other pickers in sales tickets redeemable for cash at the end of the picking/fishing season—or immediately for groceries, candy, or popsicles at Theo Berry's Dockton Store. The money was good: in 1930, a picker earned over $4 a flat. (By the 1970s, competition had eroded pay down to the $1.30/flat that Tok paid in the 1970s.)

Strawberries were a money-maker for all Puget Sound farmers in those first decades: 39% of Puget-area fruit farm receipts came from strawberry crops. Vashon's good soil, mild climate, and ready access to the maritime highway allowed Island farmers to get their crops to market early, giving them the best prices and an edge over larger-producing, but cooler, land-locked areas such as Bellevue and the White and Green River valleys. Island-ers set up packing companies, like Northwest Canning Co, Vashon Island Fruit Co, and Masa Mukai's VIPCO, and sold their berries fresh, barreled, or frozen to markets from Seattle to London, England.

WWII changed all that. In January 1942, when 125 Japanese and their children were taken off-island to war-time internment camps, the Island lost some of its most hard-working, talented berry farmers. Most, because of Japanese exclusion laws, couldn't own their farms and didn't return to the Island after the war ended; those that did, like the Matsuda's, encouraged their children to get educations and not rely on farming.

The prosperity that followed WWII offered full time, mostly off-Island jobs that paid better than the typical Island combo of farming + fishing. The improvement of mainland roads allowed first mainland farmers, and then California mega-farms, to compete with Island fruit for market supremacy. Another kind of turnover occurred across generations: as the first generation of farmers aged or died in the 1950s, they tended to pass their land to descendents or buyers in equal-but-smaller subdivisions, making profitable farming that much harder. In the 1970s, farmers' kid labor dried up as new Federal labor laws required pickers to be at least 12 years old. In 1979, the *Beachcomber* ran a story on Tokio "Tok" Otsuka, second-generation Island strawberry farmer and last of the commercial growers. He needed pickers badly, yet could only pay them $1.30 a flat for berries heading to a cannery. A photo shows bell-bottomed teenagers in his field, some bent to the task, some standing around eating Tok's fruit. He told the *Beachcomber* then, "People don't want to work on the farm anymore. The kids all want city-type jobs. They rather be a box boy at Thriftway." By the end of the 70s, all the Island's commercial fruit operations were shuttered or plowed under.

Loganberries Come Home

Still, I thought at least a FEW plants from the old days might have lingered on. When I first met Dr. Bob, I asked him whether he knew of anybody who still had remnants of the old farmed berries. He said, "You must talk to Helen Brocard: she probably knows more about the Island's old berries than anyone. AND, I think she'll let you pick a few."

I called, asked if she ran a U-pick. "Not really—it's more a personal plot, but you can come pick what I've got." She lived in Dockton, her house and shady fir grove in the middle of what once must have been working fields. When I knocked, that warm August afternoon, a dainty woman north of 70 with chin-length, salt-n-pepper hair answered the door. I recognized her from the farmers market: she sometimes sold her berries there. As she walked out, her first words after hello were "Meet my Rochester—this is the kind of peach tree that I used to pick for Mr. Morgan at his orchard on Morgan Hill. I had to send all the way to New York to get my tree." The tree, only five years old, dangled green fruit just above my head, ripening in the warmth coming off the south side of the house.

Her little fenced yard was thick with perennials and fruit. Along the perimeter were 20' trellises of cane fruit: loganberries, olympic berries, and raspberries. I asked her if she grew marionberries. "My parents tried, but they don't really work here: they're strictly an Oregon berry. I used to make marionberry pies at my restaurant; they always sold out. So—how much do you want?" she asked, frowning as her hand danced over the brambles.

"Just enough for pie," I said.

Relief flowed over her face. "Good! There's not much left, but we can probably get that much. Loganberries have a long season—40 days—but I've been picking a lot as it's been a really GOOD year."

The berries had colored blush to purple, but Helen said that anything redder than scarlet would work in pie. She asked, "Do you use flour in your pie filling?" and before I could reply, stated—"I don't: I use a tablespoon of cornstarch mixed into the sugar because it makes a beautiful transparent filling that shows off the berries' color. Flour just mucks them up. Loganberries make the best pie, don't you think?"

I'd vote for marionberries, myself, but I wasn't going to quibble with my berry benefactrice.

The vines were wrapped around a double-row of wire stetched between posts. When I sunk to my knees to pick the lower fruit, she warned me against landing on the thorns of the first-year vines lying on the ground. "Those are the primocanes: I just leave them there to grow until the 2nd-year canes on the wires, the floricanes, are done fruiting. After the fruit is all picked and done, I'll cut the floricanes to the ground. Then I'll get my long leather gloves on, lift the primocanes, and loop them around these wires. Next year, they'll produce the fruit, while the new generation of primocanes grow out along the ground."

After we picked loganberries, we visited her strawberries, picked a few. Then, eating berries in the shade of the fir grove, she told me how she came to have the berries that her mother grew, berries that had gone full circle from here to Tacoma to Bellevue and back.

The surrounding old field had been her parents' farm: in the 1940s they grew gooseberries, loganberries, and 'Red Lake' currants commercially. Her father, Ivan Kranjcevich, came from Croatia in the 1930s; once he met and married Eva, they bought seven acres to farm on Maury Island. They'd sell to Sunny Jim Fruit Processors in Tacoma: their inspector would come out to look at crops and offer a price to farmers, then later the company would send out a truck to pick up flats from all their Maury Island farmer clients. "This was all berry- and fruit-farming, back then," Helen said. Like a lot of Island kids of that era, she made her clothing allowance picking for her parents, neighbors, and for farmers like Mr. Morgan on Vashon Island.

But berry farming couldn't pay all the bills, so Ivan, like many farmers, hired out: he took a job cooking on the Dockton fishing boat *Umatilla*, captained by Lucas Plancich. Up near Cape Flattery, in the middle of a clear, moonlit night, the boat was rammed in two by the battleship *U.S.S. Arizona*. Seven men spilled into the water and were pulled out by their sister boat, the *Emblem*. The *Arizona* kept right on going until the Navy ordered the ship's caption to turn the boat around. He was tried and demoted.

Two men on the *Umatilla* died; their families were given settlements. Ivan, though severely hurt with internal injuries, was given no settlement. He could still cook, though, so he took over the home kitchen while his wife took over the farm. When he died in 1945, Helen's mother was sat down by a welfare worker and given a choice: welfare or the farm. Eva chose the farm. The family kept the farm going until, with her kids grown, Eva remarried in 1960 and moved to Tacoma. She took some berry plants with her.

In Tacoma, Eva dug up her yard, installed her berries and other plants and flowers, and kept on farming, selling produce and flowers to neighbors and restaurants. Helen married, settled in Bellevue, and started her own restaurant, "Pogachas" (which means "flatbread" in Croatian) that served California-style cuisine; it's still going strong today. And from her mother's garden she took cuttings of currants and loganberries, sticking them into pots and nursing them along for several years.

When Eva died, Helen and her brother inherited those original seven acres. After selling Pogachas, Helen moved back to the Dockton homeplace. Eva & Ivan's loganberries and currants had come home.

Helen sent me off with two pints of ruby-red loganberries. I took her advice, switched from flour to cornstarch, and after dinner carved myself the most beautiful slice of heritage berry pie.

Helen told me that she didn't want to "become a nursery," but she has propagated berry plants as part of her activities with the Vashon Island Fruit Club. Some of her loganberry starts went to Hal Green, who joined the Fruit Club hoping to restore his father's berry patch. Hal, a retired lawyer who's settled into overalls, tinted glasses, and a Derek Jacobi bob of gray hair, gave me a tour of his homeplace, Triplebrook Farm, just before it opened as part of the 2011 Vashon Allied Arts Garden Tour.

In its 100-year career, Triplebrook Farm on the lower Westside Highway has been a homestead, cherry orchard, egg & berry farm, summer place, and now a B&B. Every stone, tree, plank, and plant touched by human hands has its story, saved for and savored by the next generation—like the white star Hal had repainted over the doors of the old red barn, shaded by, yes, a spreading chestnut tree. The 1890s farm turned through a few hands before being sold to Robinson Jenner in 1929. His first entry reads—

November 16, 1929—Purchased approximately 19 acres waterfront from W. W. Prigg for $8000... Farm includes house, barn, 2 chicken houses, brooder houses for 1200 chicks, two ponies, 350 yearling hens, 480 pullets, and all tools and equipment. About 8 acres cleared part of which is in family orchard. 3-year-old Montmorency cherry orchard of 100 trees about to bear."

Jenner kept his farm and daybook for 20 years before selling to Hal Green's father, Athol Green. At the time, Montmorency cherry trees lined the driveway, with a field of cane berries on trellises on the othe side of Westside Highway. Athol wasn't a farmer—he worked as Comptroller for Simpson Timber Company—but he did cherish his fruit crops, taking good care of the pioneer apple and cherry trees and planting his own berry patch. Hal remembers, as a kid in the early 1950s, caring for the berries with his dad and picking pie cherries that Dad sold to his co-workers. But after a nasty 1950 snowstorm that kept the kids home for a month (and drove mother to her wit's end), the family moved back to Seattle. Triplebrook became a summer place, and the berries, unfenced, became deer fodder.

Hal grew up, married Molly, became a lawyer in Seattle. When he retired and they moved here in 2003, "I really wanted to restore the berry patch," he told me. "And I wanted heirloom Vashon berries. When I joined the Fruit Club, I met Helen Brocard. She said 'I've been growing Vashon heritage berries for years—I'll give you some.'"

Hal's new berry patch now holds Helen's loganberries, plus rows of boy-senberries, marionberries, raspberries, and some robust blackberries called Chester Thornless that came from Fairie Hill Farm on 204th. Along each side of the center aisle were twin rows of espaliered pear trees. I admired the way Hal had planted attractive rows of strawberries, like a green fringe, underneath his berry trellises. And Hal had trellised his loganberries in the same loop-de-loop fashion that his father, Helen's father, Mr. Jenner, and scores of Vashon berry farmers had probably done, shielded by their long leather gloves, during Vashon's berry years.

I remembered Fairie Hill Farm. In the summer of 2006, I spotted a sand-wich board on the intersection of 204th & Vashon Highway that said "U-Pick Berries" and whipped my car westward to find it. Lisa Mathias was leasing the field for a CSA and caring for the many long, beautifully kept rows of all kinds of cane berries. Here were raspberries red, golden, and blackcap, olalla berries, tayberries, blacks, blues, logans and YES! marion-berries, my personal favorite! I didn't think much of the price, though: $3 a pint, nearly what Thriftway charged, and I did all the work. The berries were beautiful and tasty, but that price was hard to swallow.

By 2010, I too was farming on 204th, sharing the vegie patch with alpaca farmer Bill Green. Comparing notes on the berries growing at Fairie Hill Farm across the street, Bill mentioned "well, this farm used to be a berry farm, too, you know. This was the Olympic Berry Farm."

"THE Olympic berry farm?" I asked, remembering all the articles I'd read in the Heritage Museum on this famous berry, a Vashon original. A blackberry 2" long, excellent for diabetics, luscious in flavor, exclusive to the tea room of Seattle's flagship department store, Frederick & Nelson.

Vashon's famed Olympic berry—where had they all gone?

Back in 1909, a Vashon farmer, Mr. Peter Erickson, took himself to the Alaska Yukon Pacific Exposition, held on the grounds of what would be-come the University of Washington campus. There he met the famous plant breeder Luther Burbank, up from California to extol the virtues of his 'Phe-nomenal' berry, his cross between a loganberry and a wild blackberry.

Mr. Erickson thought he "could do better." It is not known whether Erickson made this boast to Burbank's face, but Burbank did eventually send Mr. Erickson a plant of 'Phenomenal' to use in developing his own berry. Erickson, with the help of his son-in-law Halleck F. Greider, crossed 'Phenomenal' with a wild black raspberry of Minnesota called 'Plum Farmer' and came up with this new berry. It was large, sweet, hardy to -18°, and productive from July to October. And, because it wasn't prone to breaking and thus bleeding its juice all over everything, it was probably easier than most berries to harvest and ship.

The men named the berry 'Olympic'—perhaps in honor of their field's wonderful view of that mountain range—and in 1937 they took out a patent on the plant in Halleck Greider's name. Soon they were growing over 20,000 tons of the berries. A doctor proclaimed them perfect for diabetics. Mindful of that report, Frederick & Nelson offered to buy the entire crop off the Greider's farm. Their tea room became famed for this exclusive berry, served in sherbets, jams, and their "Olympic Berry Pie—40¢ a slice."

Erickson & Greider formed the Olympic Berry Corporation. Soon they were selling plants to other farmers, confident of a market beyond the F & N's tea room that would be hungry to have berries so famous.

Unfortunately, first Greider and then Erickson died in the 1940s, leaving Widow Pauline and little Halleck Jr. to care for a multi-ton, high-maintenance crop. A photo from the Heritage Museum shows Widow Pauline and her boy standng between tied trellises; she talks, in the article, about the rising weeds, the bald spots in the rows, the trouble of getting laborers to bring in a crop worth only a couple thousand dollars. It's a rerun Sad Song of Vashon's declining farms: too little labor, too little income from the crop.

By the mid-90s when Bill Green bought the farm, he found many rows of Olympics still on their posts and wires, in good shape. The following winters were too wet; most plants succumbed to root rot. When I arrived, the only plants left were growing out from under concrete rubble that son Nathan had piled on to protect the plants from UPS trucks.

But my, were they lucious... if only there was enough for pie.

After I blogged about these berries, I heard from Halleck Jr.'s daughter, who remembered picking the berries "at Grandma Pauline's house." Her brother, Halleck III, still grows Olympics in his Shoreline yard. And I've heard whispers that, here and there, some few Olympic berries still grow.

I've got one: the only survivor of a dozen cuttings I tried to propagate one winter. It grows slowly at the base of my raspberry trellis, someday to be loop-de-looped around the double wires, someday to produce enough for a pie. Will it be as good as a loganberry pie? As good as my mother's Oregon Marionberry pie? Surely at the rate that blackberries grow, I won't have long to wait to find out.

Mighty Tasty Strawberries

At the 2012 annual picnic of the V-MI Fruit Club, Emily Macrae ran a taste-off of strawberries grown in Dr. Bob's test rows. The berries had been frozen and sugared. I've added some notes.

Emily's Top Five—

Glooscap - flavorful, hardy, prolific with a full-on second crop in the fall
Honeoye - Big, dark prolific berry with a tropical taste. June bearer.
Albion - Best flavor of them all. Day-neutral, long season
Jewel - Beautiful and delicious. Firm fruit. Long season.
Shuksan - prolific, tasty and freezes exceptionally well. June bearer.

The Rest—

Gaviota - tastes very good, but not prolific
Diamante - good taste, but pale in color
Puget Crimson - dark, flavorful, but soft, susceptible to powdery mildew
Chandler - Bob likes this variety, but its flavor doesn't 'wow' me
Allstar - Unattractive (pale under the crown) without a redeeming taste
Tillamook - impressively big, but without great flavor, in my opinion
Stolo, Seascape, Monterey are all berries that I find lacking in flavor.

Sources: Kathy's Corner, Raintree Nursery, Sakuma Brothers

At last... Real Summer's here

Midway through the calendar's idea of summer, a high pressure system sets up over the Pacific Northwest and drives the jet stream far to the north. At last, we bask in warmth. The rain clouds disappear, timers for driplines click on regularly, and sprinklers fan across lawns the owners refuse to let brown. The weather might even turn into a drought: it's pretty common to barely have a drop of rain from July through September.

Along trails and roads, the margins turn rusty-red as madrones send their leaves twirling down in their annual leaf drop. Daisy flowers are making more impact in the borders: shasta daisies, helenium, calendula, coreopsis, and later the purples and pinks of the aster family. Columns of lilies rear into the sky to open trumpets blaring forth intense perfume. At Courthouse Square, the tan plumes of ornamental grasses are riffled by passing traffic on the highway, while in my garden the spikes from Stipa Gigantea dance like a hatch of golden mosquitoes frenzied in the afternoon sun.

Sometime in August, the much-anticipated first tomato is turning red. Maybe it's a golfball-sized Stupice, maybe it's a yellow Taxi, maybe it's the first of the tiny Sungolds sweet as candy. We clip away foliage weekly, trying to keep the vigorous bushes open to air circulation and heat. Soon the bushes of Siletz and Legend, Early Girl and Oregon Spring will be weighed down with heavy red slicers, followed by the vine tomatoes, finally the heirlooms in a good tomato year. But if it's not a good tomato year, we can sigh and depend on our green tomato recipes, especially the spicy apple-green tomato pie.

TRUE summer is here at last. And the livin' is soooooooo easy.

Summer Pruning

Shaping & training fruit trees in the summer

By the end of June, the dwarf apple trees in our community orchard—the same that we had pruned so vigorously the winter before, the same that I'd kept sprayed against scab all winter, were loaded with tiny apples.

But the cherry trees we'd headed back the year before looked very bizarre: the top of each trunk sprouted like a green feather-duster from the big head cuts made 18 months before. Michelle Ramsden had warned that we'd need to prune again, come summer, so it was time to go learning more pruning tricks from the Fruit Club.

I'd been looking forward to their annual workshop, if only to show off my chain-saw. As I'd picked berries with Dr. Bob at his berry-patch, we'd got to talking about managing wood—a topic any Islander with a wood-stove or large pruning tasks can jaw on about at length—and I'd told him about the Stihl saw I'd bought the year before. "It's got an 'EZ Start' motor that lends a little extra torque at the end of your start-up pull. I call it my Lady Saw because like most women, I don't have much arm strength, and up until I bought this thing, pulling on a chain-saw hasn't been easy."

"I'd like to try that saw," said my 80-something host. "Bring it to the pruning workshop." I promised I would.

In mid-July, 25 fruit club members and I converged on the Burton Peninsula home of Kelli and Todd Brooke to learn about pruning fruit trees in summer. The Brookes live near the center of the peninsula, neighbors to the Ostroms and their 100-year-old orchard, but these old fruit trees were probably planted after the Brookes' house was built some 50 years ago. Arching over their back lawn were four old trees at least 25' high: Gravenstein, Golden Delicious, Baldwin "with huge apples big as a softball," plus a tree they hadn't identified. The branches were arched high and criss-crossed, bristling with lichens, water-sprouts, and quite a few baby apples. Even after today's pruning, the Brookes would still have a nice crop.

I arrived with my felcos, a long-reach pole pruner and the EZ-Start. When Elizabeth Vogt handed me my name-tag at the entrance and thanked me for bringing a chain-saw, I couldn't resist giving her the same brag on the EZ Start that I'd given Dr. Bob. Then I joined my fellow fruit clubbers under the shade of the Brooke's old Gravenstein.

Dr. Bob Norton passed out a hand-out as a younger man set an orchard ladder into the high reaches of the old apple tree. "The point of pruning now," said Dr. Bob, "is to shape the tree when it has spent its vigor and is not so likely to respond to pruning by producing new growth. In summer pruning, we reduce height and open the tree to more sunlight, which helps the color of the fruit and reduces the need for future dormant pruning."

Dr. Bob made the case that one could do TOO much pruning in winter. Fruit trees in late spring are ready to burst forth "when the storage reserves of sugars and starches produced in the leaves during the last season are ready to send out the vigorous flush of growth in spring." When one hard-prunes a tree in early spring, the tree is left with more reserve than its new shape can contain; that vigor pushes out new water sprouts that shoot straight for the sky. They look terrible, bristling out from pruning cuts like Grandpa's wild eyebrow hairs. And they waste the tree's energy and potential, as vertical limbs aren't as likely to break out in fruiting spurs.

Bob turned the talk over to his trainee Paul Schuster, a 30-something redhead already gunning the motor of his chain-saw-on-a-pole. "Before I start pruning, I ask 'What is this tree used for? Is it shade? Fruit? Esthetics?' Now this (he patted the Gravenstein) is mostly for shade, so we want to keep the high arching shape by removing lower limbs. If we wanted to make it easier to pick, we'd remove upper limbs to lower the canopy to a better height for picking. So I start evaluating at the trunk and work up, noting crossed or overshaded branches, whether a branch can hold a full load of fruit."

Paul climbed halfway up the 12-foot orchard ladder and set his Echo's chain to a long interior branch, about a foot away from the trunk. By making first an undercut halfway in, then completing the cut inches further up, he released the weight of the branch. Then he sawed the stub down to the collar—the swelling at the base of the branch. Dr. Bob pointed, "Look how he's leaving the branch collar: that will heal over quickly. You never cut flush with the trunk, as that can open the tree to diseases and rot."

As Paul continued to cut, Bob talked about how shaded branches could turn unhealthy and unproductive. "If a leaf is covered by another, it loses up to 80% of its ability to photosynthesize. With most of its leaves shaded, a limb can't produce any energy reserves. It probably won't produce much fruit, and it may sicken and die." The goal was to create a dome of sunlight-filled leaves and not leave those dark clusters of overshadowed leaves.

Bob walked to an Italian plum whose branch-ends sagged from the weight of too much growth and fruit. He grabbed a spray of twigs at one branch's end and said "What I'm about to do is really winter pruning: I'm going to thin out much of this twiggy end-growth that's competing for the tree's energy." His felco clawed up into the spray, snipping into many a juncture, until the spray was reduced by 70%, with only 3-4 thin ends still dangling their baby fruit. "There's a better chance of these plums ripening now."

One of the apples had lots of water sprouts and branches that were too high to harvest easily. So Bob suggested that a select few of those water sprouts be saved, and he cajoled Kathy Ostrom to come hold onto the "savers" while the members ripped and clipped the condemned sprouts. "If you can head these savers back a little, or weight them so they are angled closer to 45°, or if you retain sprouts that are already angled closer toward horizontal, then in future years such water sprouts may turn productive. The closer a branch is to horizontal, the more likely it will fruit."

After an hour, the group moved to Vashon Cohousing, where the club and host Rick Edwards had winter-pruned cohousing's mixed orchard of apples, pears, cherries, and asian pears some months before. With time running out, Dr. Bob simply pointed out where pruning cuts should be made.

One pear, a former espalier that had been neglected, had two major branches left of the trunk and five on the sunnier right. Carolina Nurik, another fruit club founder, spoke up, "This tree needs better weight balance: if some of the verticals on this right side aren't removed, this tree could crack under the weight of a heavy fruit or snow load." Bob suggesting supporting the heavy side with a ground brace, waiting for the fruit to drag the branch earthward, then shorten the limb up to the fruiting wood. If they wanted to return the tree to espalier form, they could prune the excess verticals to the third node, in hopes new wood would grow (or could be trained) at more productive 45° or 90° angles.

A Liberty apple tree near a drip-hose had tons of fruit: 3-5 at every node, a dozen apples for every foot of limb. Bob said, "Half this fruit should be thinned, or the limb might break. What's left will have a better chance of ripening. Pinch off the small or scabby apples, leaving 1-2 fruit in clusters about 6" apart. Also, these long branches you can head back to where they are putting out laterals so the branch is less extended next year."

A youngish cherry tree had lots of fruit, most way beyond reach. Fruiting spurs develop at the base of new laterals and last a few years; gradually new spurs develop further up the elongating branch as the old ones die out, within years taking fruit and branch far beyond where you want to pick. You can renew an old tree by reducing both its height and the length of individual limbs, provoking new growth that in the next year can be thinned to shoots growing into a good position. A healthy cherry is so vigorous that you can remove nearly half its limbs in a year. Carolina Nurik talked about sawing several feet off the top, then weighing branches to bring fruit within reach. "Cherries require a lot of pruning to stay manageable. That's why the fruit's so expensive." I recalled seeing Hartmut Reimnitz's cherry tree pruned that way: only 9' tall and covered with bird netting, it looked like the skeleton of a half-open umbrella. Ugly, but pest-proof and effective: cherries covered every branch, all of them within easy reach.

Dr. Bob moved to a plum tree that had divided itself into three main leaders. "This is too many: removing this center trunk will open these two outer trunks to sunlight. Now where's that EZ-Start chain-saw? Karen?"

I pumped the priming button three times, pushed the safety bar forward, and handed it to him. He pulled on the starter cord. And pulled...

...and pulled... ...and pulled... ...and pulled and pulled and pulled...
You call this EZ? The crowd was grinning. My face was reddening. After nine hearty yanks, Dr. Bob finally got my EZ saw going, set the chain to the limb, and when it spit nothing but dust he yelled, "This saw is DULL!"

Much later, I learned from a pro that my saw shouldn't be man-handled: an EZ start engine needs a slooow pull. Nor had I sharpened it correctly. It wasn't the saw's fault: its balky performance was all due to Human Error.

I's guilty: the heedless kid who couldn't resist showing off a dangerous new toy. No wonder folks backed up when I kept coming at them with my saw, protesting "But it really IS an EZ Start! Won't you try it, plu-eeeeze?"

Schedule of Basic Care for Fruit Trees

Mid-Winter on calm, clear days—

- Start winter pruning. Prune (as much as 30%) for good scaffold structure. Remove unproductive "hangers"—branches drooping earthward, at an angle below the horizontal.
- Spray dormant oil to smother overwintering insect eggs.

Late Winter, before leaf-break—

- Spray copper or lime sulphur against peach leaf curl.

From leaf-break through the bloom period—

- Position mason bee colonies once temperatures reach 50°.
- inspect for tent caterpillar egg masses (look like styrofoam); destroy.
- Spray a fungicide targeting apple scab just prior to bloom, after petal fall, and ten days later. Avoid spraying when pollinators are flying.

Summer—

- In May, hang traps against coddling moths or put "footies" around fruit when 1" in diameter.
- After June fruit drop, thin fruits to clusters of 1-2 every 6" on branches.
- Stop scab spraying unless weather turns wet+warm for more than a day
- Summer-prune vigorously growing trees after fruit develops to achieve desired height, balance, and exposure of leaves to sun, thinning so you see as much sky as leaves when looking out the canopy. Remove unproductive branches, water sprouts, suckers, and hangers.
- Seriously consider fencing against deer.
- Irrigate: fruit trees need 1-2" a week during July-Sept's dry days.

Harvest—

- Protect from varmints: deer, raccoons, birds if possible.
- Pick when RIPE! stems detach easily from tree, seeds of apples turn dark brown.
- Bring mystery fruit for identification to the annual Fruit Show.
- Plant new fruit trees that are scab-resistant. Protect against deer.
- Consider joining the Fruit Club to learn more about fruit care.

Christmas in July

In the middle of July, I start dreaming of winter. It's not just to cool off (our heat-waves usually come in late July) but to figure out whether I can squeeze a fall/winter garden into my stuffed vegie beds.

By July, my bolted lettuce is poking its shade-cloth into the air. Cabbage heads have keeled over of their own weight. The 49 square feet of pea vines are supporting, what, maybe three pea-pods? With my spring plantings jaundiced and hang-dog in the noon-day sun, even I have to admit they're past it. Time to cook 'em or compost 'em. But maybe there's time for another crop to keep the good food coming?

Fall/winter vegetables to sow now

This question in mind, I called some more experienced gardeners, starting with Jenn Coe, who has been running the Food Bank's gardens for several years. "Before July ends, you plant fall cauliflower, root crops, brassicas—and brussel sprouts and parsnips as early as possible," she said. "Things that grow fast—arugula, mustard, radishes, lettuce—you can plant all through August and September. For a winter supply of swiss chard, get it in by September 21st."

She recommended a chart in the fall/winter catalog of Territorial Seed Company, which is also viewable online.

"You need to get plants started when there's still enough daylight get them to a decent size by the fall equinox. Then they'll sit in the ground over the winter and start growing again when the crocus bloom."

Margaret Hoeffel of Shoulder-to-Shoulder Farm told me, "People can plant beets the last week in July, and I typically don't plant spinach until August. All the mustard greens, you can plant in August and September and have a wonderful fall crop."

But it's so hot, I said. Won't the seedlings just shrivel up and die?

"If we have another heat-wave when I want to start spinach, I put the seeds in the frig for a couple days, for radically better results.

Fall gardeners has tricks up their rolled-up sleeves for sowing in summer's heat. "I grow my seedlings on a deck that has only four hours of sun," Jenn Coe said. "The ambient air is the right termperature for germination, and they would get too dry in full sun. I use an open flat without individual cells so the plants share the water."

Long-time Westside gardener Opal Montague has a good trick to keep seeds moist in high heat. "I put burlap bags over the planted seeds and keep them wet. I peek under the bags every day, because if the seeds germinate and don't stay wet, they're going to die." Another method: germinate seeds indoors for up to a week between moist towels in a ziploc bag set in a warm place: check daily and plant when the root just emerges.

Another method that keeps things moist is to use the ABS system of germination. This system of stacked flats offered by Gardeners Supply Company makes use of capillary action: a wet mat draws water from a reservoir to beneath bottomless seed-pots, where contact with soil can draw water up to the seeds. Hal Green of Triplebrook Farm uses this method to start his fall carrots, which need constant water for germination, then transplants them into soil for a good start despite mid-July's heat.

Seeds won't germinate? Still time for transplants

If your sowings fail to sprout by mid-August, you can still get a fall-winter garden installed if you resort to using transplants. Pull spring's aging plants like lettuce, cabbage or chard, then drop baby plants into their place. Unless you're protecting late lettuce starts with the shade of bigger plants, pull those old veg to give fall's plants more room. But root vegetables are best direct-seeded, and they need their space in the garden NOW.

Both Jenn Coe and Master Gardener Nancy Lewis-Williams think it's okay to direct-seed into the first week of August, leafy greens in September Beyond that, you need to plug in transplants. Luckily, growers like Langley will offer transplants for sale at local nurseries and retail outlets.

So, pull one, plant one, right? More like, pull two, plant one. Lewis-Williams has noticed that fall/winter vegetables "really do grow better if you give each one more space." Jenn Coe pointed out that with fall crops, "you can't really cut and come again: their growth is much slower. You need to make space for all the plants you'll want, because you won't be re-planting."

"Also, plants need air circulation when the rain returns. You don't want them touching each other, but to have room to dry out," Jenn advised. "Floating row covers help keep water off. Even in a greenhouse, space plants further apart to improve air circulation and discourage disease."

By mid-November's frosts, you'll be choosing which veg to harvest, which to leave to size up for spring eating. Some root veg like potatoes, parsnips, and carrots, and hardy greens like leeks and kale, are hardy and can be left in ground; just swaddle thickly with loose mulch and cover with reemay to protect against rain. Protect flimsy plants like spinach, lettuce, or peas with greenhouse film or glass held up with hoops or frames. With these protections, you'll be eating from your winter garden all the way to spring.

Timetable for a Fall-Winter Vegie Garden

FL=Sow in flat to create a T=Plug in Transplant DS=Direct Seed OW=plant holds in garden over winter, sizing up later for spring harvest.

By—	7/1	7/15	8/1	8/15	9/1	9/15	Harvest
arugula*		DS	DS	DS	DS	OW	winter-spring
beets	DS	DS	DS		OW	OW	all winter
broccoli		F, DS	DS	T	T	T	winter-spring
broccoli raab*			DS	DS			
brussel sprouts	F, DS	DS	T				fall-winter
cabbage	F, DS	F, DS	F, DS	T	T	OW	fall-winter
carrot	DS	DS			DS	OW	winter-spring
cauliflower	F, DS	F, DS	DS			OW	all cool season
chard	F, DS	F, DS	F, DS	DS, T	DS, T	T	fall-winter
cress*	DS	DS	DS	DS	DS		fall-winter
green onions	F, DS	F, DS	F, DS	DS, T	T		all cool season
kale	F, DS	F, DS	F, DS	T	T	OW	all cool season
kohlrabi	DS	DS	DS	T			winter-spring
lettuce*			F, DS	DS, T	T	T, OW	fall-winter
mustards*		DS	DS	DS	DS, T	DS T OW	winter
oriental greens*		DS	DS	DS	DS		fall-winter
onion Walla Walla		F	F, DS	DS	T	T	spring
parsley	DS						
parsnip	DS	DS	DS				winter
peas*				DS	DS	DS	March-April
radish	DS	DS	DS	DS	DS	DS	when sized up
rutabaga	DS	DS	OW				winter-spring
spinach*			DS	DS	DS		fall-winter
turnip		DS	DS	DS	OW		winter spring

plants fare better if given winter protection: thick mulches, cloches, cold frames, hoop houses.

Water-Wise

Our sole-source aquifer, rainfall, wells and water systems, salmon, water hoarders, and my heavy hand with irrigation.

Tucked into the upper reaches of Paradise Valley is an old homestead—the Singer Farm. If you turn south near the cemetery and wend down namesake Singer Road, you'll soon see their gray barn, the farmhouses on high ground, dark horses and black cows grazing right next to the buildings.

But not right down to the creek. On the pastured slopes that rise from this winding West Fork of Judd Creek, the animals have been displaced by thousands of baby-blue tubes. Each one protects a baby doug fir, dogwood, cedar or Oregon grape. There are so many—over 4000 planted every ten to fifteen feet—that the land looks pin-cushioned.

Odd as they look, these blue tubes are helping to restore a natural habitat. The stream was once tramped over by Singer's livestock, but today its banks are untrampled, its water running clear over a gravel streambed. In a few years, this sun-struck section of Judd Creek—once known as Salmon Creek—will start looking like the good habitat for salmon it once was.

"We knew that coho wanted to get up the stream that high—the Singer family had seen them," Beth Bordner of the V-MI Land Trust told me. "And there have been anecdotal reports of salmon upstream from there. Fish want shade, cool water, insects to feed on. But here, the creek was in an open pasture: little vegetation to hold its banks, no cooling shade or shelter, no logs in the water to create riffles or pools."

"As soon as we got the parcel in 2007, we fenced off the creek, as the Singer family agreed it was a good idea to keep their animals away from the water. We opted along that whole stretch to do re-forestation close to the creek, removing the Big Four Weeds (holly, ivy, blackberry, and broom) and planting those areas with conifers and native shrubs to provide a natural buffer. We left the far eastern portions as meadow: our Audubon Society has discovered that Paradise Valley is a stop-over for many migratory bird species, and they like open space with a forested edge."

Over 50 volunteers a year have helped weed and plant here since it was acquired in 2007. They've been joined by summer workers from Washington Conservation Corp, King County's Earth Corps, and the Student Conservation Association, led by the Land Trust's steward, Abel Eckhardt.

This isn't the only parcel the Land Trust has acquired: all told, 90 acres so far have been so conserved just along Judd Creek, in what the Land Trust calls the Paradise Valley Preserve. The Land Trust and King County work as partners: the Land Trust finds and initiates purchase of parcels on salmon-bearing streams, the county buys from the Trust a conservation easement, and both work on habitat restoration. The West Fork's headwaters in Island Center Forest are also protected by the county. And King Conservation District, an agency descended from FDR's Soil Conservation Service, is running several water quality projects with landowners further downstream.

All this effort and money isn't just for salmon. The quality of Judd Creek matters to us humans, too, for this valley is one of our better recharge areas for the aquifers that supply us with drinking water. The health and well-being of every creature on this Island depends on our care of the water that's here. To have high-quality water not only for humans, but for the creatures that inhabit and depend on water, we need to take care of our rain.

Storing Rain

The hydrologic cycle, otherwise known as the water cycle, is an early science lesson taught to every elementary school kid. You've all seen the diagrams: rain falls on land, then either rises back into the sky through evaporation or transpiration from plants, sinks into the ground, or drains off the land in waterways that eventually reach the ocean.

Humans tap the cycle usually after precipitation sinks into the earth. A very few humans tap the cycle before rain even hits the ground. On the north end, nearly in the shadow of the Heights water tower, gardener Ken Miller squirrels away water into 34 different containers. Six are industrial totes about four-foot square, the others 55-gallon drums. The largest totes press against the house under a downspout. When rain starts running off his roof, a side outlet opens briefly to flush particulates, then that valve closes and the rain pours on into the totes, which are daisy-chained together to fill one after the other. Overflow lines feed other tanks downslope and drip-lines laced through the garden. The tanks fill surprisingly quickly: "The rain we had last week with a quarter-inch of rain in 24 hours, I filled a 275-gallon tote in a few hours." To water his garden's 24 raised beds, he "dips and drips: I dip a watering can into a tote, slam the lid shut, and go water my beds."

Most Islanders aren't like Ken: we tap our water once it's in the ground. Some of us get water from sources on the surface: District #19, our largest water district with 1430 connections, draws over 60% of its water from the surface flow of Beall and Ellis Creeks (filtered and treated of course). Other sources are nearly as shallow: the main water source for Heights Water, the second largest water system with 700 connections, is a spring twenty feet down (though they also have two deeper wells to meet summer demand). Westside Water's 210 connections draw from a pair of 21' deep artesian wells in the canyons of Shinglemill Creek. But other wells are quite deep: some dug by Water District #19 have been punched many hundreds of feet down to reach a deep aquifer 100-300' below sea level.

But most Islanders drink groundwater that comes from a zone peculiar to the Island—those underground deposits of sand and gravel laid down by the Vashon glacier 10,000 years ago. These layers of advance and recessional outwash are natural aquifers: their coarse materials offers space for water to collect without tightly binding to soil particles (as water does with much finer clay particles) and to easily release into the wells we dig. These aquifers aren't continuous or uniform: they are a rag-tag patchwork of layers bottomed by denser clay layers that act as aquitards, slowing water's downward progression and causing the water to build back up toward the surface. The build-up of groundwater fluctuates from spot to spot and from month to month; its top surface—what we call the water table—is lower or higher depending on the perk-rate of the ground, up with winter rains, down with increased summer draws. If you could view it, the surface of our groundwater would appear more like a rumbled cloth than a calm, unrippled lake. That's why some Islanders wells are shallow, a few dozen feet deep, and others like my neighborhood's well descend more than three hundred feet down.

In the Island's hydrological cycle, about a third of our rain reaches these aquifers—a process called recharge. Ponds, marshes, valleys like Paradise Valley, and the watersheds of our creeks and ravines make excellent recharge areas because water has a longer chance in these depressions to sink into the soil. But plenty of rain just rolls off "The Rock:" it runs down steep slopes, squirts out the sides in seeps or springs, and flows into ditches, creeks, and streams that eventually release into Puget Sound. The actual amounts that evaporate, runoff, or sink into the ground have been debated since the first serious water study in 1983, called the Carr Report; the official tally, used since 2009 by King County based on most-recent hydrological modeling, estimates that the Island has, on average, 43.8" rainfall a year. Of that rain, 20" (45%) evaporates, 25% runs off into streams and ditches directly, and 13.5" (30%) sinks into our aquifers as groundwater recharge. "In comparison, the Carr Report estimated that only 11% became groundwater," said environmental educator Susie Kalhorn. "Thirty more years of study have refined the picture of our water and shown us how complex it is."

43.8" of rainfall is just an average. Some years are wetter than others, and northern sites on the Island are wetter than southern sites. King County has five rain gauges measuring rainfall across the Island: at the office of Heights Water on the North End, East Maury Park, Tahlequah, the KIRO tower on Maury, and the head of Judd Creek. Those stations reveal that the Island gets significantly more rain than the mainland, and Vashon Island about 6-10" more rain than Maury Island. In 2011, for instance, the Heights' gauge collected over 57" of rain through the year while just under 45" fell at East Maury Island Marine Park. In 2007, 2010 and 2011, all wet years, it rained most at the Heights office (61", 59" and 57.2"), nearly 10" more than measured at KIRO on Maury Island (50.6", 47.25", and 45.6"). Compare these rainfall totals to Sea-Tac's historical mean of 38 inches.

Despite our rainy reputation, our weather actually divides into a wet season and a dry season. Rain starts in mid-October, gets stormy around Thanksgiving, slacks off in January, stays dreary through February (when many of us fly to Hawaii), eases off in March, but dogs us into early summer. The Fourth of July is notorious for being rainy, and the following weekend, you'll be donning raingear for at least ONE of the days of Strawberry Festival. But after that, dry days rule until rainfall starts around Halloween.

When the dry days hit, it's nice to have water banked. At GreenMan Farm, behind the greenhouse sit what look like a pair of flying saucers. Round, black, and 20' across, they are cisterns, each holding 1100 gallons of rainwater collected off the roof of the farm's 100' greenhouse. Jasper Forrester used to worry, come late summer, that her well couldn't supply enough water to irrigate her farm. Not any more: "In a good rainstorm, these tanks can fill up in five hours." She taps the water to irrigate a pair of 45' hoop-houses that grow produce for her CSA farm.

GreenMan's and Ken Miller's systems are just for irrigation and aren't designed to provide potable water. Ken's neighbor Michael Laurie, a water conservation consultant who worked with Susie Kalhorn on the pesticide hang-cards and has chaired the Island's groundwater committee, has taken water conservation so far that his home was on the 2012 Ingenuity Tour. He has his own rainwater catchment system that stores 1000 gallons, plus drip irrigation, a green roof, rain garden, composting toilet, and low-water appliances and low-flow aerators indoors. "Most people find if they have low-water-use appliances and water accessories, 50% savings is really achievable."

Even using rain off the roof for drinking water is now possible, Laurie told me. In July 2011, King County's Board of Health approved a sustainability measure allowing for some homes, under certain conditions and caveats, to use roof-captured rainwater as their home's only water source. Perhaps more flying saucer cisterns will be landing on Vashon soon.

30 Years of Scientific Study

It's not that Ken or Michael are worried about running out of water today: they're eying tomorrow's needs and the future's changing weather.

In the 1980s, King County, also looking to tomorrow, wanted a better understanding of our Island's water supply. In Seattle and a lot of King County, much of the water supply comes from snowpack that builds up in the mountains, melts into the Cedar River and South Fork Tolt River watersheds, and is stored in reservoirs and lakes to meet demand downstream. Some people used to believe that the Island's water also came from that snowmelt, stored in a region-wide aquifer stretching from the Cascades to the Olympics. But the consultant study that King County commissioned, released in 1983 as the Carr Report, thoroughly debunked that myth: it found that most Island wells struck water at a point above sea-level—well above the depths of a supposed region-wide aquifer that, to be drinkable, would have to exist below the depths of our salty sea. They concluded that the Island was an isolated hydrologic system and that our Island's only water source is rain. The report stated—

"The only water entering the system comes from direct precipitation. Rain infiltrates the ground to the aquifers and is drawn from wells and springs for people's use. Any pollutants that infiltrate the ground will eventually affect water quality. There is only so much water, and only so many people can be supported by the water resource."

For those who sifted through its 234 pages, the Carr Report must have been an eye-opener. Not only did the report reveal that the source of our water was a "sole-source aquifer," it also looked at rainfall, subterranean flow, seasonal flux of wells, and for traces of contamination from human activity—arsenic from the Tacoma Smelter (none), nitrates from failing septics, fertilizers, and manures (slight but growing), and chloride (a sign of salt-water intrusion mostly on the North End shore.) It identified areas of highest groundwater recharge and recommended development be limited there. While the Carr Report estimated there was probably enough groundwater for a population of 13,000, it recommended the population, then around 7500, be limited to 11,000 because the water supply "is limited and vulnerable to contamination."

The Carr Report's findings were somewhat controversial: for instance, the idea that our aquifers were only getting a few inches a year in recharge probably felt like starvation rations to water and land use planners. In the 1986 update to the *Vashon Community Plan and Area Zoning*, King County rezoned the Island's critical aquifer recharge areas as zone AR-10 (one home per ten acres) to allow recharge of the aquifers. The rest of the upper plateau areas, were zoned AR-5 (one home per 5 acres), while new development was directed toward settled areas, mostly around the town of Vashon.

Thirty more years of scientific study has flowed since the 1983 Carr Report, further refining our picture of Island water. Hydrology and environmental studies. Stream flow and precipitation reports. Probes of wells for contaminants, of streams for salmon and for invertebrates as stream-quality indicators. The big generators of these studies have been King County and the Department of Ecology, but many Islanders have participated, gathering data and educating the public on study findings. By the 1990s, some had formed the V-MI Groundwater Advisory committee. In 1994, this group of concerned Islanders worked with King County's Dept. of Public Health to win an EPA designation of the Island as a sole-source aquifer. That same year, the state's Watershed Planning Act encouraged citizens and local governments to evaluate and protect their local watersheds, including providing minimum stream flows for fish. In 2000, many of these Island groundwater watchdogs were appointed by the King County Council to participate in the county's new V-MI Groundwater Protection Committee.

Studies intensified in this new century. Groundwater quality in wells was tested in 2000. King County's Water Resources Evaluation of 2001-04 studied water quantity and quality: volunteers monitored their wells and kept rainfall records, while the county installed stream-flow gauges and drilled test wells, eventually leading to new maps showing where, exactly, our water is, both above and below ground. Even the non-profit Washington Trout got into the action in 2001, partnering with Vashon Audubon Society to investigate over 80 streams; they found 19 streams with salmon or trout runs, nearly all hampered from low stream flows or man-made barriers.

Using the results of all this observation, in 2005 King County and the V-MI Groundwater Protection Committee released a *V-MI Watershed Plan.* Like reports before, it cited uncertainty about availability of groundwater, increased nitrates in some wells (three-fold increases at some sites, though still below dangerous thresholds) and potential contamination from human activities. "There is broad recognition that each water use can affect the quantity and quality of the water supply of others," the plan states. "We commit to use water sustainably so that our groundwater supply is neither diminished in quality nor quantity." Among its recommendations, "to educate Island residents about stream flows, the importance of balancing the needs of people with the proper functioning of the Island natural hydrology, and the role of water conservation in protecting the water supply."

In 2011, expanding upon their 2006 "Water Facts" flyers, the groundwater committee with the help of King County created and mailed to all Island households a 12-page tabloid, "Protecting Our Liquid Assets." What Carr *et al* said in stacks of typed pages, "Liquid Assets" explained simply in color photos, diagrams, maps, and captions. "We drink rain," Liquid Assets begins. "We're self-reliant when it comes to fresh water, so keeping it clean is crucial." It covered geology, the Island's complex hydrology, watersheds, wells, water systems, and conservation efforts. "'Liquid Assets' was our attempt to create a shared language about our water," said long-time committe member Donna Klemka, "It's a community resource we all steward." Edited by Kalhorn with design aid by graphic design diva Sy Novak, this amazing document showed how the Island's rain, hydrology, and humans together affect water quality and supply. (You can find copies of "Protecting Our Liquid Assets and the follow-up 2012 report card "Assessing Our Liquid Assets" at the library or online—a clear benefit of government transparency.)

Our Water: take care to keep it clean

Whatever gets into our water can contaminate it—car oil, pesticides, fertilizers, barnyard manures—which is why King County and King Conservation District provide funds and programs to help us protect it. Though some of our Island aquifers are protected by a lid of Vashon Till, there's plenty of cracks for polluted water to seep through, and plenty of wells and water systems that tap groundwater never filtered by the hardpan.

"We don't see how groundwater is moving underground," said Donna Klemka of the V-MI Groundwater Protection Committee. She knows, to her own embarrassment, just how easy it is to contaminate water. "My well isn't very deep—only 67 feet. I have an all-natural garden, and one year I put on a lot of barnyard manure. I didn't make the connection right away—our water is only tested once a year—but at the next testing of my water quality, there was an increase of nitrates. My neighbor isn't very far away and could be drawing from the same aquifer, so what I'm doing over my well could be affecting my neighbor's water."

Donna's is one of the Island's 1000+ private wells, making up 30%± of the Island's water supply. Most Islanders and businesses, however, get their water from Class-A or Class-B water systems. My neighborhood of 14 households is just small enough to qualify as a Class-B water system; it's one of 134 that get water to 20% of Island households. About half the Island—downtown Vashon, larger neighborhoods, camps— get their water from 22 different Class-A systems, entities like Water District #19 or Heights Water. While Class-A water systems are monitored and tested quarterly, Class-B systems must meet regulations, but have less stringent enforcement.

Our neighborhood's water manager tests our water quarterly, and he has lectured us on keeping our water clean. No hoses left in horse tanks or ponds, for fear a big draw could pull polluted water into our water supply. Upgrade to meters, check valves and better backflow preventers.

And when he's wagging his finger, I cringe a little in my chair, for I too know how "green" intentions can go awry. One summer, tired of constantly watering my sandy soil, feeling that I should be thriftier with water, I installed drip-lines. Most CSA farms use driplines—a flat black plastic tubing with slits every 2' or so—but I used what the hardware store sold: narrow, 1/4" black plastic tubes with half-gallon/minute emitters every foot. I laid the lines in grids about 8-12" apart, put the system on a timer and watered 3x a day, 15 minutes at a time, until each lettuce and tomato plant was ringed with wet soil. Regular, hands-off, Fahget-about-it watering. Sweet...

A few weeks later, our water manager sent out a terse email. "We have a leak," it read. "We're using far more water than we usually do in summer. Would everyone please check for leaks and drips?" So dutifully I added up the water from all my emitters. A vegetable bed needs about 62 gallons per 100 square feet of garden bed each week. So let's see... (number of emitters) x (1/2 gallons/minute) x (minutes/day) x (irrigation days/week). Oh dear—that's six HUNDRED gallons a week! Ten times too much!

Two years later, our water manager noticed a spike in demand, eventually pinpointing it to one embarrassed household who insisted they weren't using any more water than usual. Finally he called in a dowser—a water witch. The man came with a long L-bent metal rod he held lightly by the short end; like a divining rod, the rod rotated in his hands to point at the leak. After digging into ground that should have been damp, my neighbor found a big Doug fir had grown roots over to sip from that leaky pipe. Water in the root-zone: that's what keeps plants happy. Michael Laurie, who installs irrigation professionally, told the Fruit Club that one inch/week is the recommended amount of water for vegetables, annuals, and turf during the height of summer. Test your system's delivery rate by catching its drips for 15 minutes in a flat-bottomed can; 1/2" in 15 minutes = 30 minutes to deliver that weekly inch. But when soil is so sandy that water passes through, or so clayey or sloping that water tends to run off, then it's better to divide the week's worth into several brief waterings of 10-15 minutes each.

Water wants to flow, to bind to elements along the way, pulling sediments and contaminants into its grip. King County monitors with this vulnerability in mind. In 2013, King County is winding up a study of nitrate loading in Quartermaster Harbor, studying whether failing septic systems along the shore (along with other factors) affect nitrogen levels in the water. Already aware that failing septics were a problem, in 2012 the Washington Department of Health awarded King County with $350,000 to develop a pilot low-interest loan program for property owners in marine recovery areas who have failing septic systems. Another $50,000 was granted to help landowners with best management practices for livestock.

King Conservation District, the agency descended from The New Deal's Soil Conservation Service, can offer technical assistance to private landowners. They have cost-share programs to help farmers and livestock owners with pasture, manure, and compost management, increasing their farm's productivity while protecting water quality—for instance, they helped fund Plum Forest Farm's composting center. KCD also funds stream restoration and native planting projects. For Homestead Wilderness School, KCD kicked in 90% of the costs and sent labor from Washington Conservation Corps to help kids, teachers, and parents clear the property's blackberry-choked stream and replant with native plants.

The big payoff

Up on the Singer Farm, four years after the Land Trust had fenced off Judd Creek, land steward Abel Eckhardt walked down the meadow toward the most gravelly part of the creek. Here, where the cobbles are just the right size, he hoped to find the egg nests—called redds—of this fall's coho salmon. " Redds aren't obvious, but once you've seen a few, it's not hard to spot them. The redds are usually on the downsteam end of a pool: there the water is pushed through the gravel in the redd and keeps the eggs oxygenated. You'll see a section of gravel without an algae coating—gravel that's had its algae knocked off as the female kicks it around with her tail before and after she's laid her eggs." All told, he found seven active redds, some still being laid, the male and female "doing their dance" in their last cycle of life.

On November 1, 2012, just downstream of the 204th Street culvert, salmon watcher Kelly Keenan was sitting on a little gravel island in Judd Creek, her eye pressed to the viewfinder of her video-camera. It was a good year for coho—100 spotted just in Judd Creek. "It was raining, and I was listening to the birds, the raindrops, the water flowing, feeling like this was meditation, it is good for me. I heard it first, the tsh-tshh-tshhh of a fish coming through the culvert. Splash splash, then rest, splash splash splash, and then I spotted a tail swishing the pool below me." She flicked on the camera and shot what now appears on Vashon Nature Center's website: dark fins wiggling upstream, a roseate belly flashing coral as the female rolled over to dig. "The redd-digging makes a LOT of noise. Usually a male is hanging out nearby—they're bigger, more red—sometimes blocking the upstream water, waiting. Once she's finished the nest, he swims over her quivering his tail, releasing milt over her and the eggs she's laid in the redd."

A photographer and orca watcher for Preserve Our Islands and Orca Network, Kelly was here to observe the health of what our resident orcas eat most—salmon. Now she was having her "Circle of Life" moment. She said to me, "People don't realize that lawn fertilizers, laundry detergents, bad septics, all leach into the water salmon live in. Eat salmon, you're eating what's been in someone's yard, things that aren't good for orcas OR you."

I can't say it better than that. So be a good water steward. Care for the rain that passes through your life and your land. It's your part of a resource all Island creatures need, share, and treasure.

Do Your Part To Protect Island Water

Reduce pesticides and non-organic fertilizers
Install drip irrigation, test its delivery rate, and adjust for your soil
In your house, install low-water-use appliances
Keep manure piles covered and don't over-manure your soil
Keep open-ended hoses out of livestock water-tanks
Maintain your septic tank
Fix leaks in cars or trucks
Dispose of hazardous waste at drop-off events—don't dump!

Late Summer & Harvest

It's the dog days: slow, easy, golden August ripe as hoped-for corn. Bush beans topple over with their load of haricot vert (soon moldy if handled in the dew or rain) as the pole beans get higher than your head. Bolted lettuce must be pulled to give way for fall's sowings and transplants: cauliflower, cabbage, and carrots. By September, we sow again the salad greens to enjoy with fall's raspberries and pears.

As grape vines turn golden, wine makers squeeze fruit juice onto the glass plates of their brix meters and peer within for a reading of available sugar. Fruit tree owners without brix meters rock their fruit on their stems, hoping that ripeness will give each ready fruit its telltale quick release into a waiting hand.

In the kitchen, it's picklin' time. The largest pots are dragged out, jars washed and sterilized, and the surplus produce—cukes, tomatoes, tomatillos especially—brined in salt or vinegar before their jacuzzi bath in boiling water. If it's been a good tomato year, there's popcorn bowls full of tomatoes ripe for saucing. Fill that pantry!

A new invader, the Spotted Wing Drosophila, saws its way into ripe fruit on the vine or limb, and if you don't get to your fruit first, those tiny worms will. And the mid-August rains may bring blight to your tomatoes unless you're ready with clear tarps or bags to cover your hard-fought-for tomatoes.

As summer winds down, so goes plant energy, downward. Hardwood cuttings pulled off the main stems of perennials and shrubs will strike roots more easily, as will the plants you move within the garden. But maybe your energies also are winding down, and it suits you better to just drift through the fulsome garden, clipping deadheads and sipping ice tea or minted lemonade in these warm, balmy days.

Save and Share the Plenty

Putting up food, freezing & canning, local resources, power outages, giving excess to the food bank, and using all those green tomatoes

It's hard to see rot show up on a perfectly ripe raspberry. Mildewed squash vines, cracking cabbages, tomato vines sagging like fallen socks—these are pointed messages from your garden. They can make you feel plenty guilty for not eating all, ALL, yes EVERY LAST ONE of your vegetables—or they can motivate you.

Most of us aren't farmers or have farm-sized families. We don't have enough mouths, chewing double-time, to keep up with a garden going full-throttle. Instead, we need strategies for either spreading the wealth around or for preserving it for our own future use. Luckily, the farmers market has for several years hosted a Food Preservation Fair in mid-August. Time to buy new lids and rings for your Ball jars!

Putting Up Your Own Food

The first Vashon household I spent time in, had a pantry I envied. All winter, when we stayed over during our first house-hunting expeditions, we ate dinners created with David & Elizabeth's preserved garden produce. Their pantry shelves, packed with big Ball jars of chunked tomatoes, slim green beans, pickles and plenty of preserves, groaned with self-satisfied virtue. I was sure this was part of the Recipe for Island Happiness.

Canning is enjoying a revival all over the country. If you don't have the equipment, you can borrow it from the Vashon Food Security Group. In 2009, they created a Food Preservation Equipment Library: a dehydrator, food strainer, two pressure canners, two juicers (raw and steamed foods), a vacuum food bagger, two hot-water-bath canners, and a home canning kit with the necessary hand tools. Any Islander can reserve the equipment for three days by contacting the current librarian, signing a liability release, and making a small donation for each item. (Google "Vashon Food Security

Equipment Library" to find out who's in charge of the equipment.) For another $5, they'll also sell you a DVD, "Finding Joy in Canning and Freezing Foods," filmed at a food preservation workshop during the 2010 Vashon Food Summit. In late summer, the group puts on a Food Preservation Fair at the VIGA Farmers' Market.

If your canning books are hand-me-downs from your grandmother's day, consider updating your library, if only to enjoy the full-color photos of the post-desktop publishing revolution. For instance, the Ball Company's *Blue Book Guide to Preserving* is well organized, full color, and includes more salsa recipes than Grandma's books ever dared.

Freezing vs. Canning

FREEZING—YES!
• don't have to blanch food beforehand
• food keeps more nutrients
• decide later how to use the food
• containers are cheap: ziploc bags or used butter tubs work fine
• great for berries: if you freeze them as individuals spread on a cooky-sheet for 1-2 hours, then bag in a ziploc. Later, lets you scoop only as many berries as you need for breakfast or baking.
• freezer jams can be made in minutes, without cooking

FREEZING—No Thanks...
• a long power outage will defrost and ruin your freezer's contents
• can change the texture of high-water foods (but great for breads)
• don't want to take time to thaw food
• need a big chest freezer to handle a big harvest

CANNING—YES!
• no thawing—food's available now
• holds up in power-outages
• prettily canned produce makes good gifts
• some foods look better after canning vs. freezing, such as chunky salsas

CANNING—No Thanks...
• equipment can be expensive (you can borrow equipment from the Food Security Group's Equipment Library, if it's still a going concern)
• Boiling water in a big water-bath kettle can take hours on an electric stovetop (but minutes on a propane stove)
• limited to acidic or sugary foods—unless you use a pressure cooker
• need jars and pantry space (but jars & rings can be reused)

To Freeze or to Can?

What turns a fresh strawberry into red blobs? Freezing. Water expands when it freezes, breaking your food's cell walls. When the food is thawed, those cells collapse; losing juices and the firm structure it had when fresh.

So for freezing, choose food that doesn't need to hold its shape. Small things like berries or peas can be frozen as individuals on a cooky-sheet, then bagged and later scooped for as many as you want. Throw whole or chunked tomatoes into a ziploc for use in soups and sauces later; once frozen, they peel easily under hot running water. Sauces like spaghetti or enchilada sauces freeze well in plastic butter-tubs. Baked goods, especially bread, freeze very well; defrost in a 150° oven for a couple hours, or for a couple minutes in the microwave set on a defrost setting, then put the crisp back in the crust by heating the bread in a 300° oven for a few minutes.

If I have enough berries, I'll make boil-free freezer jam. Ball now makes a freezer-jam pectin to use with Splenda. Measured by the spoon, it can make tiny batches (down to a single cup of jam) and takes only 30 minutes.

When you want distinct chunks such as in a salsa, consider canning. Canning seems to preserve crispness a little better, as in pickles and dilly beans, provided you use produce at its peak. Fruit that's overripe makes a nice jam, but a flabby peach salsa.

I live in a household of two, and I've learned from too many jams-gone-moldy that big jars don't work for us. Unless you know you'll dip into it often, use a jar that'll be opened once, maybe twice, before it's emptied.

Most people start their canning career with hot-water-bath canning, which is limited to foods with high acidity or sugar. That's—
• anything in vinegar, like pickled beets, cucumbers, or beans
• in a sugar solution, such as peaches, pears, or cherries
• cooked down with sugar, such as jam, jelly, preserves, applesauce
• with both sugar & vinegar, like chutney.

To can low-acid foods such as squash or pumpkin, meat or fish, or pre-made baby food, you need to use a pressure-canner to obtain the higher heat that, without sugar or acid, is your last defense against bacteria. For such foods, freezing might be the easier, and better-tasting option.

Canned produce also makes nice gifts for the holidays.

Giving excess produce to the Food Bank

The local Food Bank at Sunrise Ridge welcomes donations of fresh produce and distributes all that's given, every week. Best time to drop off donations is Tuesday before noon and Wednesday before 10am. Save homemade concoctions such as jams or baked goods for your friends, as the Food Bank cannot distribute homemade goods to its clientele.

Root cellars, dry storage, and storing in the soil

Cathy Fulton of the Food Security Group told me that root cellars don't work very well here, as our high water table will give most subterranean storage areas moisture problems. Jasper Forrester of GreenMan Farm in the Dilworth neighborhood said, "It's really too wet here for most people to be able to dig out and construct a true root cellar. At our farm, the water table is so high, we hit water when we're digging post holes! I store winter veggies in bushel or half bushel baskets on shelves in one of our outbuildings. As long as we keep it cool, dry, and dark, they store pretty well."

"I believe the old fridge method would work, as long as you provide ventilation," she said. Some folks do keep old, unpowered refrigerators in outbuildings; they may be rusty, but they'll keep your squash, pears, and apples protected from critters and frost. Use refrigerator shelving so kids won't be able to cram their little bodies into a dangerous hidey-hole.

Root vegetables that have most of their bulk underground may keep just fine in the soil over the winter. A little frost even makes some vegetables sweeter, as the plant converts some of its starch into sugar to act as an antifreeze. At many a farm, kale, leeks, carrots, green onions, and potatoes overwinter just fine, providing fresh produce right into March.

What about all those Green Tomatoes?

One October, with dozens of green tomatoes on my hands, I sent an S.O.S to the Island grapevine that I wanted recipes for using unripe green tomatoes. Something besides Fried Green Tomatoes—no matter the recipe, to me they always taste like well-greased hockey-pucks (and I've tried...)

And Islanders came THROUGH! Below you'll find recipes that will take you from appetizer to dessert (oh LORD, the PIE!!!).

The old trick of dropping tomatoes into boiling water to get the skin to come off easily doesn't seem to work with green tomatoes, but then, these recipes don't require peeling. DO core green tomatoes all the way through, as the white center is tasteless.

Green Tomato Salsa Chip Dip

Thanks to Kathy Bosler, who found this at Cooks.com. This works fine fresh or canned, and it would be good with some Truly Green Tomatoes, such as Green Zebra, mixed in.

4 c. chopped green tomatoes

2 c. chopped and seeded sweet peppers (banana, red bell,: think color contrast)

1 c. chopped & seeded jalapenos, about 1 cup's worth

1 c. minced onion

2 tsp. salt

1.5 c. acidic liquid, either cider vinegar, lime juice, or combo of both

3 cloves minced garlic

1 c. cilantro, chopped

1-2 tsp. sugar, to your taste: it balances the acid bite

1/8 tsp. cumin

Chop all ingredients and place in saucepan. Bring to a boil, reduce heat and simmer for 10 minutes. Then cool, or if canning, pour salsa into hot jars, seal and hot-water-bath for 30 minutes. Makes 3-5 pints.

Green Tomato Bruschetta on spinach or toast

Inspired by an idea from Mary Freebourn, an Island "Cake Lady" who is taking the SCC Culinary Arts program. She gets credit for the Green Bruschetta idea; I added the spinach, blue cheese and walnuts.

1-2 green or pinking-up tomatoes
4 tbls. extra-virgin olive oil
1 tbls. balsamic vinegar
1/2-1 teas. minced garlic
a little sugar, salt & pepper
fresh basil, chopped into thin threads
VARIATION 1: fresh mozzarella, cut into 1/2" squares
VARIATION 2: shavings of blue cheese and diced bits of walnuts for garnish
Serve either on grilled toast brushed with olive oil, or a bed of fresh spinach

Chop the tomatoes into 1/2" chunks and marinate for a few minutes in olive oil & balsamic vinegar with S & P, some sugar if tomatoes are too tart. Cook on a hot griddle or heavy pan for 5 minutes with minced garlic. Meanwhile, into remaining vinaigrette add ingredients of either variation. Serve on the bed of spinach or on toasts basted with olive oil & garlic.

Green Enchiladas

I freeze many pints of this tomatillo sauce to make green enchiladas all winter. You can substitute up to 50% green tomatoes.

Get a bag of tomatillos (about a dozen will make a single pint, and this recipe is for making MANY pints.), about half as much green tomatoes, and about 25% that weight of yellow onion—a ratio akin to 4 cups tomatillos, 2 cups chopped green tomatoes, 1 cup onion.

Also get a few hot peppers (hungarian wax or jalapeno), a bunch of cilantro, lime juice, and garlic. You'll also need a big kettle and a food processor or blender.

De-husk and lightly wash the tomatillos; wash and core the green tomatoes; put toma/toms plus peppers on a sturdy cookie sheet and roast in a 375° oven for about 20 minutes, until skins are toasted & puckery. Pop peppers in a brown bag to steam for 10 minutes, then peel, split & de-seed, and chop. MInce onion. Using a food processor or blender, grind tomas/toms, then add peppers, about a cup chopped cilantro, the onion, a tbls. minced garlic, splash of lime juice, S & P. Pack into pint butter-tubs or Seal-a-Meals and freeze.

Chicken & Cheese Enchiladas (makes 6-8)

A pint of above green sauce, thawed
1 poached chicken breast, shredded, <1 cup/person (pork works, too)
half an onion, diced
a cup pepper bits: ideal is 1 poblano, 3-4 anaheims, 1 jalapeno, roasted & skinned
pepper jack or white cheddar cheese, shredded
6-8 corn tortillas, oiled & heated until flexible on a hot griddle

Heat oven to 375°. Mix meat, onion, peppers, and half-cup+ shredded cheese in a medium bowl. Spread 1/4 cup sauce in an 8x8" baking pan. Across the center of a tortilla, make a fat row of meat mix; over it dribble a spoonful of green sauce, roll up, put in pan. Repeat until pan is full. Over tortillas spread rest of green sauce and more scraped cheese until lightly covered. Bake for 20 minutes until enchiladas start to turn golden. Serve 2-3 per person.

Shepard's Spicy Apple & Green Tomato Pie

Though I've modified this a little, credit for this delicious recipe must go to Renee Shepard of Renee's Garden. Tastes differ as to how tart this pie should be, so if you're serving to kids, hold the green tomatoes to half-the-fruit total, slice them thin with a mandoline, and let the kids try it first before you tell them what's in that yummy pie!

Pastry for a double crust pie
2 tablespoons orange marmalade to brush inside the bottom crust
1/2 cup firmly packed light brown sugar
1/2 cup sugar
2 tbls. cornstarch
1/2 cup golden raisins
1 tablespoon orange zest OR splash of orange juice OR bit of orange flavoring
1/2 teaspoon ground cinnamon
1/4 teaspoon ground ginger
1/4 teaspoon salt
4 medium green tomatoes, very thinly sliced (use a mandoline if you've got it)
4 large Granny Smith or Gala apples, peeled, cored, thinly sliced
2 tablespoons cold unsalted butter or margarine, cut in pieces

Preheat oven to 425°. Divide pastry in half; roll out one-half pastry leaving a 1 inch overhang. Brush marmalade evenly over bottom of pastry.

In a small bowl, mix sugars, cornstarch, raisins, cinnamon, ginger and salt until well combined, then stir in green tomatoes and apple slices. Roll out bottom layer and brush with orange marmalade, pour in fruit mixture, drop bits of butter across top, then add top layer and crimp closed.. This is a juicy pie, so put a cooky sheet on oven shelf below pie to catch drips. Sprinkle pie's top with sugar/cinnamon mix, or brush with milk. Bake in preheated oven for 15 minutes at 425° F, reduce heat to 350° F and bake 25-35 minutes longer, until fruit bubbles and crust is golden. Let cool completely before cutting—this gives the thickener a chance to set up; otherwise, your pie's interior will just run out when you remove the first hot slice.

If you find juices accumulating around the outer rim of the pastry, take a turkey baster and suck some of that overflow off the top of the pie.

Making More

Fall is a good time to plant, transplant, divide, and propagate. It's also the season to plant garlic and shallots, as well as flower bulbs.

It feels good, after weeks of indoor canning and early fall drizzles, to be outside in the garden again. I'm on Colleen James' front porch on the Burton Peninsula; she's teaching me to propagate lavender. Even though her front garden is cast with shade, her yellow Victorian is a sun-catcher that warms our faces and hands. The sun pours down her slope, and the porch captures all its warmth. Pretty nice for late October.

This is the weather window to move, divide, and propagate perennials and shrubs. Though the rains arrive mid-month, they come and go until mid-November, when frosts and hard rains move in for the duration. The plants, sensing winter's approach, are going dormant, stopping new growth, hardening existing foliage. With energy moving downward, transplants, even cuttings, are heeding the call to put down roots. They'll strike roots easily in October's moisture and warmth—while it lasts.

Today, Colleen's in full propagation mode, building up a big inventory of new plants for next spring's Arboretum sale in Seattle. In her kitchen, stems with seedheads lay across shallow bowls that catch seeds as they drop. Her greenhouse is full of young, frost-tender plants, and her porch is her potting shed, lined with the gear needed for new plants—flats, bags of potting soil, trays for potting up.

She thrust a knife into a big bag of potting soil—the vanilla type, no fertilizer, manures, or hydro-gels added. "If you put a cutting into soil with fertilizer, it won't root," she said. She upended part of the bag into a big, high-backed tray, put an empty cell-flat on the soil and with both hands scooped soil across its surface. The individual cells, each the size of a bathroom dixie cup, filled instantly. "Much smaller than 1.5" across isn't enough room for the roots."

"It's important that your cuttings go into a clean environment—new soil, clean trays. I wash my used cell-trays in my big sink or the kiddie pool, adding about a half-cup of bleach to the water to sanitize. Underneath these cell-trays, which are pretty flimsy, I put these liners—" she shook an open-bottomed tray at me—"that will stiffen the trays but let water drain out. Then, once you've got the cells loaded with soil, press it down a little with your fingers so it's not so fluffy, then top off."

Once we had three flats loaded with soil, we went around back to her lavenders. "See how much growth is on this 'Fred Boutin'?" She ran her hands over its branches, each about 18' long. "We'll cut these branches back to just above the bare wood."

The hard winters of 2008-2011 have taught me that a fall haircut for some woody shrubs helps them survive a hard winter. They are not so likely to sprawl open or break under the weight of wet snow, and there's less tender plant growth to freeze. But it feels so harsh, so *wasteful*: there you stand with half the plant in your hands, feeling guilty for scalping your beloved. Colleen feels the same: "I just hated pruning my plants so hard. But once I learned how to turn all these sticks into new plants, I felt better."

Once Fred had his haircut, we proceeded to a nearly-white spanish lavender. The flowers, pale rose-violet at this point, were unlike the deep purples I associate with spanish lavender. Here, clearly, was something different. "I wish I knew what this variety is," she admitted."Isn't it beautiful?" The foliage was so ghostly pale, it reminded me of dusty millers when they first became popular.

Back at the porch, Colleen grabbed a handful of trimmings. "The best cuttings are from wood that's not dead bare, but not young green either—wood that's in-between, just starting to stiffen. So go up the stem just past where it's bare, clip there and throw away that dead part of the stem."

She then took a single stem and scraped off the foliage from the trimmed end, about an inch or two. "See these bumpy rings around the stem? From these nodes, the roots will emerge. By ripping off the leaves or branchlets around a node, you expose a hormone inside the bark that, once it feels soil contact, goes into survival mode and puts out roots. So clean the foliage off the first one or two nodes."

Taking a multi-stemmed branch, she tored back a branch so it peeled free with a cuticle of bark hanging off the end. "That's a heel cutting, and it will root well because there's lots of inner plant exposed to contact the soil."

Above the stripped-down stems of our heel cutting,s she left two nodes' worth of foliage about 2" long. If the cutting was already multi-stemmed, she trimmed all the little stems back, leaving each 1-2" of foliage. Every cutting, whether single or multi-stemmed, ended up about 4-5" long, each with two nodes stripped naked below, two nodes with leaves above.

Into single cells she plunged each cutting until the naked end touched bottom. Then she firmed the soil around it with her fingers. "You don't want the stems TOO long especially if the flat will be outside, because the wind could move them around and open up air-holes around the new roots, which will kill them. This firming-down helps prevent that, and it gives good contact of soil against the cutting."

She lightly watered the flats. "I water them through winter only when they are really dry." Sounded like a good idea to me: I had recently killed all but one cutting in a flat-full of Olympic berry cuttings when I'd let the rain of the day before accumulate in its liner.

I told her I'd long had a copy of the Arboretum's book, *Cuttings Through The Year*. "That's the best book," she replied. "And if you look under the section for October, you'll see it has a really long list of plants that can be propagated now. It's a good time anyway—who has time in spring? But things are slowing down now, so I have the time. And if I lose garden plants to winter, I'll have a whole bunch of replacements ready."

Hardwood Cuttings to take in October

Here's just 25 of the 85 shrubs that "Cuttings Through The Year" says can provide hardwood cuttings this month. These are commonly planted in Island gardens.

Artemesia, aucuba, berberis, camellia, heathers, rock rose, cotoneaster, daphne, escallonia, euonymus, fuchsia, holly, honeysuckle, juniper, bay laurel, lavender, phygelia, pieris, rosemary, salvia, sarcococca, skimmia, vaccinium, viburnum, vinca.

Cuttings Through the Year, the Arboretum's popular how-to propagate booklet, is in its fifth edition. It is available in the Arboretum Shop or by phone or mail order for $8.50 each (2011 price). To order, call 206-325-4510, or send check (payable to Arboretum Foundation) to: Cuttings, Arboretum Foundation, 2300 Arboretum Drive East, Seattle, WA 98112-2300.

Good to Divide Now

This is a good time of year to divide perennials, Colleen had told me earlier when she invited me down to help propagate. Her advice: look for plants that aren't blooming as much as before—it's a sure sign the plant wants dividing. "Lift the whole plant and, if it's gone hollow in the center, chunk off a couple daughter divisions with a shovel, sharp knife, or by teasing it apart between your hands. Big perennials like daylilies may take two big garden forks, back to back, to pry the plant apart. Put the mother plant back in place, refreshing the soil with some compost and watering in. Then move the new daughters to new sites, also tucking them in with compost, lots of water, but no fertilizer: you want the plant to recover, not put out new growth that will soon be killed by frost.

Some of these plants will still be blooming, so use flowering stems for your flower vase. Cut off any other dead foliage, then divide the plant.

Layering: a less disruptive way to propagate

If you have leggy plants or shrubs you don't want to disturb, you can try layering. Bring a branch down to the soil, scratch the bark away around a node or branching crotch, then pin to the soil with a landscape staple, length of wire, or big cobble. After several months, the branch may have set new roots at the point of soil contact. You can then clip free the rooted branch and transplant the newly rooted "daughter" to a pot or spot in the garden. This works well for hydrangea and lavender.

Perennials for Fall Division or Transplant

achillea (yarrow)	hemerocallis (daylily)
agapanthus (lily of the nile)	monarda (bee balm)
alchemilla (lady's mantle)	paeonia (peony)
arisaema (jack in the pulpit)	penstemon
boltonia	polygonatum (solomon's seal)
brunnera	rudbeckia (black-eyed susan)
coreopsis (tickseed)	stachys (lamb's ear)
echinacea (purple coneflower)	saponaria (soapwort)
epimedium (bishop's hat)	

A reminder from Lutherans and Vampires:
Plant Garlic no later than Halloween

In mid-October, James Dam, a long-time Island gardener who first told me how to chit seeds for early, guaranteed germination, showed up at the Food Bank with the last of the Lutheran Church's bean harvest. "Sorry we're so late, but we've been planting garlic lately."

Both the Food Bank Farm and the Lutheran Church plant garlic for their clientele. Jenn Coe, the Food Bank Farm Coordinator, tries to get it in the ground by mid-October, but it's very easy to remember the growing season as "From Halloween to Fourth of July." I planted mine in a dahlia bed where I'm going to let the dahlias overwinter; by the time the dahlias start to emerge, the garlic will be pulled and gone.

Garlic wants good, non-soggy soil (perhaps enhanced with a little aged compost, 5-5-5 fertilizer, or alfalfa meal) and at least half a day's sun. Divide a bulb into cloves, leaving the paper wrapping on, and stick the clove pointed end up about 2-3" into the soil and 3-4" apart. Quite hardy, garlic should make it through hard freezes with some protection from a cover crop, row cover, or fluffy mulch, its first leaves emerging by the new year.

For the learning experience, I harvested garlic with fellow food bank volunteers on July 11, 2009 (a good growing year). Even though the field had gone to grass, the garlic didn't seem to mind the competition. I learned that you harvest when half the plant's leaves have gone brown. Though you can cook garlic "green" as soon as you harvest, it will keep only if you cure it in a warm (around 80°) shady place with plenty of air circulation. I arranged my garlic on a rack in our workshop, where it cured over the summer and lasted nearly until the next harvest.

So once Halloween's vampires are back in their coffins, remove that garland of garlics from your door and go plant the cloves in the garden. Garlic is SOOO worth planting: it's much fresher, more mild, and more flavorful than store-bought garlic. You can grow a LOT in a small space that's not being used over the winter. With a whole head from a single clove, it gives a return of 12-20%—an excellent investment. And if you plant before Halloween, no vampire will come anywhere near your garden.

The Case for Daffodils (and other bulbs)

When you plant garlic, consider planting other bulbs like tulips, daffodils, crocus, and that garlic relative, the lily. Our sandy loam soil in the
non-hardpan areas is ideal for growing bulbs. In fact, Vashon had at least
two bulb enterprises in the 1930s: the Sheffield Dahlia Farm south of the
old Mitchell Tree Farm on the south end, and the Annual Croft Lily Festival
(put on in June, oddly enough, considering Croft Lilies are Easter Lilies).

Daffodils will do fine under deciduous trees and shrubs that leaf out after daffodils fade—for instance, under Indian Plum, one of our first native
shrubs to put out spring growth. Daffodils naturalize well on sunny roadsides (but not under evergreen trees), the edge of woodlands or in groves of
alders or birches. Daffs are heliotropic and will face the strongest light—so
unless you prefer them with backs turned, put them where their light orien-
tation works with and not against your garden's design.

The bulbs should be planted 6-8" deep: on the deeper side if you've got
sandy soil, on the shallower side if you want the bulbs to divide and naturalize. If you've got clay soil, lay the bulb with the nose (the tapered point)
pointing sideways so that water doesn't collect inside the bulb. An easy way
to plant is to scoop out a shovel's worth, toss in some bulb food (a 5-10-20
is good) and an odd number of bulbs arrayed around the hole, then replace
the scoop of soil.

My first order for daffs was to Washington Bulb Company (www.tulips.
com), hosts of the Skagit Valley Tulip Festival and the largest bulb company
in the U.S., with 500 acres in daffodils. Local stores carry bags of 'King
Alfred' and white 'Mt Hood' in autumn. Mary Ann Roberts likes to order
bulbs from bulb growers Brent & Becky's ("Their catalog is full of color photos and information"), Van Engelen, or John Scheepers.

Daffodils are deer-resistant, but tulips and lilies are not. Tulips can rot
from too much winter rain, so turn them on their sides when planting. Lilies, while they don't like soggy soil, are uniquely able to pull themselves by
the roots to the soil level they prefer. Dahlias are marginally hardy left to
overwinter in the ground: their survival probably depends on whether your
soil drains well or hangs on to winter wet.

Reaching Brix

Can Vashon's maritime climate produce wine–worthy grapes?
A handful of hobby viticulturists are testing that proposition.

Golden October sun raked over golden vines in the vineyard. A breeze fluttered the yellow and blue tablecloth, as our hostess set down a tray of artisan cheeses. The local baker arrived with a duck confit, a cassoulet, and a huge loaf of bread shaped as a cluster of grapes. Friends yammering in French raised glasses of ruby-red to toast the hosts who invited them to help with harvest. It feels like Provence, but it's Maury Island, October 4, 2009, and we're here to pick pinot gris grapes at Maury Island Winery.

Bill Riley had his equipment arrayed on the deck: a red steel crusher, wooden-slatted press, and three big glass carboys. On the lawn, a little John Deere tractor was loaded with shallow yellow bins. Around 3pm, the "crew"—some toting along not-quite-empty wine glasses—walked uphill to the six rows of pinot gris. Bill, passing out red Felco hand pruners, said, "You'll looking for grapes that have red and blue tints—leave the clusters that are still yellow." We spread down the rows, dropped to our knees before fan-espaliered vines and started snipping.

It didn't take longer than 30 minutes to harvest all six rows and fill up the John Deere tractor that hauled the grapes to the press. Bill weighed each bin before dumping its contents into the crusher. The total yield: 293 pounds. The brix had reached "around 20," he said, "which is a little less than for traditional pinot gris, but since I want to turn much of this crop into a champagne-style wine, I want less sugar and more acid, more tannin: it makes the wine less explosive."

We sat around the picnic table, watching as the slightly-mashed grapes were transferred them into the press. Bill knuckled down on the first grapes, and the juice ran free and thick into a big kitchen pot. He dipped a small glass under the spout, then held it to the light, revealing a translucent amber glow. I took a sip, tasted honey-water and apricots. Delicious and refreshing right NOW—just pass me that camembert cheese, please.

Early Vineyards and Wineries

Grape-growing in Puget Sound began in earnest on an island, though not our own. In 1872, Lambert Evans, a Civil War vet from Florida, took a homestead claim on a sun-warmed slope of Stretch Island in the south Sound and planted grapes and apples. In the 1890s, Adam Eckart bought some of Evans' land, started raising grapes, and rebranded a strain of "Campbell's Early" (a Vitis Labrusco Concord hybrid) as "Island Belle." By 1918, after he had published a guide to growing grapes and established the Island Belle Grape Growers Union, his 'Island Belle' became the most planted grape in Puget Sound.

Though Prohibition in 1920 killed the state winery business, the Volstead Act's exemption of 200 gallons of homemade wine per household created a demand for grapes. (In California, grape plantings jumped 700%.) On Vashon, Paul Billingsley, a man with mining interests in Alaska whose father, the Rev. John Billingsley, had bought property on Back Bay in 1919 from the Sherman family and named it "Still Waters," planted several acres to Island Belle in 1925. These vines, bought from the Werberger Winery & Vineyard on Pickering Pass, were scions of plants grown by Adam Eckart, that father of the Island Belle. (Gene Sherman, who grew up a neighbor of the Billingsleys, found a document stating the Billingsley planting began in 1935. That makes more sense: with the end of Prohibition in sight, a planting in 1935 would have given Billingsley a legal crop by 1937-1938.) Upslope from the Billingsley's place, the Dunn family also had ten acres of Island Belles on their land west of 216th & Monument Road.

When Prohibition ended in 1933, Stretch Island—which in the supposedly "dry" years had rebranded its main town as "Grapeview" and its ferry "Island Belle"—immediately saw the opening of St Charles Winery, the first to be bonded by the state. Billingsley sold grapes to that winery. Soon he had most of 80 acres planted in grapevines.

In 1936, Maury Islander Harley O. Hake started the Island's first bonded winery and the state's 27th. He grew loganberries on 13 acres on Hake Road and from those made a sweet wine of 14-16% alcohol. He also made dandelion wine and bought grape concentrate to make a table wine. In-law descendant Sue Knight told me, "He was a smiling, sweet man. One of his granddaughters nicknamed him 'Whistling Poppi.' He used to take the ferry to Tacoma, walk his wine around to the hotels and restaurants. But he wasn't a businessman: he had a LOT of friends, gave much of his wine away, I heard. Finally the state liquor board, who had to send out inspectors every year, said his annual payment didn't cover the cost of inspection. So they came over, took away his license, and broke all his bottles."

Sometime before WWII and perhaps as early as 1935, Paul Billingsley, encouraged by St Charles Winery and aided by Aaron Sherman, procured Vitis vinifera cuttings from Rudolf Werberger's vineyard. These translucent green-gold grapes, often pictured in Old Master still lifes, were Chasselas Doré, an ancient variety used for table grapes and to make a light, floral white wine. St Charles Winery blended Back Bay's grapes with a red for sacrament wine. At some point, the vineyard acquired an Indian moniker, Tsugwale, pronounced Chug-Wall. Billingley died in 1962, and the vineyard went fallow for 15 years.

Washington's Vinifera Revolution comes to Vashon

After Repeal, the state's wine industry continued to make the kind of sweet, fortified wines that homebrewing households had gotten used to during Prohibition. But after WWII, tastes slowly began to shift. GIs who had served in Europe returned with fond memories of European wines. A younger generation, educated, prosperous, and also Euro-traveled, wanted a quaff with more cachet. To supply it, California vintners started to make and export drier wines made from vinifera, which Washington's liquor board promoted as a boost to the state's sales tax revenue.

By the mid-60s, when sales of table wine first surpassed that of dessert wines, state ag researchers were trialing wine grape varieties in Eastern Washington. Pommerelle and NAWICO, the state's two largest fruit wine and fortified wine makers, had been bought out and refocused toward fine wine, eventually becoming Ste. Michelle Vintners. A group of academics and doctors making a little hobby wine in their garages grew tired of buying California grapes and found some land in Sunnyside, WA to plant their own vines. Taking the name Associated Vintners, they would become Columbia Winery, one of the two largest in the state.

Gradually the realization that the state could make world-class wines began to take hold. When Washington wines started winning prizes, local media noticed. Stan Reed, food writer for the *Seattle Post-Intelligencer,* wrote in 1970 after tasting an Associated Vintners gewurztraminer that "A new industry has been born in Washington."

Around 1974, Gene Rosford, son of Island bus driver Harlan Rosford and then renting a cabin at the Billingsley farm, looked uphill at those old vines and thought, "How cool it would be to bring that vineyard back to life. The Chasselas vines were 40' long, as the owner's cows had been eating just the fruit, not the vines. On the hilltop, the Island Belle/Campbell's Early vines were so overgrown with blackberries that, when they were yanked and burned, the bonfires were so big, they frightened even the firemen."

About two acres remained in Chasselas Doré. At first Gene ran the Tsugwale vineyard as a U-pick, but later wholesaled the grapes to Manfred Vierthaler, a German restauranteur and vintner in Sumner. Vierthaler made Chasselas Doré wine, which Rosford claims was, in the mid-70s, the first commercial wine made with Western Washington vinifera. It's hard to prove that: Ron Irvine, who wrote a history of Washington state's wine industry, says a vineyard in La Center near Vancouver, Washington was planted in 1971 and their first wine, a Pinot Noir, was released in 1976. Vierthaler released what he called Riesling in the 1970s—one of which did have "Tsugwale" on the label—but the labels are tellingly void of vintage years.

The 70s ferment

The 70s saw a boom of vinifera planting in the PNW, mostly east of the Cascades, but a bit on the maritime side. Mt. Baker Winery east of Bellingham planted its vineyard in 1978, sourcing some cuttings of Chasselas from the vineyard on Back Bay. Destination wineries Chateau Ste. Michelle and Columbia Winery were built north of Seattle. In British Columbia, the government, not proud that its local wine industry was dependent on California grapes, imported 4000 vinifera vines in 1974 and invited Germany's Geisenheim Institute to trial cool-climate varietals in the Okanogan Valley and on the Saanich Peninsula.

In the 60s young New Jerseyite Bill Riley came out west with his pal Rudy Marchesi "to do wine." Rudy's grandfather had introduced them to his homemade wine, and Bill, like many students then, had picked up the taste for wine while bumming around Europe. After getting a degree from Stanford, Bill came north in 1974 to work the vineyards at Sagemoor Farm near Pasco. Six years into its vinifera plantings, one of the earliest east of the Cascades, Sagemoor would soon have 466 acres in wine grapes and become the largest supplier to wineries in the state.

In Mt. Vernon, Dr. Bob Norton at the Washington State Extension's Research Station (yes, the same Dr. Bob of our Island Fruit Club) started trials in the mid-70s to find cool-climate vinifera that might thrive in our maritime climate. Islander Les Street —who as a lad had snooped the abandoned Hake Winery with an adventurous uncle—attended some of their seminars. With that knowledge, he drove to B.C., following a rumor there were some interesting vines left in limbo at the Saanich, B.C. horticultural station.

"All the imported cuttings had to come through quarantine at the B.C. station," Street told me. "They didn't know what they had because their inventory was only by numbers, not by varietal name, and the man who'd made the list had retired. So we figured, why not just call him up and ask if he still had the list of varietals? He did; we went and got it, gave it back to the quarantine station, and left there with many clean cuttings."

Street planted those grapes on Maury Island, many of which were the first of their type in the state. On another acreage on the hilltop above Manzanita, he planted vines gotten from the state's agriculture department, including Chardonnay, Muller-Thurgau, Pinot Noir, Siegerrcbe, Madeleine Angevine, and Gewurztraminer. He also grew french hybrids (a 70s experiment that didn't pan out). As excitement grew in the state over the potential for a wine industry, his "Northwest Company" (in partnership with Jim Wilson) supplied vines wholesale for new vineyards, to retail nurseries Furneys and Molbeks in Seattle, to Vashon's Country Store, and to locals. His first sale, in 1977, was to Gerard Bentryn of Bainbridge Island Vineyard & Winery, who was then teaching grape/wine seminars and promoting Puget Sound as its own AVA. Among Bentryn's students: Jeff Jernegan, Steve Synder, and Bill Riley.

Vashon Winery and the Back Bay Vineyard

In 1975, with just three wineries in Washington State, Ron Irvine with partners opened up the Pike & Western Wine Shop in Pike Place Market. Interested also in hard cider, that year he was also elected President of the Hard Cider Society. In 1989, he leased land from Wax Orchard and from Will Gerroir & Karen Peterson of Vashon Winery to create his own hard cider. Soon he was working part-time for them.

Will Gerroir and Karen Peterson had opened up Vashon Winery in the mid-80s and, in 1986, released their first wine, a Chardonnay, with grapes sourced from friends who started the Portteus Vineyard in Zillah; that vineyard still provides grapes for Vashon Winery.

Jim Stewart, of Seattle's Best/SBC Coffee fame, bought the Back Bay vineyard property from Preston Nibley around 1985-87. Manfred Viertha- ler was still buying the grapes—which he referred to as "Golden Gutedel," one of the German names for this grape—off that vineyard, making a wine Stewart tartly referred to as "medicinal" in taste. But a year later, Vashon Winery asked to buy his harvest. Stewart says, "With the Chasselas Doré, Will Gerroir produced a bone-dry Semillion-style wine. It was wonder- ful!—light and summery, went great with oyster shooters, and it would age well because of the high acidity."

"In most years, we could get a harvest of about 500-1000 lbs off the vineyard," Stewart said. "If we hit 16 brix, we're lucky. Some years we didn't even pick them, thanks to a combo of birds, weather, and deer. Once I put the fence in, that kept the deer out. But we have to harvest before October 10, because every year like clockwork, a flock of tiny birds arrives and, by the third day, every single grape is gone." He says Irvine, who eschews add- ing sugar to wines, prefers to hold off harvest in favor of higher brix, which results in a more acidic wine (at least to Stewart's tastes).

Though Vashon Winery would put most of those grapes into its own product, Stewart would be paid for his grapes with about 200 bottles of wine. Stewart had himself some fun with his stash, convening "the Buffalo Skull Ranch Men's Club" and commissioning a bottle label from designer Sue Hatch. He told me, with some pride, that a case of "Buffalo Skull Ranch Private Reserve" was once bid up past $900 in a Rotary Auction years ago.

"More than a case from Andrew Will?" I asked. "More than three times more," he said with glee in his eye. "Blew 'em right out of the water."

In 1990, Ron Irvine bought Vashon Winery from Gerroir and Peterson so they could retire down in Belize. He published his 456-page opus on Washington state wine history, *The Wine Project*, in 1997. Vashon Winery's most recent release of a Chasselas Doré was 2006.

Wine Grapes take hold on Maury Island

In 1998 at Bertryn's class on Bainbridge, Islander Jeff Jernegan met Steve Synder of Bellevue. Synder, who had an epiphany during class "that this was something I wanted to seriously pursue," kept in touch with Jeff and, that summer, joined Jeff in a scouting expedition across the Island. "He shows me this abandoned vineyard he'd found on southern Maury Island. I remember tromping around with my wife and Jeff through the blackberries and scotch broom looking for grape vines and found a ton of them." They'd discovered the abandoned vineyard of grapes from the Washington State Ag Department planted by Les Street and Jim Wilson twenty years before.

" They probably had 50 different grape varieties there from table grapes, to french american hybrids to Cabernet Sauvignon and Chardonnay. This was like a dream come true—a ready made vineyard. Jeff found the owner, Jim Wilson, who was happy to lease us the land. So in the winter of 98-99 we spend a huge amount of time clearing out the blackberries, scotch broom and old vineyard trellis posts and start planting a new vineyard of vines that had a history in Puget Sound."

"We called it 'Maury Island Vineyard.' We also planted some experimental grapes, many of which we got from the WSU Mt. Vernon Research Station. I think we tested about 20 different varieties. Our plan was to use the grapes for our own consumption and make wine for our own use, and then when the vineyard matured we would sell grapes to wineries that wanted them. At the same time, I was formulating a plan to start a winery and considered using all our grapes there. At one time, we had about 3.5 acres under cultivation."

With Steve commuting from Bellevue on weekends, the two men got their first harvest in 2000. But by 2003, with health issues in the Jernegan family and a new baby for the Synders, they decided to give up their lease. Wilson eventually sold the parcel to a bonsai nursery; their vines, all their hard work, was mostly ripped out.

Shortly after, Synder bought land in Hollywood Hills near Woodinville and planted Pinot Noir and Chardonnay in early 2004. The first wines from his own grapes were released in April, 2008.

When asked what lessons he learned from his Maury experience, he said, "It taught me to be patient, and also all the ins and outs of running a vineyard. Of all the grapes and clones we experimented with, only Pinot worked well except for a grape called 'Regent' which I have been pushing these last eleven years."

Steve Synder now sits on the Board of Directors for the Puget Sound Wine-Growers Association. For the past three years, he has held a very popular day-long class, "Growing Grapes in a Cool Climate" and is on faculty at the NW Wine Academy at South Seattle Community College, teaching viticulture classes at night.

In 1980, inspired by Bentryn's seminar on Bainbridge Island, Bill Riley planted vinifera vines he'd bought from Les Street on his five-acre plot on Maury Island. His land is a warm, southwest-sloping site on Indianola soil— a site that should be ideal for grapes. Riley tried 13 varieties, including French-American hybrids, "hoping a few of them might produce decent wine if I tended them properly and didn't mess up... But in 2000, I ripped them all out and started over. Too many mistakes, too many lame varieties, and too much really lousy wine. I went back to Bainbridge Island Winery, took their seminar in grape growing, and bought Pinot Noir and Pinot Gris cuttings from them (Pommard clones)."

"I decided to finally get serious about this grape-growing/winemaking thing. I bought a real tractor, drilled a well, cleared away more blackberries and dying alders and fenced in the whole property. And I applied for a winery license." He got that in July '08 from the state and the ATF. In 2008, he planted two Dijon clones of Pinot Noir and two Ruhlander clones of Pinot Gris—two grapes known to ripen in cooler temperatures. In 2011 he planted another half acre of Pinot Precoce, an earlier ripening variety known in Germany as Fruhburgunder or early Burgundy. Some of his new plants are from his old friend Rudy Marchesi, who owns and runs Montimore Vineyards in Forest Grove, Oregon, the fifth largest vineyard in that state.

From his Pinot Gris grapes, Riley makes a "Crémant"—a French term for all sparkling wines made outside the famed Champagne region. (As sparkling wine can be made with grapes of a lower brix, it's a go-to strategy in cool-weather climates when a typical summer keeps grapes from reaching their full potential.) He also produces an estate-grown Pinot Noir and a rosé called (punning on the Italian) "Amauré."

Today's grapes and wine aspirants

Though a Puget Sound AVA (American Viticultural Area) was recognized in 1995, only 1% of Washington's grapes are grown in this region. Of the three Island wineries now in operation—Palouse Winery, Andrew Will, and Vashon Winery, only the latter uses grapes from Western Washington— barely enough for 5-10% of the winery's output.

Our climate is challenging. Every summer, Island grape growers ask themselves: Will my grapes get enough warm days—in wine-speak, enough "accumulated heat-degree days"— to ripen to a high enough "brix" or sugar level to ferment well? Mt. Vernon's WSU Extension publication, "Growing Wine Grapes in Maritime Western Washington," claims only a few grapes, Siegerriebe and Pinot Noir Precoce among them, will ripen with less than 1600 heat-units. Over a dozen including Agria, Regent, Madeleine Angevine, Zweigelt, and Pinot Gris can ripen with less than 1900 heat units.

In Ron Irvine's estimate, at least eight small vineyards have been planted since 2000. Most are hobby plantings: quarter- or half-acre plots planted by Islanders who either make their own vine or are hoping Ron will offer a grapes-for-wine trade.

Northward on Cedarhurst, retired psychiatrist Chuck Torrey planted a vineyard around 2003 and pressed his first vintage in 2008. Half is Pinot Noir; the rest is Zweigelt, Agria, and St. Laurent. To measure heat units, he uses a digital Hobo device in a solar shield mounted among the vines at grape level. His site has reached heat-units ranging from 1459 in cool years (2011) to 1769 (2009, an excellent year). "We're on the edge of 'can't do it here,' but I'm determined to make it work."

Steve Buffington, perhaps the youngest of the new growers, also has the youngest vines. But he's "made grapes" for years. "From 1996 through '03, I used to go over and pick grapes and prune in Prosser."

He found a site on Wax Orchard good for both orchard and vineyard: "I knew the quarter-acre between house and road would be good for grapes. It has hot, poor soil, good sun, no hardpan, was somewhat protected from the wind." He said you need a lot of time and money: "I budgeted about $3000 for the trellising, vines, and wiring." He also attended conferences at WSU's Extension Research Station in Mt. Vernon, "They've got cool-weather specialists, instead of the California transplants where nothing applies."

He planted "mostly whites: Sauvignon Blanc, Chardonnay, Pinot Gris, and some varieties all the rave in New York: Corot Noir and Noiret. I'm probably the only one who didn't plant Pinot Noir," he said.

But Henry Haselton did, inspired by a 2008 *Beachcomber* article about Vashon Winery's 2006 Pinot Noir made from grapes grown at Monument Farm. When Haselton realized that his place on 216th was just uphill from Monument Farm, he called Irvine. "I said, here's all this land, it has good exposure, sandy loam soil that drains really well. Ron said he was already thinking this spot would be good for wine grapes." Haselton planted a quarter-acre in four varieties that prefer cooler climates: Pinot Noir and Pinot Noir Precoce, plus two whites: Chasselas and Siegerrebe. He doesn't want to make wine himself—he'll let Vashon Winery do that.

Vince Nordfors of Piner Point took Steve Synder's wine-making class and, taking Synder's recommendation, planted seven rows of "Regent" grapes on his south-facing acreage in 2010. His must be the southern-most planting on the Island, and it is just south of Les Street/Steve Synder's old vineyard, now that bonsai nursery.

On land once farmed by the Hoshi family, Damon Lanphear and Rebecca Alli Lanphear have planted Chardonnay, Pinot Noir, and other varieites on another south-facing slope in Dilworth. Once interns at Hogsback Farm, they extended their learning on a bike tour of Europe's wine country and at WSU Extension classes before planting vines on their land.

Tony Raugust and Joe Curiel of Monument Farm have produced what's probably the most publicized grape harvest so far. In 2003, after chatting up Ron at Vashon Winery, the two realized they owned a perfect site for grapes—and in-house expertise with Tony's degree in horticulture. Encouraged by Ron's mentorship and his longing for an Island-grown Pinot Noir, they planted 450 plants on a third of an acre, keeping it fenced, netted, pruned, watered, and perfectly weeded.

The first harvest came in a year early, in 2006—according to Torrey's heat records, a warm year. With those grapes, Irvine created what he called his "Holy Grail: a 2006 Pinot Noir, Monument Farm Vineyard—the first commercially produced Pinot Noir made from grapes grown on Vashon Island." Released in May 2008, the supply of only 25 cases quickly sold out.

Can Your Site Grow Grapes? Here's how to find out

Despite his enthusiasm for the grape, Ron Irvine has no vineyard of his own. "What I call the Sunny Slope on Monument Road has good sun, wonderful drainage, all sand. But my soil has hardpan: it's heavy and wet."

"If you were to say to me, 'Gee, I've got a great site, what do you recommend?' I'd say, it depends on your site," said Irvine. "You need sandy, draining, not-too-fertile soil, and good sun not just in July/August, but all through the growing season, March through Halloween."

He suggests using a weather data-logger that, for under $200, will count up accumulated heat units over a site's growing season. This device measures, on each day over 50°, the temperature rise above that and assigns that day a number of heat units. These units, accumulated over an entire season, reveal how much warmth—ripening power—the site provides. And microclimates can make a real difference: for instance, an open south-facing slope such as Bill Riley's can raise heat values by 25%.

"Plug it into your computer and track temps for a year or two," Ron recommends. "You want at least 1600 degree days, with a best-case scenario around 2100." WSU Extension's publications on grape-growing in Western Washington give average heat-units for Puyallup at 1755 and Sea-Tac Airport at 1863; Irvine claims Pinot Noir requires at least 1900. From what data I could gather from three Island sites (Maury Island Winery, Chuck Torrey's northend vineyard, and Monument Farm) heat units here range from 1495 in cool years to 2389 in warm years. Brix ranges from 16 in cool years to 21.5 at Riley's site in warm 2009.

Watching for Ripeness

With a little help from his friends on October 4, Riley's few rows of Pinot Gris were harvested, crushed, and pressed, yielding over 250 lbs of juice. A week later, he harvested his Pinot Noir grapes.

"I'm very happy," he told me. "The brix was up to 21.5, and I got more grapes than ever: 650 pounds. And though this is the first year I've tracked heat degree days, this site achieved 2389 degree days."

Growing wine-grapes on Vashon IS like a Holy Grail quest. You have to have a favorable aspect and soil. You have to buy a lot of expensive trellising, netting, fencing, and gear. You hope for warm weather, hope you get to the fruit before the deer/coons/birds/bugs and diseases do.

But, by ripping out failed early experiments and replanting with earlier ripening vines, by fencing and bird-netting and jumping the hoops of ATF bureaucracy, Bill Riley earned his just reward. In 2011 at the Seattle Wine Awards, Bill's estate-grown Pinot Noir made from those wonderful 2009 grapes won a Double Gold.

"Growing wine grapes on Vashon?" he said. "It's more than possible."

For more information on growing wine grapes in Puget Sound, visit http://maritimefruit.wsu.edu/ and read their pdf "Growing Wine Grapes in Maritime Western Washington."

Kudos

In the summer of 2012, Ron Irvine was named by *Seattle Weekly* as the best Winemaker of 2012 in their Best of Seattle awards. That summer, after an 80-day drought with no rain and warm-not-hot temperatures brought on a bumper crop of wine grapes, Jim Stewart with help from Ron Irvine, Joe Curiel, and Anthony Raugust were able to pick enough of Back Bay's chasselas doré grapes that October for 200 bottles of wine.

For more information on growing wine grapes in Puget Sound, visit http://maritimefruit.wsu.edu/ and read their pdf "Growing Wine Grapes in Maritime Western Washington." Also visit Cloud Mountain Nursery's website, from where many of our growers got their vines.

Fall into Winter

The Fruit Club puts on its Cider Fest at the VIGA green, making hard and sweet cider with apples from local orchards. Later, the club hosts their Fruit Show, with speakers, tastings of up to 100 different apple varieties, and experts on hand to identify your mystery apple.

Apples and pears ripen, and windfalls start to litter the ground, your driveway, even along the highway. If it's a good year, boxes groaning with excess will mysteriously appear at the Food Bank. Jenn Coe will email for volunteers to help with a burgeoning harvest at the Food Bank Farm. Mid-season tomatoes will be ripening on indeterminate vines—if it's a good tomato year, heirlooms like Brandywine.

As corn tassels brown on stalks, proud gardeners will squeeze their corn cobs in hopes of finding ripe ears to run indoors to a boiling pot. By night, raccoons will be making the same patrol for the same delicious corn, leaving bent and keeled-over stalks for an annoyed gardener to discover the next morning.

Our stores stock up on bulbs for sale, as well as flats of winter pansies, pots of chrysanthemums and ornamental kale. It's time to plant garlic and cover crops, tuck in some last transplants to winter over. The dahlias are still so beautiful, you consider leaving their barely-hardy tubers in the ground just to enjoy the blooms as long as possible.

Rain shows up occasionally in October, then powers up in November, bringing "pineapple express" monsoons from Hawaii and the first power outages. The first frosts blacken basil and flatten callas. But on sunny days, raking leaves makes you feel invigorated, virtuous, as you fold last year's garden life, come full circle, into next year's gardening.

All the Ways We Compost

*Compost Fest, composting at Plum Forest Farm, plus a C/N ratio
chart, Island sources, and the Over-a-Barrow Compost Sifter*

It was a cool, threatening-to-drizzle October morning, not a great day for hosting a public gathering in your front yard. But I was one of dozens walking toward the 2009 Compost Fest, the Island's first, hosted by Cathy Fulton of Mariposa Gardens. And it looked like this outdoor symposium on decomp was drawing a good crowd.

Walking up the drive between a half-built cob hut and a tic-tac-toe of bamboo poles fencing a shaggy yard, I spotted the entrance greeting table with its banner "How Many Ways Can We Make Compost?" Inside the fences were many 3'x8' beds cut into the grass; in one, chickens were scratching the soil, cooped there in a hoophouse of pipes and scrap deer-fencing. "Chicken Cultivators—an organic Weed & Feed operation," declared the sign. Brewing in a still nearby was Stinging Nettle Tea, "stimulating for the immune system of plants," "aids the microbial life in soil, roots, and leaves," and smelling "absolutely disgusting." Next to the apple tree, a bearded man in muck boots was wrestling with a pair of bars painted siren red; as he fell backward, long fangs reared out of the soil.

Quite the operation you got here, Ms. Fulton.

In pallet bins were demonstrations of hot composting, cool composting, and composting of animal waste. On the ground variously heaped were the cardboard-layered lasagna beds, the industrious chicken "tractors," and a heap labeled "hugelkultur" that looked like a nest a troll would like to sit on. Nettle tea brewed stinkily in its plastic still, worms sashayed through the kitchen scraps in a big tupperware chest, and a fellow in a Crocodile Dundee hat and overalls seemed to be making cowboy coffee over a homemade metal-bucket campstove.

I'd come to this strange symposium to improve my composting technique. For years, I've been practicing something very like her demonstration of cool compost: casual layers of kitchen scrap, cut grass, and garden weeds that are collected over time and take months to compost. Because such a pile layers up slowly, it doesn't build up enough heat to kill weed seeds—and I have learned the hard way that weed seeds survive cool composting to sprout another day. Once I realized my compost was bringing weeds to my garden, I tried to stoke up my compost by watering it more often, layering greens and browns when I had them, chopping chunks up, adding horse manure and even my own pee (I'll let you imagine how...). But I couldn't seem to get the pile to peak much more than 90°.

In contrast, the hot compost demo clearly had this problem fixed. Boxed in a neat corral of old pallets on edge, its layers of grass, horse manure, and apple cider waste steamed like a hot racehorse in cold air. I checked the compost thermometer: it read a weed- and germ-killing 110°.

A woman in a white sailor's cap walked up. "Interested in hot compost?"

"YES! How'd you get that to COOK?"

"See how everything's shredded? It helps to break up the big bits so there's plenty of surface area and broken areas for the microbes to chew on. Here, give the pile a shot." She handed me the noozle of her garden hose. "You have to keep the pile moist as a sponge. And here you see how I've got everything layered?" She pointed at a 2" layer of reddish goo. "That's the apple pomace I got from a friend who makes cider. But you could add okara— that's tofu waste from Island Spring— or grass clippings or chicken manure, anything with lots of nitrogen to really stoke up the pile. "

That's how I met Cathy Fulton and her many ways to make compost.

What makes a compost pile COOK?

You probably already know that compost wants oxygen, water, and layers of "greens" (nitrogen-rich materials) and "browns" (carbon-rich materials) to provide fuel and food for organisms—large, small, and micro—that come to dine at the compost feast.

The most easily seen are the larger creatures like worms, sow bugs, slugs, centipedes, etc. They move in and chew down larger particles, leaving pieces small enough for microbes and fungi to attack.

The heat is created by the activity of microbes: clans of single-cell bacteria that each have their preferred temperature range. First up are *psychrophiles*, which live in temperatures from 0° to mid-60s. They chew on carbons (your

browns), release amino acids and generate a bit of heat, making composting happen even in mid-winter, albeit slowly. Also at work are fungi and
half-bacteria/half-fungi beasts called *actinomycetes* that establish their grayish webs around the fringes of a pile; these work on carbonous browns such
as paper, leaves, sawdust, and wood.

When the pile goes over 50°, *mesophiles* take over and multiply. Their
populations can double in 30 minutes—millions in a single gram of compost. They favor carbohydrates such as sugars and starches, and like carb-fu-
eled athletes, their energetic activity can raise the pile to over 100° within a
few days, setting the stage for the arrival of *thermophiles*. (And they'll return
during the cool-down phase of composting.)

Thermophiles chew on the tough stuff: paper and wood, fats, and proteins. It's a Roman bacchanal in there: all that eating, pooping, and repro-
ducing can stoke temps past 120° (where pathogens and weed seeds start to
die), past 130° (earthworms start to die...), and if it gets over 160°, better
hose that pile down before the soil self-sterilizes. When the heat peaks, you
turn and water the pile, whih starts a second burst of activity. After a couple
of temperature peaks and turnings, the thermophiles will exhaust their food
supply and die off. As the temperature drops, the mesophiles revive and tear
into the last rough bits in your bin. After this point, your compost will be
ready in a week or so.

That's the science behind composting. But there's many ways to do it. So
let's take a tour of the stations of Cathy's Compost Fest.

Make a Hot Compost Pile

According to the interpretative sign tacked on Cathy's hot compost bin,
this method makes good compost in a few weeks. It's material- and labor-
intensive: you have to have all your materials at hand (including a compost
thermometer), it will take about an hour of sweaty labor to build, and you
will have to turn the pile at least twice that month to encourage those heat-
loving microbes to attack your weed seeds and woody scraps.

The layering of nitrogen-rich "greens" and carbonous "browns" is important: the microorganisms and creatures in compost use carbon (think
"carbs") just like we do to fuel up, and they use nitrogen (think "proteins")
to build body structure and to reproduce. Brown materials are dry, fibrous,

and have lost their fresh "greenness": examples are dried hay, straw, autumn leaves, newspaper, or coffee chaff. A pile dominated by fibrous browns will have lots of air pockets for water and oxygen, but not enough nitrogen to build up microbe populations. Greens such as fresh-cut grass, vegetable scraps, fresh okara or spring manure are plump with water and nutrients that microbes need to build their cell structures, but a pile with too much "green" may collapse, squeezing first oxygen from the pile and then ammonia gas from dying microorganisms. A pile that's gone anaerobic will stink of ammonia, signaling that it's losing nitrogen and needs some carbs mixed in. To help you make good blends of carbon & nitrogen-rich materials, you'll find a table of sources and their C/N ratios later in this chapter.

Cool Composting

In contrast to the neat and well-layered hot pile, Cathy's cool bin was downright shaggy: bristling with bean vines and hay stalks, swaddled in damp sheets of cardboard, leaning a little to the left.

"Here is the quinessential compost pile," explained Cathy's sign—just put all your weeds, kitchen scraps, and garden refuse and let it rot in its own time. Such a pile may take two years to turn into compost. Avoid adding fresh grass clippings all at once because they mat down and can create that smelly anaerobic condition. If you use a wire enclosure, weeds can actually sprout out the sides, so line it with flakes of spoiled hay or cardboard. Cover with a tarp in the rainy season to prevent nutrient leaching.

The good news with this method is that it needs little maintenance beyond occasional watering in the dry season, and you can add materials as they come to hand. And because it's a cool process, nitrogen gas isn't being burned off into the atmosphere —if it was, you'd notice that ammonia smell. If you have a big screen, you can get good, fluffy compost out of a cool pile by sifting the rough stuff over a wheelbarrow (see plans at the end of this chapter) then throwing the chunks back into the bin and wheeling the rich, fluffy siftings straight into the garden.

The bad news is that a cool pile doesn't get hot enough to kill pathogens or weed seeds. And if the container has openings large enough, varmints like crows and raccoons can get in and raid your kitchen scraps—one reason many islanders have switched to worm bins.

Composting Animal Waste

Occasionally at Mariposa, comes the time when chickens meet their end. Sometimes, blame the raccoons. But sometimes, it's an official community Slaughtering Party with the "WhizBang Chicken Plucker."

Cathy's sign read, "This compost pile started out as a place for me to park the used bedding from my chickens, so the straw would have plenty of time to rot before being put on the garden. When we started hosting community poultry processing days here, I wanted to compost the waste from the slaughter. This bed provided the perfect place."

"We dig a hole in the bedding compost, empty our buckets of waste and feathers from slaughtering 20-30 chickens, then cover the offal with a generous amount of sawdust that we acquire from the Forest Steward's mill. We occasionally add bedding from our neighbor's goat shed. It is best to build this kind of pile away from traffic and visitors: the odors can be strong at times! Use a large amount of sawdust—at least a 3" layer on top of the chicken waste—to reduce odor and flies. With so much sawdust, this pile has to compost a long time, maybe as much as two years."

After living with her offal pile for a couple years, Cathy later told me that the smell does linger for a couple weeks and can be noticed from twenty feet away. And no matter how well you cover the pile, the raccoons will find the pile and tear it apart, so she advised keeping lots of sawdust around to rebuild the pile. She never turned it (and who'd want to get that close?)

Sheet-Mulching—aka Lasagna Beds

Under Cathy's fruit trees, a carpet of dried grass covered the earth, with corners of sheet cardboard poking out from under. These were her sheet-mulches; they're also known as lassagna beds, composting in place, the "no-till" or "no-dig" method. Since you don't have to dig at all, it's possibly the easiest way to create a new garden bed.

Pick your site, whack down its existing vegetation (though you should uproot scotch broom, blackberries, bindweed, or quackgrass), wet the ground thoroughly, lay down sheets of cardboard or newspaper sections on top of the knocked-down vegetation, and top with thick layers of organic material—manure, hay, straw, grass clippings, animal bedding, seaweed, food industry by-products, anything that will compost. It's best to do this in late summer or fall so everything is decomposed before you plant in spring. Weeds that do emerge will be easy to pull. Because you don't disturb this bed after it's built, soil microbes will thrive. Worms seem to love gathering under cardboard, but raccoons know this and will toss your new bed like salad to get at those wormy delights.

My neighbor Jason sheet-mulches with the manure and bedding from his chicken coop. Around the New Year, he works into the topsoil of his raised beds a 3-4" layer of coop sweepings, then tops this mixture with a thinner layer of clean straw and lets the microbes work. Within a month, the bedding has transformed into a dark humus that's surprisingly fluffy, ready by March for the transplants he grows in his greenhouse.

Hügelkultur heaps and trenches

In one corner of Cathy's garden was a 3' high heap shaped like a half-buried brioche—a big bun with a smaller bun on top. This curiosity was a hügelkultur heap, which translated from German means "mound culture."

Cathy got this idea from a permaculture book by Toby Hemenway called *Gaia's Garden*. He writes, "To create hügelkultur, pile up branches or brush a foot or two deep in a mound 4-8 feet long. Stomp on the pile to compress the branches, then toss on compostable materials—grass clippings, sod, straw—into the pile. Sprinkle some compost on the mound, and top with an inch or so of soil." If dug as a trench, you heap the material about 12" above grade: the material will sink as it decomposes.

Cathy had several hügelkultur sites going in both above-ground piles and below-grade trenches. In other permaculture books, I've seen this method adapted as swales dug across slopes to absorb runoff. The weave of sticks within the pile create spaces for oxygen and water, and the wood as it rots will hold water like a big sponge. Some people cover the bottom of a trench with rotting logs or lumber scraps, with sticks and compost on top.

Later, when she sent her illustration (next page), Cathy said, "I think that if the material would have been placed more in the proportion as is shown on the cross-section image, it would have done better. It is difficult when dealing with tree limb debris to smash everything down solid before topping with weeds, manure, leaves. Still, last year I planted broccoli and cabbage there and it needed very little watering. The hügelkultur trench has not sunken lower than the surrounding area. It's not a good idea to use madrone branches—they take FOREVER to decompose."

Hugelkultur Trench Cross Section

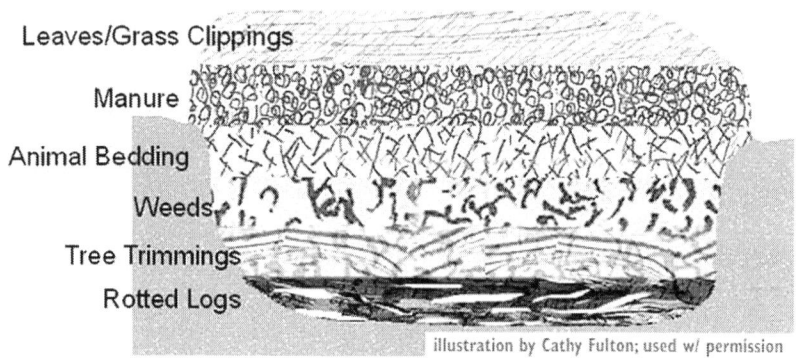

illustration by Cathy Fulton; used w/ permission

In 2013, the fruit club started a hügelkultur at their Sunrise Ridge demonstration orchard. The 20' trench was dug two feet deep, piled with old logs, sod, and vegetative trimmings, and topped with composted manure and biochar made from blackberry brambles. A log on its shady end was inoculated with mushroom spores for "a more celestial fruiting body," said coordinator Gloria Bradford. The plan is to grow berries and can fruits, along with perennials and annuals to keep the mound from eroding. Gloria said, "We'll see how it grows—it's sure to be an amazing polyculture."

Nettle Tea

According to Cathy's sign, nettle tea improves plants' immunity to diseases and infections from insect predation. When used as a soil soak, it also gives soil microbes large doses of calcium, copper, iron, nitrogen, phosphorus, and potassium—like giving them vitamins.

To make nettle tea, cut a bunch of nettles at about half-height, preferably before they're setting seeds. Wear gloves! Mix the cuttings with water in a large container and cover the lid because the tea smells pretty foul. Allow the brew to ferment 1-3 weeks—it'll slowly bubble and froth—until this fermentation stops, then strain (probably with a clothes pin over your nose). Store the infusion in clean plastic or glass containers in a cool spot. Dilute the tea before using: for a soil soak, use 1:10 tea to water, for a foliar feed dilute 1:20. (Stronger, and the brew becomes an herbicide.)

Biochar: a way to deal with sticks & twigs

Ah, those sticks & twigs: we've all had to deal with them after a storm, a tree-felling, or when opening up the forest for new garden space. They're a pain, frankly, especially madrone and hemlock. But Ken Miller, the guy in the Crocodile Dundee hat, had come to the Fest to show Islanders how to transform sticks and twigs into something good for the garden—biochar.

Into his homemade combustion chamber (a metal bucket blackened by fire) Ken had stuffed alder sticks topped with tinder. Once it was filled, he put a match to the tinder, capped the growing flames with a metal lid held slightly aloft on metal cross-bars, then stood a 3' chimney stack on top. He explained: "The top and bottom of the bucket have slots to let in air for the intial combustion. Once the chimney goes on, the heat can build up to 800°, and it eats up all the smoke. In less than half an hour, the burn is down to bright-red embers. At that point, you exclude all the oxygen—otherwise your biochar would all turn to ash—and the wood turns to charcoal."

If this sounds like the reason peasants burn the Amazon forests to create fertile fields, you aren't far wrong. The Amazon region has large swaths of "dark earth" or "terra preta" that are thousands of years old—soils that, long ago, were seeded with charcoal to increase fertility. The native soils are lean on nitrogen, but these "dark earth" soils are 9% carbon and highly fertile.

He handed me a chunk of biochar that looked exactly like the vine charcoal I've used in drawing class. "This is biochar made of blackberries—see how it doesn't soot up your hand?" he said rather proudly. "You can biochar all your bones, scrap wood, berry vines, sunchoke stalks, all your sticks and twigs. For Islanders, it's a way to process wood scraps and woody brush, raise acid soils toward neutrality, and provide a long-term soil amendment that resists leaching from rain."

Biochar becomes most useful as a soil amendment when it is "charged" by soaking it in a tea made from compost, nettles, or manure. Fire gives biochar a honeycomb cell structure that holds liquids easily—and shelters soil microbes. I saw biochar's benefits to the soil when I visited Ken's garden later that year; in biochar-enhanced beds, the plants were noticeably larger. Not only does he dig biochar into his beds, he seeds biochar chunks right into his compost piles, figuring they will absorb nutrient-rich liquids as he keeps his compost watered. And here's one last benefit: on top of the little biochar stove he uses in his own yard, he can brew up a nice cup of coffee.

Worm bins, not piles: a popular alternative

You'd think many Islanders would compost, but no—in a casual survey of classmates and blog readers I did last year, many said they'd given up composting because of varmints.

Julia Lakey once had a stacking compost bin from King County at home. "The coons jumped on the roof to collapse it, so I put wire around it and a temporary lid—it became quite the contraption. Then there was the time I tossed in kitchen scraps and a rat flew into the air, did a U-turn and disappeared." She gave up composting and now buries her food waste.

About 20% of the gardeners I surveyed had either worm bins or fed their kitchen scraps to chickens. A good worm bin acts like a safe for kitchen scraps. Make it big, make it heavy, and the critters can't get in.

"Mine looks like a coffin—a 2'x 4' box with hinged lid and a handle to lift the top," said garden club member Deborah Teagardin. She commissioned hers from the Worm Guy, Mark Yelkin, who also sells his "Wiggle Worm Castings" through True Value. "The bin is very heavy, but it works so well that when we moved, we emptied it and took the system with us. It keeps the raccoons and rats out. And it gets rid of our kitchen scraps."

The chest is partitioned with 1/4" hardware cloth into two halves, both filled with moistened worm bedding (shredded newspaper works well). You add kitchen scraps to one side: the worm dine there for months until that side gets too full of castings and the worms migrate to the other side. "In the summertime the flies and pill-bugs get pretty bad, so I just do the 'Open-Throw-Slam-Walk Away' routine without looking," she said. About twice a year when one side's been filled to capacity, she'll pull out the old bedding full of worm castings and use it as side-dressing around garden plants.

Another friend, Vicki Clabaugh, made hers out of an old chest from Grannie's Attic. She told me "I do not use much of the actual worm bin compost because it is full of seeds from tomatoes, cukes, melons, etc, and these seeds sprouted EVERYWHERE the first year I used the compost. Now I fill 3-6 pails halfway with compost and then top with water. Stir daily for a few days. Then I use this tea, after straining it through an old screen, to water pots and my raised bed, especially when planting seeds and starts. I dump what's left in the bottom of the pails back into the worm bin."

Mark Yelkin told me, "Worm tea is like 'Red Bull' for plants, it has so much microbial activity." He once ran a worm compost service, offering "2 buckets of scrap for 1 bucket of worm compost" to subscribers and restaurants, filling large composting arrays with their output. But personal difficulties and "too much silverware and junk" from certain restaurants, plus a closure of the Dirt Yard where he was based, put an end to Worm Guy enterprises—though he's willing to make more worm bins. Or try using two Rubbermaid tubs, one within the other: you'll find plans online.

Worm bin wigglers are not your standard 6" earthworms. They are *Eisenia fetida*, also known as Red Wigglers, and they are adapted to living in dense populations in the warmer temperatures of rich organic rot, rather than earth. You can collect them yourself if you have a compost pile or exposed dirt: just lay a big square of moist cardboard on top, wait a few days and you'll find scores of red wigglers gathered on the underside. You can also get worms from Yelkin, or from Ann who demonstrated her worm bin at Mariposa Garden's Compost Fest. She sells them for $15/lb; you can contact her at anneonvashon@comcast.net. Or you can get them from her favorite website on the subject, www.redwormcomposting.com. There's a lot of information about worm composting on the Internet.

Ann said you need about a pound of worms for every square foot of bin volume. They'll eventually multiply into gazillions of worms, but they will not reproduce more than the space in your bin can handle. Be patient: worms don't so much EAT your scraps as suck on the slurry generated by decomposition, so it's a good idea to let moist bedding and scraps moulder for a week or two before introducing the first worms.

Plum Forest Farm's Composting Facility

If you want to make organic compost to the national organic standard, you need it to reach 131-170° for several days. (That's in a "static, aerated heap"; in a windrow you aim for the same temperature, turning it five times, over 15 days.) To achieve his organic certification, Rob Peterson of Plum Forest Farm built his composting facility to that standard, using the compostables generated on his own small farm.

I first saw his composting station in 2010 when Rob was building it (with financial help from the King Conservation District, which is concerned about managing runoff from lifestock). The facility, set up next to his chicken coop and cow pasture, has three 9'x9' bins and a shed roof that partially covers a 20'x30' concrete pad.

During what he calls "the collection phase," Rob dumps weeds, clippings, any organic material that comes from his farm's planting beds and stables. Then he tops this pile with hay (grown right there in Paradise Valley) to tempt his two cows, Golden and Clove. Once the gate's throw open, his two Scottish Highland cows amble in and start nosing through the hay. They pull, they shred, they grind and stomp, and they add in some nitrogen in the form of piss and poo. When this cow-churned pile is high enough (and a bin becomes open), Rob sweeps the chicken manure and bedding from the coop onto the concrete pad, fires up the Bobcat and turns this stinky, coarse roughage into the open bin.

"We're not certified yet, but we WANT to meet that standard," he told me (they did achieve organic certification in 2012.) He checks the temperature of the new pile daily; once it gets above 131°, he turns it with the tractor and adds water if it's dry. He will turn it 4-5 more times over next two weeks until the temps ease off from 131°. Then he lets it sit and cure, covered, for several months. It makes a compost fine enough to take straight to whatever bed he's preparing for planting; he doesn't even bother to screen.

I asked him if he ever used leaf mold. "I plan to in the future—part of the compost station has an area set aside for leaf mold," he said. "I've also used okara—it really heats up a pile. It's a bit stinky, but it's great if you have enough carbon to offset it. If I found somebody with lots of leaves to give me, I'd add okara to it and that would compost great."

Putting it all together in my own compost bin

Back in my own garden, inspired by the Compost Fest and what I'd seen in other gardens, I built a new pile with old bean vines, garden trimmings, coffee chaff, leaves, and barely composted grass from my older compost pile. Five days later, stabbing into the pile hopefully with my compost thermometer, the warmest temperature I could find was 90°. I told myself I was halfway to the kill-zone, but days later, it was back down to 60°. How deflating... I added mowed alder leaves (you'll read about that in the next chapter) and green manure, and then, quintessentially passive composter that I am, I forgot all about it.

But composting happens, folks, as sure as death and decay. In March when I was rebuilding my bins in the Fulton style (pallets from the tofu factory), I forked into that November pile and found it had turned into finished compost, brown-black as chocolate cake and earthly fragrant. Inspired, I drove off for some spring horse manure (green), gave my garden and frig a clean-up (more greens), layered those with leaf mold (browns), used the finished compost as inoculant and watered as I layered. Four days later, 110°. I'd gotten to at least WARM...

A year later, I started bringing home bucketfuls of okara from the tofu factory. My new layering technique became brown/green/okara white, and within a day, my new pile heated past 140°. This okara-driven warmth was quite noticeable in my garden beds, too: a tomato bed fed shovelfulls of okara was warm to the touch days later, and my young lettuces top-dressed with okara jumped in growth compared to non-okara'd plants. The boost in protein-rich nitrogen produced plenty of macro-organisms in my new composts: worms writhed a-plenty, and I found thousands of tiny silvertails, an invertebrate that looks under a magnifying glass like a white shrimp, clustering on the underside of my compost bucket. All this heat and activity by organisms began to produce a richer soil amendment that didn't seem to harbor so many potent weed seeds and did my wanted plants a lot of good.

At long last—good home-cooked compost!

Compost Ingredients and how they rate

We Islanders are lucky to have so many sources of good compostables. Okara is a very high-nitrogen by-product that Island Spring Tofu Factory is happy to give away by the bucket or the truckful—but it gets stinky over time, so you'll want to mix it into soil or compost the day you get it. Grape lees and cider pomace, the pressings from wine or cider, are available around Halloween. Seaweed makes good compost or mulch; if you're worried about salt, let rain wash it off. Minglement Roasterie offers coffee chaff and spent grounds. Just ask permission before you haul away.

Then there's all this manure lying around. When you first visit a farm to get manure, ask how to act around their animals, especially dogs. You're a strange presence to them: they might be nervous, curious, even aggressive. You don't want a stallion stomping you for stealing his territorial markers.

In spring, the fresh green grass grazed by large animals such as horses and cows pops out as a lush, high-nitrogen nugget of nutrients. But when that grass dries out in summer, what comes out the nether end is a dry, fiber-laden wad full of carbon—like adobe. NW garden expert Steve Solomon (*Growing Vegetables West of the Cascades*) points out that composts made with these summer manures aren't as full of nutrients as general-interest garden-ing books would have you believe. But spring manure, gotten while grass is green and not topped with seeds, can be worth the labor. Some of the most beautiful soil I've ever seen was created in upper Gold Beach by Julia Lakey, who top-dressed her flower garden with horse-apples every late winter.

Discussions of the "proper ratios" is confusing: writers talk about bal-anced compost having a carbon to nitrogen ratio of 30:1, but they aren't talking about 30 lbs of carbon materials to 1 lb of nitrogen—they're talking about the strength or concentration of C or N in the material. Think of the ratio like partners on a see-saw: if one partner is heavy, the other partner must be farther out on the see-saw to keep it in balance. To achieve compost balance, the heavier an ingredient is in nitrogen, the more it needs a partner with a high concentration of carbon. For instance, chicken manure is very high nitrogen (C/N ratio is 3:1) and needs to be balanced with something high in carbon such as sawdust (210:1) or shredded paper (400:1). To find how close your compost ingredients would come to the proper ratio of 30:1, divide the carbon number into the nitrogen number. For instance, a pile of chicken-poo + sawdust has a C/N ratio of 70:1 is heavy on carbon, and benefits from more nitrogen (throw on the poo!) to cook all that woody dust. Once you've found ingredients that complement each other, pile on those green and browns, those Cs and Ns, in roughly equal quantities. Well-balanced compost should fire up past 100° within a couple of days.

C : N Ratios of Common Compost Ingredients

Nitrogen-rich GREENS: C/N ratio

URINE 2:

POULTRY MANURE * 3-7:1

BLOOD MEAL 3:1

FISH WASTE 2.5-5:1

SOYBEAN MEAL 4-6:1

COTTONSEED MEAL 7:1

OKARA * (tofu waste) 8:1

SPRING GRASS CLIPPINGS * 9:1

ALPACA MANURE * 9:1

PIG MANURE 9-19:1

VEGIE PEELINGS * 12:1

ALFALFA HAY 13:1

GRAPE LEES (after wine-pressing) 14:1

LEGUME HAY 15:1 More nitrogen in spring hay; use summer grass as a brown

SHEEP MANURE * 16:1

TURKEY MANURE 16:1

COW MANURE 18:1

SEAWEED * Anywhere from 5-27:1.

LLAMA MANURE 20:1

SUMMER GRASS CLIPPINGS * 20-30:1

GREEN PLANT TRIMMINGS * 20-40:1

HORSE MANURE * 22:1 (higher N in spring when they're eating spring grass)

Carbon-rich BROWNS: C/N ratio

COFFEE GROUNDS * 20:1 6.2 pH; provides phosphorus, potassium, magnesium, copper.

ALDER LEAVES * 25:1

WOOD ASH 25:1 Good source of calcium & potassium, but very alkaline

NON-LEGUME HAY 30:1

APPLE POMACE 48:1

OAK LEAVES 50-80:1

STRAW * 80:1 Decomposes very slowly: good for heavy clay soil. Often used for animal bedding, comes with manure

PINE NEEDLES 85:1

HARDWOOD BARK 115-435:1

PAPER & CARDBOARD * 150-200:1 Shred first

COFFEE CHAFF * 200:1 (?)

WOOD CHIPS OR SHAVINGS * 21-1300:1 shredded wood of deciduous trees, while heavy in carbon, is said to promote helpful soil fungi in our types of soils

SAWDUST, ROTTED * 210:1

NEWSPRINT * 400-850:1

SAWDUST, RAW * 500:1

* Easy to find on the Island.

My Favorite Composting Tools

Composting Thermometer: The only way you'll know if your compost is cooking. Also good for testing soil temperatures in spring.

Aeration Tubes: Laid between layers, these tubes with holes let oxygen into your heap. I use PVC pipes, 2" wide, with 1/2" holes drilled every 2". Pipe that comes off a spool is curved to a pile's rounded shape.

Garbage Can of Finished Compost: I keep a garbage can of sifted, compost nearby so when I need mulch or soil amendments, compost is ready to go. If it's a can on wheels, you can pull it to your work site.

A Great Compost Sifter: You KNOW there's good compost in that cool pile: how to get it out? Here's my husband's great design for a tool that sifts the good stuff from the unfinished.

Bob Dale's Over-a-Barrow Compost Sifter

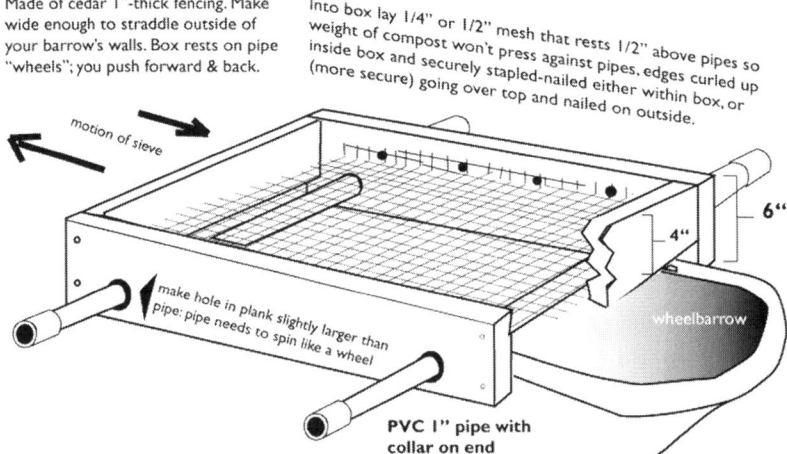

Made of cedar 1"-thick fencing. Make wide enough to straddle outside of your barrow's walls. Box rests on pipe "wheels"; you push forward & back.

Into box lay 1/4" or 1/2" mesh that rests 1/2" above pipes so weight of compost won't press against pipes, edges curled up inside box and securely stapled-nailed either within box, or (more secure) going over top and nailed on outside.

motion of sieve

6"

4"

wheelbarrow

make hole in plank slightly larger than pipe: pipe needs to spin like a wheel

PVC 1" pipe with collar on end

We made our first from 1x6" cedar fence planks; it's lightweight with eased-over edges. Make sure the INTERIOR of the box is 1/2-1" wider than the EXTERIOR of the barrow, and that the mesh is high enough over the pipes so the weight of compost will not press the mesh against the pipes.. You want as little resistance as possible so the box glides rims easily. Once the "fines" are through, toss the chunks back into your bin. Another use: with a flat-sided piece of wood, to grind horse apples into innocuous "fines." (Make box with whole 4 sides: the cut-away is just to show detail.)

ˈrees and Autumn Leaves

*⸲ remier Island trees, including some that give good fall color.
And a gardener goes mad for leaves and making leaf mold.*

If the weather cooperates, autumn on the Island becomes a tapestry of deep, dramatic color-play. Along my favorite forest trail, the color is so stimulating, I take my camera on walks to capture interesting color mixes. To the usual palette of bracken, lichen, salal, leaf, and tree trunk, add wheat, gold, copper and chocolate, emerald, teal, lime green and plum-gray.

 In my studio's view of Maury Island, I can see a single red maple shining out from the native canopy of dark fir and maple gold. Closer to Vashon-town, there's a lot more color: maroons, purples, fire-n-smoke tones. Each deciduous tree shows itself individual, blazing amidst the evergreen pack. That makes late October/early November an excellent time to go tree-spotting. And as birders have their Life Lists, I think it possible you could check several off your Life List of Trees just from sightings around the Island.

In 1992 (and updated in 2007), a group of tree-mad Islanders from our local Audubon chapter went looking for, in spots along the highway or easily accessible, the biggest and best of Island trees. They compiled a list (still posted online at www.vashonaudubon.org/media/HighwayTrees.pdf) that starts at the north end ferry dock, travels south down the highway, diverts to the cemetery, up Cove, and onto the Burton Peninsula, and comes back along Quartermaster Drive. Among the nearly 100 significant trees they found, two were "largest in Washington State"—a set of bolleana white poplars along the road at Monument Farm and an Italian cypress across the street from the movie theater (rather dwarfed by its neighbor, a big sequoia). If you print out the "Highway Trees" list, you can easily (though perhaps dangerously) scout these trees while traffic's backing up behind you.

To that list, I'd like to add a few of my own favorites. Outside the library's front door are three snowbell trees (not whitebeams, as the list declares) yellow now, but in late spring full of white danglers that look exactly like snowbell flowers. The parking lot is edged with red maples, Acer 'Red Sunset.'

(Whether these trees are still here after 2013's library renovation remains, as of this book's publication, an open question.) Across the street, Windermere Real Estate has young ginkgos, bright yellow now, along the highway.

Turn east at the town's main intersection to find several ash trees, Fraxinus oxycarpa 'Raywood,' along the street in front of Cafe Luna and Frame of Mind; its somber fall coloration differs from year to year, sometimes running through olive green, wine-red, and deep plum at the same time. A big monkey puzzle is across the street from the Senior Center. The removal of an overgrown eucalyptus fronting the pharmacy's parking lot revealed a husky strawberry tree, Arbutus unedo. Across from the movie theatre is the largest Italian cypress in the state—though that significance is rather dwarfed by the towering sequoia standing next to it.

Red maples, so striking in autumn, are much planted: find more of them in front of Vashon Physical Therapy and along the road to Island Lumber's back lot (where, if you look to the NE corner house, you'll see a tamarisk). South of town, the PGE utility property is fronted by more sunset maples, with a row of red oaks along its driveway. 188th's white colonial, once the Cherry Hill B & B, is surrounded by a small arboretum, including china firs, copper beech, sourwood, a collection of big camellias, and a sequoia in back. The gas station/athletic club also has some fine trees: a liquidamber that's stunting a sourwood to its immediate south, a pair of silk trees next to the gas station's sunroom, and across 192nd, a sequoia, oak, holly, and chestnut crowded together on the SE corner of the intersection.

At the intersection of the highway & Cemetery Road, a pair of black walnuts loom over the old Fuller store on the SW corner. They mark where one of the Island's leading families had its start. In the 1890s Philip McCormick, a young plant salesman from Woodburn, Oregon, sold these black walnut trees to the Fuller family. At some point in the transaction, he fell in love with a Fuller daughter, Isabelle, and moved here in 1898.

The cemetery itself has a fine collection, many planted by the Island's Japanese families. These include bristlecone pine, linden, noble fir, eastern arborvitae, hinoki cypress, trident maple, Italian and golden yews, campersdown elm, knobcone pine, and a silvery holly and, at the Steen plot, a weeping variegated holly (unfortunately, the maintenance crew trimmed up "the weepers" in 2011).

At the Country Store, owner Vy Biel has a collection of trees and shrubs planted in the 1980s. Shrubs include parrotia, fothergilla, daphne, calycarpus, cotoneaster, corylopsis (winter hazel), and at the store's NE corner, a european hazel that's the largest in the state. Her trees include oak, ash, magnolia, cutleaf alder, catalpa, and paulownia. Across the little footbridge, you'll find Chinese mountain ash (Sorbus hupehensis) and Viburnum opulus dangling deep-red, translucent berries. Many specimens are labeled, though you might have to search around and in the plant to find the tag.

At Sunrise Ridge, soldiers stationed at the (then) Nike Missile Site during the Cold War planted trees; pin oaks line the entrance drive, a tulip poplar is next to the health clinic, some yews and a Harry Lauder's Walking Stick stand around the furniture annex, and a big liquidamber towers over the old Harmeling orchard site. At the back of the campus next to the llama farm, Mary Jo Barrantine, granddaughter of Philip McCormick and frequent docent at the Heritage Museum, has a bald cypress, sequoia, catalpa, and a 20-year-old larch from Montana.

With big acreages and a tree-friendly climate, it's no surprise many Islanders have their own arboretums. Nearly to Burton, at that big A-frame overlooking the inner harbor, Merle & Ruth Sauer planted (from SE corner close to highway) a cedar, monterey cypress, and trident maple, with a laburnum, tulip polar, and catalpa uphill. On their west slope, there's (from bottom to top), Austrian black pine, cherry, nootka weeping cypress, magnolia grandiflora, gingko, Japanese maple, and crytomeria. Garden tours often reveal these private arboretums, so take your Life List or tree guide.

Down Cove Road at the hostel grows a colony of unique "Wineleaf Maples" distinguished by a burgundy cast to the underside of their leaves. Sharon Munger, who used to host the "Barnworks" art show across the road, says she was once visited by two brothers who grew up at her place; they said the seeds of these maples were handed to their father in the 1910s by a fellow from Germany's Black Forest who was hanging around the Cove area. She would be more than happy to let you dig up some of those seedlings, but before you do, ask yourself if you have room for trees so large.

Finally, all the way past Burton at the north end of Magnolia Beach is a tree perched all by its magnificent self on the point of a bulwark. In perfect symmetry, it stands silhouetted against the silvery entrance to Quartermaster's outer harbor. In autumn, its leaves make a net of gold over black branches. I didn't know what it was until I stopped and the homeowner said "It's an elm." Exactly which elm is a mystery. It may be an American elm—tree shape, bark, leaf shape, and fall color all point that way—an exciting idea, as the trees are rare thanks to the Dutch Elm disease that wiped out the Midwest's millions of American elms. More likely it's a Siberian elm, a fast-growing tree that's somewhat invasive; I know of two mishapen specimens that sprouted in the riprap shoreline of Guv's Lane and upper Shawnee Beach, just north of there. Could seeds from the good-looking tree been carried by the tide down the Burton shoreline? Possibly...

So before the leaves fall, check out our local trees. If you want some for your own back 40, check out local nurseries and plant centers, plus Trees of Legacy on lower Wax Orchard Rd. and Colvos Creek Nursery at the Country Store (where you might find Mike Lee, Colvos Creek founder and partcipant in the "Highway Trees" project, on Saturdays). The Land Trust has an annual sale of native trees and shrubs, and the Fruit Club often sells young fruit trees at the farmers' market.

Leaf Lust: There's GOLD in dem dar leaves

With the return of wind, rain, and that tree hormone that detaches leaves from their branches, soon there will be blankets of gold, rust, or red leaves on the ground. Such riches, lying there wasting away—they ignite at something covetous in my soul.

One reads, in gardening books, about the benefits of leaf mold. When added to garden beds, leaf mould can double soil's ability to hold water while cutting in half its need for fertilizer. You can grow seeds in it: you can feed your compost with it. If you mow leaves on your lawn, you will feed the soil, encourage microbial activity, build up a water reserve in the soil and thus help your lawn stay greener next summer.

And this time of year, a stockpile of shredded leaves is immediately useful, as shredded leaves make a good-looking mulch to protect your plantings over the winter. You should get the blanket of leaves OFF your plantings anyway so they won't be smothered. When you're weeding next spring and find yourself with bucketfuls of compostable "greens," you'll already have a stockpile of "browns" ready to mix with them into a new compost pile.

One October, I was driving by a neighbor's house when I noticed the motherlode of maple leaves carpeting her big lawn. I got my rake, big baggies, big boxes, and lawn-mower, threw them (well, the mower took more of an "Ally-OOP!") into the back of the truck and drove down to that neighbor's house. Knock knock. "Hello there. I'd like your leaves."

My neighbor was surprised but delighted. "Go right ahead—we can't seem to get anybody to do it for pay anyway." (Moral: they'll never say No if they can pay you in leaves...)

It was quick work to mow the leaves right on my neighbor's lawn—plus I loved the notion that I was capturing some of the grass's green nitrogen to fire up decomp. The carbon in leaves is surprisingly resistant to rotting—which you'll find out if your compost shovel ever tries to cut through a matted layer of still-identifiable leaves—but by shredding the leaves, you largely break the carbon, helping molds and fungi gain a foothold.

I tried raking the leaves into windrows before mowing, but quickly found that if the rows were higher than 6 inches, the mower's engine died. The leaves reduced down so much, I worried there'd be nothing left to gather, but a wide-tined plastic rake coaxed the fine shreddings out of the grass and into my bags and boxes. I filled seven garbage bags within 90 minutes, enough to cover a long perennial bed AND fill a wire bin four feet high.

A pickup full of bags of gold—I felt RICH. So it was deflating to find that, within days, the leafy soufflé of my leaf bin had fallen to a quarter of its former fullness. More—I must have MORE! I raked another neighbor's leaves. I raked along the highway. I even went to PSE and raked the leaves under their Sunset maples. The neighborhood never looked so good.

When raking the verge of a busy by-way, you need to be careful. I had thought of using a leaf-blower, but then I read about a park worker in Bellevue who'd been killed by a car while using one: maybe the machine was too noisy, maybe he was wearing ear plugs—at any rate, he never heard the car coming. So I stuck to a manual rake and made eye-contact with oncoming drivers. Once I even set my truck's emergency flashers a-going—bad idea—within the hour my battery was dead and I was stuck there until a passing neighbor picked up my mental "S.O.S!" and stopped to give me a jump off his car battery. The next time I went raking along the highway, I borrowed an orange cone (won't say where from) and parked it about 100 feet in front of my working spot to forewarn oncoming motorists.

Not all leaves are fit for compost. Some leaves, like those from apple trees afflicted with scab, could re-infect plants. If your fruit trees harbor any fungal diseases, rake away all dropped fruit and leaves and don't discard in the compost pile unless you are certain your pile will reach the hot kill zone over 130° for several days. Rose leaves with black spot, hollyhock leaves with rust, tomato leaves with late blight—burn these, don't compost them.

Then there are those allelopathic plants that exude the chemical hydrojuglone to suppress growth of nearby plants. When exposed to air or soil, hydrojuglone changes to juglone, which gets into all parts of the host plants and is toxic to a variety of other plants. Black walnuts are infamous for the level of juglone their roots exude, leaving the nearby earth bare of understory plants; their leaves also carry lesser amounts of juglone. Pacific madrones are somewhat allelopathic, as are eucalyptus, tree-of-heaven, manzanita, oak, pine, cottonwood, black locust, and forsythia. If you have leaf litter from such plants, composting it can remove the juglone over time; first shred leaves to promote decay, then segregate the stuff in its own compost bin. When it's thoroughly decomposed, you can test for juglone's presence by planting tomato seedlings in that compost, as tomatoes are highly sensitive to juglone and will die if the chemical is present.

When it was too wet or too much trouble to take my lawnmower on a leaf-run, I'd often just bag the leaves whole, then up-end the bags onto my asphalt parking pad and mow there. In about an hour, mower and me could shred 7-10 bags' worth, then scoop the shreddings into a wheelbarrow and distribute them around the garden. I was in leaf-heaven, that year, mad with leaf-lust. Two weeks and 39 bags later, I had a beautiful coppery orange mulch all over my garden beds, two completely full leaf bins, newly layered-up compost piles, and a very toned torso for a 50-year-old. I felt rich, I felt fit, I felt virtuous, and it was all free. There's GOLD! in dem dar leaves!

Cider & Sauce

In the kitchen, at the Fruit Club's annual Fruit Show, or at our two commercial ciderhouses, Islanders make good use of all those apples

It looks so English, this rain-glazed country lane with the small green fields and black cows. I spotted the "VW" letters on the red barn and parked the car on the grassy verge. There's Ron Irvine, pushing a handtruck loaded with crates of yellow apples. On the concrete apron in front of the barn, Verne Johnson is hosing down a red-n-blue array of equipment, buckets, and racks. This is apple-pressing day at Vashon Winery, and I'm here to see what one can do with a whole mess of apples.

In 2011 and 2012, our state enjoyed a record-breaking crop. On the Island, old apple trees were laden, the ground carpeted with windfalls, fruit lining driveways, rolling onto the highway. By November, people were phoning the food bank, pleading for volunteers to pick or take their surplus fruit. Crates of fruit were on shelves, on the floor, stacking up in the donation shed in the dead of night. What to do with all these apples?!

With this in mind, I snagged an invitation to join the gang at Vashon Winery to see how they make hard cider. Ron had an epiphany about cider 30 years ago while eating his lunch on a London park bench. In a memoir he writes, "I had bought some cheese and bread and a hard cider, probably Bulmer's Strongbow. I can still smell that heady aroma, pungent and fruity, smelling of baked apple followed by a tart, powerfully intense apple, almost winey flavor." As manager of Vashon Winery and past president of the Washington Cider Commision, he set on a Holy Grail quest to recreate and bottle that flavor, making blends and single-varietal bottlings from Cox's Orange Pippin and Kingston Black, two classic cider apples. In recent years he's made his "Irvine's Vintage Cider" as a semi-dry blend of both eating and cider apples, using fruit from the WSU Extension's cider orchards and from apples bought both on-island and in Eastern Washington.

But this year for the first time, the Island has enough apples for him to make an "all-Island" blend. On a pallet were 18 boxes of apples from Carolina Nurik: eating apples Liberty and Keepsake, and cider apples Dabinett, Porter's Perfection, and Yarlington Mill. Ron was fetching another 18 boxes from the orchard out back: Yellow Transparents and Rhode Island Greenings, the King of Tompkin's County, Gravenstein and Golden Russets with their "leathercoats" of brown russeting. When I bent over to take a yellow windfall, he said, "Don't do that: we get deer grazing through here every night and they bring the chance of e-coli." So I pitched it into the bushes.

Verne came over, leaned over a box of Liberty apples. "Ummmm..." he sighed, "Smell that appley perfume!" Verne grew up on Selah, Washington, the "Apple Juice Capitol of the World" and worked for TreeTop and Hi-Country as a lad. A smiling, 40-something man in Carhartt overalls and knit sailor's cap, he topped off the kiddie tub with fresh water, lifted the first crate of Porter's Perfection and tumbled the apples in. Ron jokingly confessed to me, "Verne's here to tell ME what to do."

As Verne, oar in hand, paddled the apples around their rinse bath, the winery's marketing guy Tim Kehl flipped the switch of the hopper and started pitching apples into its maw. Then Verne turned to what they called the "cheese press"—to me, more like a giant flower press. On top of a hydraulic press sat a square steel plate; on it, Verne laid a white 18" square plate of plastic, criss-crossed with ridges and valleys. On top of that went a square metal frame, draped over with an over-sized cheesecloth, industrial grade and browned by apple juice. When the collection bucket under the apple grinder was full, Verne grabbed it, shook the apple grindings onto the cloth, wrapped the four sides over the apple pomace to make an envelope, eased away the metal square, then topped that wrapped "cheese" with another white corrugated divider. Frame, cloth, pomace, wrap, and layer, repeated as new buckets came from the grinder, until twelve layers of "cheese" were stacked, each oozing juice that dripped down the drain-hose into the cider barrel. It looked like a 12-layer German chocolate cake, and when Verne hit the switch for the hydraulics to start the squeeze, the "cake" drooled from every corrugation rich glazings of honey-colored cider.

I asked Ron what percentage of Vashon Winery's output is cider. "A tiny fraction," he said, enough for the winery, Vashon Thriftway, Metropolitan Market and one wineshop in Seattle. "A barrel will create about 500 six-ounce bottles, and I'll be happy to get a barrel's worth."

Here in the U.S.A, we distinguish between cider, a sweet unfermented drink, and hard cider, a beverage that after fermentation becomes very dry and contains from 5-14% alcohol (because of liquor taxes and state rules, most hard cider aims for just under 7% alcohol). All you need to make a jug of hard cider is a gallon of juice from 11 lbs. of apples, a very clean glass or plastic vessel with about 20% headroom (air space) above the juice for the fermenting head that will develop, a clean pail, and a clear syphon tube about 2-3' long.

Native yeast, that magic not-animal/not-plant that gives us risen bread and bubbly alcohol, lives in the air around us: it piggybacks into the cidering process on the skins of apples. Because it's wild and thus unpredictable, most cider-makers instead use cultivated champagne or wine yeasts, killing off the wild yeasts first with sodium dioxide, then introducing the domestic yeast. Yeast eats the sugars in the apple juice and converts it to alcohol, farting out carbon dioxide gas (CO_2) as a by-product. All this farting gas creates a growing head of foam on top of the juice, plus gas that must escape the vessel les it blow up. So, you close off the vessel with an airlock—the simplest being a clear hose with its upstream end going through the jug-stopper and its downstream end in a pail of clean water. This airlock lets CO_2 gases escape, while the water keeps bacteria, fungi, and bugs from reaching and infecting the juice (you want cider and not vinegar, right?)

Indoors, the rising foam of fermentation may start within 24 hours or, in a cool space, several days. It'll bubble along from a few days to a few months, then wind down as the last of the fructose is consumed. When there's less than a bubble per minute coming through the airlock, the ferment is done: all sugars are converted to alcohol, and the cider is ready for sampling. It will probably be very dry and taste less like apples and more like wine or champagne (if you're very lucky). If you want a sweeter, more apply drink, you can top with fresh cider or add a bit of sugar (one tablespoon per quart of liquid), but you must then keep the cider refrigerated to prevent fermentation from starting again. Commercial cider-makers often do secondary fermentations, or add sugar and a shot of CO_2 to boost apple flavors and carbonation, and then pasturize the bottles with a brief dip in boiling water to kill the yeast, any bacterias, and—perhaps most important of all—to prevent re-started fermentation from blowing up a customer's bottle.

With all this new knowledge, I was a little sad that I'd missed the Fruit Club's annual CiderFest. Some 200 had attended in 2012 and taken home hundreds of gallons of cider for their own use, perhaps even for their own home-brewed hard stuff. Inspired to have crates-worth of apples to play with, I went driving back to my community's own orchard, the one I'd worked so hard to keep sprayed and pruned. Would all my hard work have paid off? Would I have apples to harvest? And what variety would they be?

Alas! No record-breaking crop on our community trees! Despite all my spraying against scab, the introduction of mason bees, the summer pruning, our two dwarf apple trees had a tiny crop: 23 apples on one tree, slightly more on the other. Scabby, too. Still, it was something, and I drove up to the orchard after the winery visit, anticipating ripe fruit—and found but one apple on the near tree, high and out of reach. Great crackling expletives! roared out my mouth—but then I saw the fringe of broken branchlets a'dangle and the carpet of deer droppings underneath. Ah... it's become Bambi's Snack Bar. Should have fenced.

To Burton, then, for Plan B. Back in the summer of 2010, I was cruising around the Burton Peninsula when I spotted a woman and her tottler picking up windfalls under a large tree. I popped out and asked if she could spare some apples. "Oh, could I!" she said, thrust a bagful into my arms, then, reciting her recipe for applesauce, she and Sonny helped me fill two more bags. So, remembering that tree in November 2012, I thought my odds of scoring some apples were pretty good. And was I right: the new owner, Penny, had crates of fruit on her front stoop, a carpet of windfalls on the ground, and was out of ideas on how to deal with it all. So I shared that recipe, and later took her a pint of applesauce to prove what an asset her tree was. Too many apples is a good problem to have.

I filled a big pot 2/3rds with slices of apple, added an inch of water, turned heat to medium-high. Within 30 minutes, the slices had softly bubbled into applesauce, the taste enhanced with splashes of lemon juice, cinnamon, and a couple cups of sugar. This apple made a good pie, too—so what WAS it? I wondered, just as I wondered about the lost identity of the orchard apples back in my community. So I bagged up some representative apples and took them to the Fruit Club's Annual Fruit Show in early November.

Emily MacRae, de facto event coordinator, called out hello as she buzzed between the Senior Center and the lectures at the Land Trust Building. Walking into the Senior Center, I found Dr. Bob Norton, Dr. Al Watts of Appleyard Farm, and hobby orchardist Doug Tuma behind a room-long table holding over 100 island-grown apple varieties. Each plate held a cultivar, an identification card (created by Mary Ormstead and sister Jean Williams of the Peninsula Fruit Club) with the name, characteristics and points of interest ("Esopus Spitzenberg—Thomas Jefferson's preferred apple!")

On the other side of the room, stooped under a lamp like a Dickens bookkeeper, Sean Shepperd from Portland's Home Orchard Society was kniving open mystery apples, looking for traits searchable in his enormous apple database. When I handed him one of our scabby community apples, he noted the green-n-red coloring and called out, "Another Jonagold!"

Well! If Jonagold's dead common, I hope this next apple stumps you! I handed him the three yellow apples from Burton and watched his brow knit just a little. "Hummm... let's see ... My! This is a Belmont—quite popular in the 19th century." Dr. Bob's ears perked, and he called out, "Who's brought the Belmont?" I was so proud to shoot up my hand and say, "I did!"

Lunchtime arrived: the experts took their lunch and I took their place behind the sample table, beckoning over new arrivals to come try these island-grown apples. From the tip of a paring knife I offered slices of spicy Belle de Boskoop and Karmijn de Sonnaville, juicy Hawaii, tart Liberty, rotund Gloria Mundi, seedless Gravenstein, the pineappley Holstein and Winter Banana, the tiny Lady apple that, according to Tuma, "was in olden days carried by ladies in their little purses against bad breath" (we all immediately bit). When I exclaimed over my new favorite, a tiny yellow apple called "Tolmans Sweet," Dr. Bob said, "You KNOW that tree—it's growing next to the donation shed up at the food bank."

Down at one end were all the cider apples and pears. When I insisted on tasting "Vilberie," the pucker on my face showed why Wes Cherry, cidermaker, called it "vile berry"—it tasted like cotton wads dipped in iodine. Quick—another Lady apple!

Of these 100 varieties, Doug Tuma had brought 30—and those were only the late ripeners like Melrose, Winter Gravenstein, and Arkansas Black. A tall man with a bowl of gray hair and a pirate-y "Rrrrr!" in his voice, I first met Tuma around 1997 when my homebrewing husband was invited to Doug's annual cider party. Driving west on Cove Road and down a forest driveway, we came to a red barn with, in the field behind, walls upon walls of wire-trellised apple trees. As we explored the orchard, we passed guests staggering back to the barn, schlepping pails full of apples they'd just picked. The grinder screamed, beer, wine, party talk and fresh-pressed cider flowed, and as apples perfumed the air, we could hear Tuma's voice rising over the racket, marshalling his wayward guests to "Get those apples into the GRINDER!"

In three planting binges between 1976-1980, Tuma planted over 400 apple trees of all kinds: dessert, cooking, heritage cider. He grafted most himself with scion cuttings from the Western Cascade Fruit Club, the WSU Research Station, or "anyone willing to give me scion wood." Though some of the trees are standards, most are on M26 and M7a dwarfing rootstocks, trained to horizontal wires to encourage earlier fruiting. And because his land stays wet from a water-table a foot down, he plowed deeply, heaping up the soil in rows where he would eventually plant his trees.

His biggest problem remains the deer that graze his unfenced orchard; they eat most of the apples, forcing him onto a ladder to reach the ones they leave behind. He starts picking in August and ends in mid-November. Now here's a man who's figured out how to deal with his apple surplus—over 1500 lbs from the 300 trees he has left. A few friends buy apples in quantity from him, and for the last two years he's sold 750-lb bins of cider and table apples to Wes Cherry of Dragon's Head Cider. He fills a freezer with frozen cider, drinking it all year around. He gives cider to family, friends and neighbors, and he still throws those parties that dispose of cider by the gallon. I took home a gallon myself, all those years ago, enjoying its chill-of-November, mouth-filling flavor to the last jug-shaken drop.

Because he doesn't spray, he recommends scab-free varieties: Williams' Pride, Liberty, Spartan, Holstein. As I settled into my seat in the Land Trust conference room and looked over Dr. Bob Norton's handout, "Fruit Varieties for Vashon Island," I saw that many of Doug Tuma's preferred apples— Liberty, Williams Pride, Spartan, Jonagold, Melrose, Holstein—were also on this list. (You'll find a complete list at the end of this chapter).

Walking to the front of the lecture hall, Dr. Bob Norton lined up a dozen apples on the table in front of us. He described his own orchard: on Russian B-9 rootstocks, planted on 8' centers and kept to 8' high with summer pruning "because my wife won't let me get up on a ladder anymore." He started with the August apples: Centennial Crabapple, William's Pride. Then he pulled out a knife, cut one around the middle to expose the star-shaped seed compartments (called carpels), and held one up. "This one's seedless," he said in his squeaky voice. "Anybody know what this is?"

"Gravenstein!" shouted many.

"CORRECT!" barked the man who loves to teach. "The only one that's seedless. Vigorous, probably the best for applesauce: gets scab though."

He went through his list in order of ripening. Akane, that holds its fruit well but is prone to apple maggot. HoneyCrisp, "can grow here better than ANYWHERE!" but gets scald if kept in 38° cold storage too long. Elstar, a great pie apple, and Macoun (pronounced MaCOWin) his favorite eating apple. Of the Fuji apples, only Early Fuji can ripen here, but develops water-core on the tree. Spartan and Liberty, both scab-resistant, are heavy fruiters much planted here. Belle de Boskoop has a complex spicy flavor. He also recommended Holstein, Karmijn de Sonnaville, Esopus Spitzenberg, Melrose, Jonagold, and King, "a common old variety."

"Anybody else with a favorite?" he asked. Ron Weston, one of the fruit club's founders, answered, "Chehalis: it's scab-free, hangs on the tree well."

To save us from temptation, Dr. Bob also warned us about popular apples that don't do well here. "Gala, Golden Delicious, Ginger Gold, Empire, all get scab. Pink Lady—doesn't ripen until mid-December. Same with Granny Smith, Fuji, and Cameo." (Later he told me he didn't get any Pink Ladies at all—the raccoons got to them first.)

While awaiting the next speaker, I fell to talking with Susie Kalhorn, my seat neighbor. "Oh, this so reminds me of my first job," she commented. "I used to operate the jug-filler at Wax Orchards."

I was surprised: "I thought you were an environmental educator?" I replied, thinking of "Protecting Our Liquid Assets," of the "Garden Green/ Drink Clean" hang-tag project described in the "Bees "chapter.

"That's what I *became*," she explained. "But I got a job at Wax Orchards right after college. I used to pick apples and work on the cider-line."

I remembered that cider: a rust-brown sweet juice sold in soft-side plastic jugs and bottles, kept on ice in the Thriftway produce section. It was locally produced, even to an extent made from Island apples—and always tasted like it was pressed the day before. Susie told me that it probably was.

On the Island's high plateau at 240th with a great view of Mt. Rainier, Robert and Betsy Sestrap ran a fruit-processing company that once employed hundreds in their orchards, fruit-packing plant, cidering and fruit spread manufactury. Betsy's parents started the operation in 1929 when August Wax, looking for a better climate than his frost-pocket in Covington, bought 60 acres here for a cherry and chicken farm. When his daughter Betsy married a cattle rancher from Alberta, their wedding gift was a 20-acre parcel of Wax land. Eventually the combined family farm topped 270 acres, with cherry, peach, apricot, and apple trees plus currants, an 11,000 sf processing plant with a 2000 sf freezer, housing for family and workers (which peaked at 400 during big harvest years), an airfield, and an arboretum of trees from Betsy's landscaping business around the entrance drive.

The Waxes soon dropped the chicken business and expanded beyond cherries into fruits of all kinds. Their cidering started with a crop of Gravensteins ruined by a hailstorm; Robert, who had a genius for invention, converted an old wine press and turned those apples into cider. When the fresh, unfiltered cider proved a market hit, Robert installed a huge freezer and froze enough apple pulp to create a year-round product, augmenting his own harvest with 55-gallon barrels of apple pulp from Eastern Washington. Betsy, who co-wrote a recipe book on cider, developed a line of fruit-sweetened, fat-free fruit spreads and marketed them all over the country.

In 1978, Susie Kalhorn, fresh out of college, got her first job there. She remembers: "We would pull out the drums of pulp to defrost a couple of days before the pressing; the amount depending on the orders for the week. The cannery was unheated, so we would have to break the ice sometimes to set up the press." [By then Robert had built a larger press similar to the one Vashon Winery uses.] "I ran the jugger, filling six jugs at time and putting the lids on with a soft hammer. At that time, the juice sold was not pasteurized. Leftover jugs that didn't sell would ferment over the week. There was nothing better than grabbing a jug of hard cider, going next door to get some fresh marinated/grilled tofu from Island Spring and heading out to the sunny orchard for lunch." (Island Spring later moved closer to town.)

Sestraps blended sweet and sour apples to create their signature flavor. Their oldest daughter Anna remembers: "We'd crush and freeze each variety separately, so later we could pull out to blend, say, a drum of Golden Delicious and a drum of Granny Smith." They trucked in hundreds of bins of apples from Eastern Washington, which proved so convenient that they gave up on their own apples, pulling the south orchard out in the early 2000s.

The Sestraps were proud professionals who valued academic advice—at least in their early years. But in the 1960s, they pulled out half their cherry orchard on the advice of a university consultant who said their trees were past bearing age. On the rest, they removed all the branches and left the trunk, a style Robert called "de-horning." Two years later, when those trees burst into fruit, the Sestraps realized the "advice" had cost them millions.

In March, 1979, Dr. Bob Norton, then a research scientist at the WSU Research Station at Mt. Vernon, brought a group of fruit enthusiasts to tour Wax Orchards. Comparing notes, this group realized that they were too reliant on advice from Eastern Washington experts; what they needed was experience from growers in the westside climate and region. Together, they decided to form the Western Cascade Tree Fruit Society to help fruit growers cultivate varieties that will thrive in our own climate. Vashon's fruit club, started by Dr. Bob and other Islanders in 2004, is one of eight chapters of this region-wide organization.

Robert died in 2003, Betsy in 2012. They had sold most of their acreage, including the airfield, to Tom Stewart of Misty Isles Farm in 2000; he and his family died in a helicopter crash in 2010. The name and recipes were sold in 2008 to a Seattle company that makes the products in Oregon. While Wax Orchard products are still sold on Island, there are no more fruit trees at Wax Orchards Farm.

But in 2010, the story of commercial apples on Vashon began again...

A New Orchard, Planted in Cider Apples

Behind the podium in the Land Trust, a tall 40-something man with a surprising resemblance to British actor Colin Firth clears his throat nervously. At his left side, a ponytailed, wide-eyed blonde in an Eddie Bauer parka holds a sheaf of hand-outs. Wes and Laura Cherry are about to reveal how they planted 1000 apple trees and plan to plant another 450—most of them too bitter to eat.

Wes and Laura make Dragon's Head Cider, a traditional semi-dry cider done in the English style. Wes had been fooling with fermenting cider ever since a post-college beer-tasting trip to Europe made him realize he preferred hard cider. After careers in our region's high tech (she was a consultant, he a Microsoft programmer), they decided to shift gears, start a family, move to "a rural area with a progressive community." They started shopping properties, found 30 acres of pasture that had once been part of Masa Mukai's strawberry empire (the old packing plant is next door), and as Laura put it, "Suddenly what had been a 5-year plan happened in five months: the place, the apples, and the cider-making fell into place very quickly."

But why plant cider apples? As an aspiring cider-pro, Wes makes several points: cider apples are scarce, they don't have to be pretty to be useable so our local susceptibility to scab isn't an issue, and the weather, temperature, and growing conditions here mirror that of Somerset County, England's premier cider and apple-growing region. It helps that a local agriculture business center is promoting cider apples and cidering as a potential growth industry; the Cherrys took the classes offered there and through WSU's Extension service, and of course solicited the advice of Dr. Bob.

The first trees they planted two years ago are all over today's Powerpoint presentation. The trees, still young 2-year-olds, stretch taller than Wes can reach, their height resulting from the care Wes put into the ground before planting. On the advice of Dr. Bob and Doug Tuma, he brought in heavy machinery to sub-soil the hardpan and build up mounded rows so the roots wouldn't drown. He got the soil tested, added lime, potassium, and phosphate, installed irrigation lines and deer fencing, stakes and trellises, even made rodent guards out of drainage tubing. The prepwork done, he contacted Cummins Nursery in Ithaca, New York, a family nursery famous for its work with rootstocks, grafts, and disease-resistant cultivars, and placed an order for 500 trees. Then he e-vited a few dozen of his closest friends for an orchard-planting party.

On a chilly December day, Wes, Laura, and all those friends planted a host of traditional French and English cider apples. Bittersweets Dabinett, Brown Snout, and Yarlington Mill, plus crabapples, for the good mouth-feel that high tannins give. Bittersharps Kingston Black and Stokes Red, two classic cider apples that can stand alone without blending. Golden Russets, for the aromatics and sweetness that a good eating apple brings to the blend. A few others like Harry Masters Jersey and Vilberie—though why would anybody want that iodiny flavor to their cider? Wes even admitted to locating some old, abandoned pear trees around the Island— "I'm not telling you where!" — to add to the blend and to make his own pear cider.

The first orchard was all on Geneva11 dwarf stock, planted every 8 feet next to individual tree stakes to be grown as central leader forms. The second planting got the trellis treatment: planted every 4-6' with wires at the half-way and top points, with the intention to keep the trees around 10' high. Driplines were hung at about knee-level so that Wes could mow the mixed flower and clover groundcover planted under the trees; that groundcover, he admitted, became a hassle to mow, and so he's letting native grass take over.

After the Fruit Show, I stopped by Thriftway and picked up a bottle of Dragon's Head "Traditional Semi-Dry." Jim Hills, in charge of that section, told me, "We just started stocking Dragon's Head last August. But folks seem to like to buy local—it's our best-selling hard cider."

At home, I pulled a fluted glass from the cupboard and popped the cap off the brown bottle. When poured, streams of bubbles trickled up through the golden liquid; as I brought the glass up to smell, bubbles of apple perfume broke against the tip of my nose. But that perception of apple-ness fled once the flavor hit my taste buds: this was a dry quaff more like champagne than apple wine, as snappy as a quick inhale of snow-chilled air.

Yet as I imbibed, I felt a smile growing inside my mouth. Perhaps it was those tannins from the crabapples or the bittersweets. Or perhaps it was just me drinking in hope, happy to be partaking of an apple bounty and a new start, perhaps, for a commercial fruit crop on Vashon Island.

Dr. Bob Norton's "Best" Apples for Vashon Island

This listing names some of Bob Norton's favorites, new and old, which may be easier to grow and fruit on Vashon, based on their resistance to diseases or ability to set fruit in our cool, humid climate. To make the best decision as to which varieties best suit your particular site, he recommends WSU Extension Bulletin 0937, "Fruit Handbook for Western Washington," available at http://pubs.wsu.edu. (some notes below I added from this bulletin).

RESISTANT OR IMMUNE TO APPLE SCAB

AKANE: Striped red, mild flavor, dessert apple. Blooms early, ripens early-mid September. Keeps its crispness for a month if left hanging on the tree, which holds well. Susceptible to apple maggot.
BELLE DE BOSKOOP: A complex spicy flavor. Scab immune. Ripens in late October. Vigorous tree. Fruit remains tart even after storage.
BRAMLEY SEEDLING: Comparable to Belle de Boskoop as excellent pie apple. Large, firm, crisp, with good natural resistance to apple scab & mildew.
HOLSTEIN: Complex flavor, sweet tart, dual purpose, scab-free. Ripens in late Sept.
KARMIJN DE SONNAVILLE: Requires storage for best quality. dual purpose, wonderful spice.
LIBERTY: Vashon's best apple: white flresh, stores well, a Macintosh type. Scab resistant, gets some mildew. Easiest to grow. Heavy fruit set: must thin. Hangs well. Ripens mid-October.
WILLIAMS' PRIDE: good cooking apple. Scab-free, but gets mildew. Ripens by early August.

NOT SCAB IMMUNE, BUT HIGHLY DESIRABLE

GRAVENSTEIN: No seeds. Tops for sauce: sweet-tart with strong apple flavor. Pollen sterile: plant two other varieties with it to pollinate all three.
ELSTAR: Great pie & dessert apple. Productive; fruit starts tart, mellows in storage.
ESOPUS SPITZENBURG: Tart: more Vitamin C than lemons. Fruit ripes in October.
HONEYCRISP: Grows better here than anywhere else. Great dual-purpose apple. Can scald (turn brown) if kept in cold frig for months.
EARLY FUJI: (Beni Shogun, Sept. Wonder, Auvil Early). Sweet table apple, ripens early September. Develops water core if left too long on tree. Long storage life.
MACOUN: A "Mac" that ripens by Oct 1, Bob's favorite eating apple. Say "maCOWin"
MELROSE: Ripe mid-October. Keeps well.
SPARTAN: Small, deep red dessert fruit. Heavy fruit set, resistant to coddling moth & apple maggot. Stores well.
RED JONAGOLD (Rubinstar strain): Dual purpose, large, tends to scab.
GRIMES GOLDEN: Late ripening, tends toward scab.
KING: Most common old variety, some scab, gets "greasy."

POPULAR, BUT PROBLEMATIC HERE

YELLOW TRANSPARENT: short life, drops fruit, but good for sauce & pie
GALA, GOLDEN DELICIOUS, GINGER GOLD, and EMPIRE: all scab-prone
CAMEO, PINK LADY, GRANNY SMITH: Ripens as late as mid-December.

Putting the Garden to Bed

Fall Clean-up, Overwintering Plants, Mulching, Green Manures

I usually don't find November calling to me to come outdoors. But this particular November was holding on to the qualities that had made it a good tomato year—still warm and dry, the garden yielding and productive, the out-of-doors comfortable instead of sodden and cold. I could clip down spent perennials without soaking my gloved hands or getting chilled to the bone. Leaves, manures, seaweeds were dry and light, without the autumn wet that makes lifting them a herculean effort. For once, I was about to put the garden properly to bed for the winter.

Perennials to prune by late fall

To trim, or to let stand? Swaying stems loaded with seedheads may be appreciated by overwintering birds, but start to look fairly tatty after months of rain and wind. Many perennials groomed of dead top-growth may regrow a green crown of foliage by winter if you get them early enough: these would include columbine, artemisia, brunnera, peonies, lady's mantle, verbena bonariensis, feverfew. Other plants get their haircuts when new growth appears at their base after flowering, such as late-blooming asters and toad lilies. Hardy geraniums can be pruned hard after first frosts. Some plants, such as trilliums, hellebores, crocosmia, solomon's seal, and balloon flowers, look much better after dead foliage is cut away. Big foliage plants like hostas or calla lilies need cutting to the ground, or frost will turn them to mush.

The less hardy the plant is, the more plant you leave untouched through winter. Be aware, as you clip, that hollow stems will collect water. That water pools in the crown and, with a hard freeze, can kill a plant. So if you find hollow stems when you're pruning, pocket the clippers and just bend those stems over without breaking them.

Tall roses without supports should be brought down to 5" high so that winter's wind doesn't tear them off their roots.

Pots and Potted Plants

Terracotta pots don't handle freezes well. Even the pots with drain holes have porous walls that retain water. Once a freeze comes, the expanding water molecules will calve off a big chip of ceramic—it's called "spalling" in the trade—and that chip can be as large as a whole side of your pot. Any unfinished or unsealed brick or ceramic can spall as well. So if you care about a ceramic pot, bring it indoors during the winter.

Half-hardy potted plants like pelargoniums, fuchsias, begonias, and coleus need to come indoors, too. Once, finding a stand of "Adopt Me" pelargoniums on offer down 192nd, I ended up talking with Rachel Lydecker of Farm Candy Nursery about keeping Martha Washington geraniums alive through winter. She told me, "The Number One thing is, don't let their roots freeze. An unheated room in your house would be okay, but not in a shed or garage that's vulnerable to freezing," she told me. "The perfect situation would be sitting at your brightest window in the house, with a little bit of watering every 2-3 weeks, with a light feeding of houseplant food and perhaps a little epson salts (1 tablespoon per gallon) after the New Year."

"When the temps reach the low 40s, you can start acclimatizing the plants to the outdoors. If they're left out on a cold night, frost will make them pretty ugly, all the leaves will fall off, but the roots may still be alive. And if they get leggy indoors, you can always pinch the growing tips back."

Mulches, Green Manures, and Covers

Cathy Fulton tells a story online about the saving of her Christmas potatoes, thanks to a heavy mulch. She used to advise friends on whether root vegetables would survive winter by saying, "Just cover them with hay or straw and they will be fine." But then Snopocalypse '08 came along and had her wondering, "Will I be caught in Thriftway buying carrots and potatoes for the rest of the winter?" But digging under a foot thick layer of hay, she found the soil unfrozen: her Rio Grande Russets popped out fine, as did the carrots and beets, as good as ever and even more appreciated.

A good winter mulch is loose enough to provide plants with some air circulation, but will cut dessicating winds and prevent rain from packing the soil down. So hay, branches from your Christmas tree or from windfalls, and mixtures of manure with leaves (preferably mown up) will work very well. I've known gardeners that buy a bale of hay handy, ready to break open and spread around plants before a big freeze (hay brings seeds, though, so they get to do some extra weeding during the next gardening season). Slugs also can take shelter under a loose mulch, so you might want to put down some Sluggo or go hunting for those tiny pearly clusters of slug eggs.

Manure is said to help keep soil open, without a crust developing on the surface. And because it shouldn't be applied when you are growing eatables, I have applied fresh horse manure onto garden beds in the fall—sometimes mixed up with leaf mold—so that any winter freezes would help break down the horse apples. I have to say that horse apples in fall are solid little rolly-polly things: it can be embarrassing to take a visitor around the winter garden and have a horse apples roll out and under their toes. So I've taken to grinding them through my barrow-sifter into finer particles: they look TONS better on the ground and blend right into leaf mold.

Another way to keep the soil open and protected from too much rain is to sow a green manure (otherwise known as a cover crop.) These are grasses / peas / bean mixtures of seeds that will thrust long roots into the earth; its canopy of green leaves will absorb some of the impact of rain. Most green manures need to be sown by Halloween, but winter rye can germinate in the 40° weather we have through most of November. Let green manures grow through February, then about six weeks before you intend to sow seeds, you hoe the cover crop under and let the soil microbes break it down. A cover crop with peas and/or legumes in it will add nitrogen to your soil, and the mass of roots will give your soil in a fine, crumbly texture.

Don't forget to drain your hoses and water-lines thoroughly: stretch out a hose so its far end is downhill from your water tap, then unscrew the hose connection to the water tap to release any suction. Put freeze protection on exposed pipes, faucets, and water-taps outdoors. Bring your pressure-washer into a heated space: its hoses may still hold water that can freeze and swell an aneurysm in your hose that will blow during next spring's cleanup.

And finally, bone up on cocoa for those nasty, comfortable, indoor days by the fire. Whatever winter brings, you're ready.

From a Blizzard Born

The arrival of foul weather. Rain & Snow. Gardening you can do in the depth of winter. And a winter's inspiration that led to this book.

Snow has come. I'm inside my tiny greenhouse, banging on its ceiling with a rake, trying to knock some of this snow off. Eight inches have fallen, making its flimsy roof of wire and plastic droop like a swayback horse. If I don't knock some of this weight off, I know what *could* happen...

I'm thinking of Snowpocalypse 2008. My latest phase of garden mania had just kicked in. I'd spent November putting the garden to bed, then cobbling together this greenhouse from 2x2s, chicken fencing, and hoophouse film. When rain drove me indoors, I sat down with the tools of SketchUp, Google's 3D design software, and gardened on my computer. New rock walls, perhaps? A little kitchen garden to go with the greenhouse?

Cozy inside, cold and dreary outside. Our climate's usually at its worst in early December: Pineapple Express monsoons with 2" of rain in 24 hours, early freezes, snow threats, and—most gloomy of all—darkness on both ends of a day's commute. But this year would be exceptional. On the evening of December 4th in UW's Kane Hall, Professor of Atmospheric Sciences and KPLU Weather Commentator Dr. Cliff Mass gave a lecture and signing for his new book *Extreme Weather of the Pacific Northwest.* The hall was packed and probably steamy from wet clothes, as the audience had gotten here through a downpour that would drop 5" by day's end. My neighbor, returning from West Seattle that evening, saw a manhole cover go surfing down Fauntleroy Avenue, popped by the flooded storm drains: it went careening down that slick street like a killer ninja frisbee.

Nine days later, weather reports forecast an Alaskan freeze headed for us by the weekend. Nighttime temps into the 20s, maybe a little snow. Peeling myself off the couch, I went out and drained the hoses, covered spigots, and piled autumn leaves over the roses. For a bit of snow, I was prepared.

And it was a bit, at first: about 2" of snow covered the ground by that Sunday morning. Outside my living room window, everything but the seed stalks of echinacea and pointy New Zealand flax was mantled by snow. I wasn't too worried about my plants—a snow cover keeps plants at 32° and protected from the cold, dry wind that sucks moisture from exposed leaves. A combination of loose mulch and snow can keep soil from freezing and, in the kitchen garden, keep your hardier vegetables like carrots, parsnips, and potatoes naturally refrigerated—as Cathy Fulton found when she went out to her garden for Christmas Day dinner and found her potatoes perfectly fine under their thick mulch of hay and snow.

The days stretched into a snowbound week. Oddly enough, the power didn't fail, enabling plenty of online shopping in those pre-holiday weeks. Amazon.com couldn't keep enough copies of Dr. Mass's *Extreme Weather* in stock to meet demand.

Books kept me going, too. My mornings started with a long stare out into the white world, coffee cup in hand, before I settled into the couch and the color-drenched world of my gardening books. As day after white day passed, I drank in (along with many cups of coffee) photos of leaves filled with June's golden sunlight, roses billowing an imagined perfume, pergola beams casting shadow patterns over brick or stone paths. These books gave me a place to go, ideas to try. When I read about sowing poppies in snow, I got out my seed box, ripped open a packet of shirley poppies, and sprinkled seeds over the snow. Melting snow pulls them into the soil, while the cold gives this biennial the chilling it needs. Works with sweet alyssum, too.

Garden books can be as stimulating as candy to the garden obsessed. After a couple hours of reading, I became twitchy to put all these good ideas to use—make sketches, collages, PLANS. I turned to SketchUp, Google's downloadable CAD program (luckily, the power was still on), and got serious about learning how to use its drawing tools. I was bewitched by the program's potential to mimick a real landscape: it's 3D, with walk-through and sunlight features that help you imagine the look and feel of the garden you've sketched up. So I measured out a space equal to my backyard, drew a 2D line that I extruded upward into a 3D back wall of my garage, then borrowed from SketchUp's object library some windows that poked see-through holes in that wall. Trees imported from another library cast the shade I knew would lie on my ground, come summer. "Walking" into my virtual garage and looking out those faux-windows, I could "see" those trees across my virtual backyard. Cool! A garden in my computer!

Spellbound, I was soon laying down bed after bed, Saving As plan after slightly-different plan. And it wasn't enough to design the ground plane: in version #4, I started building upward. If I can sketchup a greenhouse, can the program help me visualize where it will look best? Making virtual 2x2 lumber set plumb and square wasn't easy—the pieces spun and jerked as if handled by a baton twirler—and took me hours to learn how to place them in position. But, within a few days, I had the simulcrum of a kitchen garden: greenhouse in the corner, a bench next to it, with a square of four triangular raised beds criss-crossed by two paths creating a central axis where there would be, undoubtedly, a fountain. During these same days, my actual garden became as white and empty as a new file's pasteboard, objects buried under a tabula rasa that hid their positions in my real garden. Looking out the kitchen window at that white-washed world, I could easily picture it with the objects now populating my SketchUp experiments.

Though some may be puzzled by the fun I had, virtual gardening, I think a lot of us 50-somethings will get it. I came into my working years just before computers entered the workplace; wanting freedom from the 9-5, I quickly bought a Macintosh and laser printer to start a desktop publishing business. My Mac and I joined the Entrepreneur Boom and the legion of other women my age who were setting up home offices for small businesses, consultancies, or just to work from home. But a day working in front of those early, slow computer screens was hard on the eyes: by mid-afternoon after staring at a screen all day, I needed to do something ELSE that was still within reach of my phone and printer. Gardening my yard became the perfect complement—nay, antidote—to computer work. And I'm sure I wasn't alone. I believe our region's groundswell of interest in gardening was driven, in part, by computer users who discovered their green thumbs while giving their tired eyes a break in the yard.

Once my SketchUp dreams were done, I moved to planting, it too on-line. Googling up "garden planners," I soon settled on GrowVeg.com. Here you can lay out your garden beds, rows, or pots, then virtually "plant" them with plant icons dragged from an alphabetized plant palette. Each drag-n-dropped plant can be stretched out to fill the alloted space, its label renamed with the seed variety, its "Notes" section filled with whatever you need to remember. As you add plants to your garden, the program compiles a list with a calendar of when to sow, transplant, and harvest each planting. I soon filled my raised beds with tiny, labeled squares of flowers and veg.

Now that I knew what I wanted to sow, did I still have good seeds? Pawing through my seed box, I saw my inventory was aging—plenty of seed packets were labeled 2005, 2001—wow, here's one from 1998. Allium seeds only last a year or so, most other seeds germinate well up to three years, but many of my seeds were even older. So here was yet another garden task the snowbound gardener could do: I could run a seed germination test.

I pressed 10-12 seeds between damp layers of paper towels, rolled them up and sealed the towels in a plastic bag, then parked the packets in the dark warmth around my water heater. Within 24 hours, the dry, wrinkled pea seeds plumped up; within 48 hours, they sported several long white shoots and looked rather like tiny albino octopi. Fascinating...

The power started flickering off for hours at a time. I took to moving my test packets from the warm water-closet to near the woodstove to keep the seeds at a temperature in the 60-80° range. After a week of seed-hatching, I ran the numbers: of pac choi, beets, carrots, peas and lettuce seed, most achieved 90% germination—the exception being the lettuces, running at 75%. Trustworthy seedhouses will put the expected minimum germination rates either on seed packets or in the company catalog, But if you're using older seed and suspect your germination rate will be low, you can always sow into transplant trays and use what plants come up. Personally, I planned (hurray!) to shop the catalogs for more lettuce seeds.

Completely snowbound, I'd created a bubble of gardening for myself. It couldn't last. A howling snowstorm on the 20th cut power and raised the snowcover to nearly a foot. The earlier snow compressed into ice and made the roads treacherous: our neighbor tried to descend our hill in his 4-wheel Jeep and did it turned sideways. Across the Island, trees started to break— and so did structures. The heavy weight of snow, pushed by wind, tore apart the plastic hoophouses at Island Meadow and other farms. Cindy Thompson, sister of garden tour host Cathy Crouse, watched her glass greenhouse sag, bulge, and finally explode under its burden of wet snow. At GreenMan Farm, Jasper Forrester inspected her vintage glasshouse—the reason she'd bought the place—and found the ridgebeam cracking. "The whole 25x50 ft. structure looked about to collapse, so I had to get up on an orchard ladder to scrape the snow and ice off the roof with a rake on an extension pole. It took me almost eight HOURS." But that greenhouse was saved.

On my birthday December 21, my husband gave me a copy of Michael Pollan's *The Omnivore's Dilemna: A Natural History of Four Meals*. Between then and Christmas, I'd daily shuffle down to the community's water system shed, charge my laptop on the generator that kept water running to our houses, then shuffle back to the house to read. My mind, already churning with thoughts of chard and lettuce and basil, was primed for Pollan's investigation of what goes into bringing food to the American table. I was ready to be appalled by his exposé of the energy wasted in the industrial food supply chain—of reading, for instance, that for each 80-calorie box of baby lettuce mix, 4600 calories of fossil food energy is used to grow, clean, wrap, transport, and market that lettuce. I read for the first time about cattle feed-lots, chickens whose "free range" was a dog-door to the outdoors they never used, about organic farms now owned by agribiz, their produce grown for mechanized harvest and trucked every bit as far as non-organic food. Pollan's book was an exposé nearly as off-putting as Upton Sinclair's book, *The Jungle*, an account of the early 20th century meat-packing industry that put me right off hot dogs back when I read it in my teens.

But what really got to me about Pollan's book was not what he wrote, but *how* he wrote it. Here was a guy who didn't write from a position of expertise. Instead, he took himself to the experts, hung out with them, listened to what they had to say, pitched into the tasks they did to make their farms, gardens, and lives work. He showed me (and everyone else who read this best-selling book) places like Joel Salatin's Polyface Farm that worked with his land's resources, acted as if the well-being of animals and plants mattered, assumed that the quality of the food the farm produced would take extra care and draw, because of its quality, extra appreciation from their customers. Because of how Pollan wrote, I got to see this quality of lifestyle in action, learn from it, taste it, be inspired by it.

Snowbound and by then somewhat cabin-fevered, I found Pollan's model inspiring, even galvanizing. Vashon has expert gardeners, farmers, conservationists, yet their wisdom only occasionally appears in newspaper articles soon thrown away. Why not tell their stories in a Pollan-like fashion?

Now you might say this is another garden dream all underlaid in white, this notion that a housewife, oil painter and part-time copy-editor could take the Pollan idea and run with it. I'm just a home-body in her own garden, learning on her own as best she can with limited time and tools. But we're all in that situation, aren't we? We're all busy, highly-scheduled, modern individuals, unable or unwilling to spend hours with an elder picking up whatever gardening tips they might drop—even if we had such an elder in our lives. We're far more likely to gain our gardening wisdom from books, our enthusiasms from articles in magazines or online, base our choices on blurbs in seed catalogs. So if that's how we roll, led down the garden path by a blizzard of words on a page, wouldn't it be great to have pages full of OUR gardening experiences? If Michael Pollan can make out of his questions and hanging-out something as good as his book, why can't I?

On Christmas Day, I was outdoors with a square-blade shovel, carving a snow garden into that 11" of snow, warming myself body and soul. My husband thought I was nuts, but this crazy exercise turned out helpful: what had been virtual 3-D was now REAL and revealing. When I could finally move around beds and paths carved per the plan, I found those paths too tight, the beds too small, the whole plan too cluttered for comfort. Out would have to come those perimeter beds and yes, the central fountain. My plans were no substitute for the real thing in the real world.

The snow melted, at last, on December 29th. A month later during one of January's calm-weather thaws, I broke ground on my kitchen potager. At the end of February, I met Michelle Crawford, Ken Miller, and Julia Lakey at a bookstore salon on kitchen gardening that Michelle organized; the group talked a blue streak all that Sunday afternoon. Soon I heard of an Island vegetable-growing workshop so popular, the coordinators scheduled a second to take the overflow. I called the *Beachcomber*, where I'd worked and written before, to ask editor Leslie Brown, "Do you think the newspaper would run an article about how Island gardeners start seeds?"

So that's how this book was started: in the white-out blizzard of Snowpocalypse 2008. Sometimes we need a winter inspiration—black seeds scribed across a snowy white blank—to show us a path that leads through white-out into new growth, new beginnings, a new spring.

Epilogue: a last look around

Revisiting many in this book at the end of the Great Recession, we see an Island that's still very much a cultivating kind of place.

In December 2012, Laura Cherry invited me to help them plant their final 450 cider apple trees. Though it had been rainy, the weekend forecasts promised clearing. For once, early December's weather looked good.

On the day before, I stopped by to see how Wes might have prepped his field. I expected to see more rows trenched and raised, but not this time. As we walked into the field, Wes told me, "King County came by, saw my earlier trenching, and told me 'no more: your land is at the head of Judd Creek and we don't want to change its drainage pattern.'" So while the land of the first orchard rippled like corrugated roofing, this new orchard was going into flat ground. And soggy ground, too, I could tell as our booted feet splished across the sodden grass. He had already opened the sod down a dozen 4'-wide rows. A string-line, hip-high, ran down each 100' length to help tomorrow's helpers keep the trees in a line, each planting spot marked with circle of lime dust every 10 feet.

The 2-year-old trees, wrapped by a dozens in black garbage bags, leaned in a teepee formation at the edge of their parking lot. French apples from Normandy's Calvados region: Bedan, Medaille d'Or, Noel des Champs, Muscadet de Dieppe, and Bulmer's Norman, another bittersweet that traveled across the Channel to become an English cidering favorite. Classic English apples like Yarlington Mill, Stokes Red, Kingston Black, and the lumpy-bumpy conjoined apple with the compensating name, Porter's Perfection. Once popular American apples like Golden Russet, red-fleshed Red Field, and the 18th-century favorite Harrison—the last known tree discovered in 1976, scion-wood taken from it just days before the tree was felled.

Wes peeled a bag back, saying "This is interesting: I bought interstems this time. Most of these trees are on MM111 rootstock that's nearly full-size: they have big, hardy roots that will withstand wind and wet ground better. This—" he pulled out a tree and pointed to the scars of a V-cleft about 6" above the roots— "is the dwarfing stock, and here—" pointing a little higher where the top-growth grew out of another scarred joint —"is the graft of the cultivar. My hope is that these dwarf trees won't need stakes or trellising because they'll have nearly full-size roots to hold them in place."

When I returned the next day, I realized this planting operation might take more than a little string to keep everybody in line. About twenty 30-somethings in parkas and boots milled around a white pavillion tent, chomping on Northern Spy apples brought by Doug Tuma and eying the sky. Rain had been falling for two days straight, but this morning had dawned bright and fair. Still, as Wes grabbed a tree and a shovel and shouted "Follow me to see how I want these planted," a light rain began to fall.

Pointing at the lower graft, Wes explained, "You want to backfill the soil about one hand's width below here, an inch above the roots. Partner up: one of you digs the hole" (a friend, on cue, thrust his shovel through the marker of lime-dust) then, while your partner holds the tree at the right level, top graft pointing north, trunk touching this string-line, you'll flip the sod back into the hole and— SHOOT..." In the half-minute he'd been talking to us, 48 hours of rain backfilled the hole completely; his flip of sod slopped muddy water all over his carhartts. "Well then, looks like we won't have to water them in," he chuckled.

The men from Redmond, the blonde from Bellevue, the moms with kids and the musician all the way from Oakland fanned out down the first row, trees in hand. Two tree-mistresses doled out the trees per a planting guide on a clipboard, as the dogs Cocoa and Jazz ran up and down the rows nosing into us and each other. Every hole quickly became a swimming hole: someone joked "Got snorkels?" One gal, after planting her Golden Russet, stamped her backfill hard: her foot sunk to within an inch of her boottop. As onlookers laughed, Wes said, "Maybe we should put a cone of sod in the hole FIRST—spread the roots on that to keep them a little higher."

The first row was done within a half-hour: that seemed quick until I realized we had eleven more rows to go before early December's sunset. I headed out for errands and lunch in town, returning to a sea of muddy shoes around the entrance to the kitchen that made me feel guilty for wandering off. As the planters, now fed, spilled out of the garage, grabbed their shovels, and poured down the row with Harrisons in hand, the sun broke through a tattered sky and turned the misty air into diamond dust. By the time the rain returned an hour later, we were done, the last of the "Yarlies" dropped into an empty space in an old row. We headed for the ciderhouse, where Wes ladled out samples of cider from his fermentation tanks for his eager helpers, until Laura came out calling "Come in outta the rain—my cocktail bar's better than his!"

As I finish this book, four years after beginning "Garden On, Vashon," the Island and the country are emerging out of the Great Recession. And when you look up and down the main stem of our Island, you see a community that, for the most part, came through it well. We lost some shops including a long-running bookstore (Books by the Way), but King County is building us a larger library (though its entrance snowbell trees fell victim to the renovation). Vashontown added a bakery cafe (Snapdragon), a sports shop, new pizza joint, and Thai restaurant, plus a credit union with perhaps a second one on the way. At Blooms, Carol Ahlfors just started teaching flower-arranging in "the BloomRoom" behind her shop. On Saturdays, the farmers market is bigger than ever, with 15 farm tables, 37 nonfarm vendors, and Karen Biondo's pizza truck serving up slabs of pie made with her own tomatoes, vegies, and herbs.

We lost a few, but in good ways. Cathy Fulton of the Compost Fest turned Mariposa to her kids and made plans to travel. Chandler Briggs of Island Meadow Farm moved to Walla Walla to learn how to farm with draft horses. Helen Brocard moved to Seattle, but made sure some of her heritage berries went to Islanders. The daffodil barn's door was repainted with an Asian Pear, better reflecting owner Jim Gerlach's passion for making perry (pear cider).

And we almost lost Kathy's Corner. In winter 2012, after three hard years of bad weather, theft, injuries, and poor sales, Kathy Wheaton took stock. She saw "a somewhat tired, understocked, not-quite-clean nursery...Not the place it had been and could/should be." She knew that consumers all over weren't spending, that nurseries were closing. "I could NOT sit and watch 40-plus years slowly slide away," she wrote to hort trade magazine *Green Profit*. "If we were going to go out of business, it was going to be on my terms. So with no savings left, no credit line left, and only half our staff of three years ago left, I decided to gamble." She hired new staff, told them to

"CLEAN, STOCK, AND SMILE!" She hired a landscape crew, filled the shelves with fresh plants, fired a vendor who wouldn't negotiate new terms. "We quit being afraid," she wrote. By spring, business was up 80%. And her letter became the inspiring lead story of *Green Profit's* October issue.

At the old Fuller Store, former VIGA market manager Rebecca Wittman started her own clothing line called "The President of Me." Across the street, VAA will build a new Arts Center (major funding provided by garden club doyenne Kay White). On the northwest corner, Minglement Roasterie bubbles on as The Locavore Social Club, offering Island-roasted coffee, Island-grown produce, island-made ZuZu's ice cream, Cliff's Beer, Dragon's Head Cider, and Imagine Take-Out made right in my neighborhood.

Among the locavore offerings at Minglement are local strawberries. In 2013 Dr. Bob Norton switched his U-picking bribe to "You pick four pints for me to sell to Minglement, I'll let you pick a pint for youself." With Emily MacRae coordinating, his pickers harvest dozens of pints a week that reach Minglement by 1pm M-W-F, where they often sell out. Joe & Celina Yarkin of Sun Island Farm also sell their Maury-grown strawberries all summer at the farmers' market and their self-serve cart on the Burton Peninsula.

Both the Yarkins and Dr. Bob lost their 2013 cherry crops to a new pest, Spotted Wing Drosophila. This tiny asian fruit fly arrived in California around 2008 and has worked its way north, supplanting the old fruit fly because of an evolutionary advance: a sawtooth ovipositor. These flies don't wait for fruit to soften to lay their eggs, but *saw* their way into fruit at any stage of ripeness, launching 3-5 generations a season. Oregon's seen crop losses of blueberries and peaches; in Dr. Bob's case, they got to most of his Bing and Sweetheart cherries—a value of $2500. In his July talk on SWD to the Fruit Club, he declared, "We'll have to promptly harvest our soft fruit because, if infested, the SWD maggots will drastically shorten its shelf life." Jokes about added protein in our fruit followed, along with disconcerted talk about lack of controls. The only one shown to work so far is spinosad, an attract-n-kill brew made by fermenting bacteria unique to (of all places) an abandoned rum distillery in the Caribbean (which explains why Bonide, Inc. named their spinosad "Captain Jack's DeadBug Brew Concentrate.") "SWD is here to stay—but don't get discouraged," Dr. Bob continued. "New bugs and diseases are always invading us—and we learn to adapt!"

Down the road during the school year, the high school kitchen might be receiving a delivery from local farms Sun Island, GreenMan, Island Meadow, or Carolina Nurik's orchard. When the school district asked for local produce back in 2011, these farmers responded by reviving Vashon Island Producers' Coop (VIPCO, once Masa Mukai's cold-storage farmers' collective). They don't try to feed 500 kids a day: instead, their contribution is highlighted on that day's menu, teaching kids "how your food is grown."

At the old Mukai farmhouse and barrel-packing plant a crow's flight northwest, two historic preservation nonprofits (one Island-based, one flown to Texas years ago) vie for control of these historic buildings that stand witness to the Japanese experience in 20th-century America. The farmhouse still has the remnants of a beautiful garden created by the second wife of B.D. Mukai, Kuni Mukai, one of the few in the country created by a Japanese-American woman and significant enough to help it obtain King County Landmark status in 1993. The fight over control of these historic properties is now in the courts. But one Friend of Mukai, Cindy Stockett of Froggsong Farm, is now raising a precious few 'Marshall' strawberries—the variety that once made Vashon's and the Mukai's family fortunes—brought by her from Bainbridge Island (another former berry-based economy) in hopes of reestablishing a 'Marshall' patch at Mukai. And while the full story of Japanese strawberry farmers on the Island has yet to be fully told, Mary Matsuda Gruenewald published her own family's story in a wonderful book, *Looking Like the Enemy* (available at the Vashon Heritage Museum).

Next door, on the field that once grew Mukai strawberries and now grows Dragon's Head cider apples, Wes Cherry in 2013 made eight times as much cider & perry as the year before (1000 cases for sale at Thriftway, Minglement, and a few stores in Seattle) and plans to build a bigger ciderhouse this coming year. As for those poor trees planted in sodden soil, Wes lost only 10%. "Not bad, considering the conditions. And we have a truly tremendous crop of apples developing on our 2.5-year-old trees. It's very exciting!"

Every Tuesday this summer, as part of my Food Bank run, I turn at 204th and head to GreenDale Garden. Changes are I'll already find Bill Green up to his elbows in the squash patch, catching zukes before they're too big to fit in the car seat. Together we'll load a crate or two full of cole and root crops, salad greens and herbs. Maybe this year, after wrapping a double-strand electric fence around the corn patch, we'll have enough corn to share with the food bank instead of Rocky Raccoon and his gang of thieves.

When Bob and I pull into the Food Bank parking lot, Verne Johnson, man on the apple press at Vashon Winery, hops out from behind the wheel of the Food Bank's delivery truck and hails me. "Hey, you know that apple raspberry hard cider I made last fall? I took it to the Washington State Beer-Stock in Orting last month—23 homebrew clubs attending—and it won 'Best of Show for fermented non-beer beverage.' Cool, huh?"

My fellow volunteers are already at work unloading the truck, loading up grocery bags for delivery, weighing the produce that's coming in from gardens like the Lutheran Church. From the food bank garden north of the parking lot are coming fresh beans, chard, cukes, cabbage, and basil. The farm on Wax Orchard is going into a cover-crop and back into its owner's control, but the board of Sunrise Ridge has given permission for the food bank to open up another patch of sod on the southwest corner of the campus. Someday soon vegetables where now there's only grass.

And there's an orchard now, next to the food bank garden. In 2013, the fruit club planted and set up a number of fruit-growing projects. There's a hugelkultur bed, some fruit trees being trained into espalier and columnar forms, a compost bin fortified with Ken Miller's bio-char, a planting of stone fruits to see which varieties are most resistant to peach leaf curl, a comparison of pears to see which varieties thrive on our Island. Dr. Bob, ever the researcher, gained funding from Western Cascade Fruit Society to test the compatability of different stone fruits with the Adara Plum interstem, a hybrid of a Spanish wild plum that will (unlike most fruit wood) accept grafts of wood from peaches, apricots, and cherries sweet and sour. After obtaining scionwood of Adara from Oregon, Dr. Bob grafted it to plum or cherry rootstocks, then onto the Adara grafted peach, apricot, plum, almond AND cherry. He literally created a "Fruit Basket" tree—and he gave the first ones to two very special women.

On May 11, 2013 in the dedication ceremony for this demonstration orchard, the fruit club invited Dorothy Johnson and Opal Montague to stand up and be honored for their work establishing the campus on Sunrise Ridge. Way back when, this was a fruit orchard owned by the Harmeling family, but in 1956, the Army Corps. of Engineers acquired it to build a Nike Missile control base and barracks (the silos, long ago decommissioned, are buried under the Paradise Ridge Equestrian Park.) The army soldiers planted many specimen trees here—pin and red oaks along the entrance drive, yew trees, tulip poplars, liquidamber, maples, and a Harry Lauder's Walking Sick by the furniture annex. In the 1970s Job Corps, a federal employment program for youth, also planted trees around the campus.

In 1970, the Island Community Council, then led by Leo Montague and Dorothy Johnson, surveyed Islanders and discovered a crying need for better health services. Only two doctors worked on the Island, and one was about to retire. Faced with this great need, in 1972 Leo, Dorothy, and others formed a nonprofit, Vashon-Maury Health Services, and opened a clinic in Burton with three nurse practitioners hired out of the brand-new UW Nurse Practitioner program. In 1976 when the Army decided to surplus the Sunrise Ridge campus, they offered it first (as was traditional) to the state, then the county, then the city. No takers. Discovering this, Dorothy spearheaded a proposal to the Army Surplus dept, suggesting they consider handing over THIS surplus property to a nonprofit organization. The Army agreed to this novel idea, signing a lease with V-M Health Services for the whopping rate of $1/year for 30 years.

This was just the first innovation by this remarkable group of volunteers. Leo and his wife Opal Montague later were instrumental in bringing Group Health to the Island. Tired of going to the mainland for Group Health's services, the Montagues spend three years persuading Group Health to associate with a satellite clinic. "Finally they signed a trial 1-year contract with our little Vashon nonprofit: our doctors would use Group Health's protocols and, when necessary, refer patients to Group Health specialists on the mainland," Opal told me. "Within 3-4 months, nearly 1000 Islanders switched their primary care to Group Health at our Island clinic. Group Health was so impressed with the level of participation —and the tiny capital costs to them—that they came to US to sign a FIVE-year contract at the end of that first year. Then they started developing satellite clinics all around Puget Sound," said Opal. "But we were the first."

Sunrise Ridge is now run by a volunteer Board of Directors. Granny's Attic, the Food Bank, the Health Clinic, King County Parks (admin of the sports fields), and the fruit club are all leasing tenants. When the fruit club approached the board about leasing 3/5 of an acre for a demonstration & research orchard, the board recognized their project as another way the public could use and benefit from this community property. And so, on that warm May day, Dr. Bob stood up and dedicated his first two multi-graft "Fruit Basket" trees to Opal and Dorothy. And wagging his finger at the amused audience, he declared, "Though I know our fruit club members will stay away from these ladies' fruit, maybe others won't be so considerate. So for each tree, I've made a sign with the name of its owner. Ladies, come have a look at YOUR Fruit Baskets. The rest of you can come over in a little bit, and I'll be happy to tell you all about them."

Yes, 2012 was a good year for fans of the apple. A year after the Tire-Swing King on Monument Road was lifted back on its feet, smiling Joe Curiel and Tony Raugust picked 700 lbs. of apples from it and its brother apple tree. They had so many, they gave half to the Fruit Club's 2012 Cider Fest.

In our community orchard, the 26 apples that I now knew were Jonagolds plumped up, turned yellow then red—and were eaten by deer. I only realized that when I discovered the apples vanished and a whole lot of deer droppings beneath the tree. C'est la vie. But after a hard pruning of the Rainier cherry a year later, the Honeycrisp apple behind it burst into bloom. In 2013 as this book goes to press, the three apple trees in our community orchard are laden with dozens of apples—maybe hundreds. They aren't all scab-free—I missed a spraying during a rainy stretch in June—but they look mighty presentable to my eye. Now if I can only muster the willpower to put up a deer fence in time...

When I look around my hole-in-the-woods garden, I see one that's profited from three years of its owner writing about gardens. I see a potager of raised beds that's yielded tender spring greens, spikey green onions, chubby cabbages and cucumbers, bright flowers and savory herbs. Basil plants and a 'Northern Delight' tomato thrive in pots against a brick wall, so much so that I dream of an espalier or two: apples certainly, maybe a 'Frost' peach? And I've got a start on a fall-winter garden, with young lettuces, cabbages, green onions, and kale growing into a size that can stand up to winter weather. My husband's making a set of bamboo-framed screens for the raspberry bushes to keep out the ravaging birds, but I still have to build a Fort Knox for the June strawberries. So far no critter has discovered the more elegant and everbearing alpine strawberries bought from Langley Fine Gardens last spring; their tiny, tasty berries make a plain ol' bowl of corn flakes taste like fine dining at Dale's B & B. And my one surviving Olympic berry is growing out its primocanes, next year to be looped around the wires of the raspberry trellis. Maybe someday, there'll be enough for pie.

I know that, thanks to writing, I've become a better gardener. I can see it here, at GreenDale Garden, and now at a new garden on the north end. This spring, I got a phone call from a part-time Islander who wanted to keep his new garden in good shape for his summer-time vacation renters. "Would you come help me plan and sow?" he asked. So once a week on Thursday mornings, I work at what we call together "GlennDale Garden." In between, I use www.growveg.com to plan what's coming next—a plan he can look at from Seattle, thanks to a shared password. As Bill Green has mentored me, I'm mentoring another gardener. And what pleasures this new space gives! To plunge my shovel into yet another soil of Vashon—loamy and seemingly endlessly deep, basking in westside sun—and see raspberries and strawberries, flowers and veg, rise out of yet another rich Vashon garden.

In this last season of writing this book, I came to realize that self-publishing this 250-page book would take all the savings I had left after three years of part-time, then UN-employment. But then I thought of Karen Biondo's crowd-funding campaign to get her pizza truck: her community pledged over $38,000 dollars to help her bring that wood-fired pizza to Vashon. If this book is about my community and how we garden, maybe this same community will help me KickStart my book into the world.

So I cobbled together a very amateur video with my pocket Canon and iMovie, wrote a too-long description of the book and why I needed funding, and registered my campaign on www.Kickstarter.com. I friended every Islander I knew on Facebook, gathered emails, starting writing pitches, stood up and announced to every captive audience I found myself in. But what people seemed to respond to most was the book itself: when I sent out chapters, pledges came in. I did a reading, and more pledges came in. Slowly, then slower... and when the last days of the campaign arrived and my fingernails were bitten to the quick, my neighbor Sherene Zolno—yes, THAT Sherene—sent out an email shout-out that took the campaign over the top. Well over eighty Islanders—including one who pledged from her trip in *Africa*—have helped put this book into your hands. And since nearly a hundred folks gave me their garden tales, plus those many hosts of the VAA Garden Tour, you could say you're getting stories and advice from hundreds of folks who garden on Vashon and Maury Islands.

And that's as this book should be. While I never could keep my own experiences off these pages, in truth I wanted this book to be not about me, but you. About how you garden and cultivate—and I don't just mean in the soil. We are a community that cultivates EACH OTHER: in our many arts and service organizations, our churches and schools, clubs and nonprofits, small ensembles and solo acts, we are nurturing, feeding, supporting, and harvesting new endeavors all the time.

Just read the newspaper, any week—you'll see our needs, beliefs, and talents flowering in new expressions of our wacky wonderfulness all year round. Feeding the Hungry. Putting on a Show. Teaching the Children. Learning Something New. Hoeing a Row Together. Playing in a Band. Building a new Center. Giving our Bounty To Each Other. And always, always, growing something good, beautiful, and useful from whatever seeds the Island places into our many open hands.

And so I hoist my glass of Island homegrown brew and say to you all—

Garden on, Vashon!

Sources

Much of the information in this book came straight from interviews and visits with Vashon-Maury Islanders. However, other resources helped me build a fuller portrait of the Island yesterday and today. I did not create a formal bibliography because some of the info comes from changeable online URLs or from notebooks of news clippings / ephemera.

The Vashon-Maury Island Heritage Museum (particularly its White Notebooks organized by topic and the histories/ interviews done by Mary Matthews).

King County records, particularly about water resources (Google any topic).

Kevin Freeman and Vashon College 101: the Geology section.

U.S. Geologic Survey map, *the Vashon 7.5" Quadrangle* by Derek B. Booth and Kathy Goetz Troost, 2007.

V-MI Beachcomber archives kept in their office.

Frank Shride, catalog from Beall Greenhouse Company, 1970s.

Vashon Audubon pamphlets on Island trees.

Ron Irvine of Vashon Winery for his researches into the history of Vashon apple trees, local cultivation of wine & cider, and his book, *The Wine Project.*

V-MI Land Trust and their maps on groundwater.

The V-MI Groundwater Protection committee and its publication *Liquid Assets*

Vashon Nature Center

V-MI Library, of course

Blanche Caffiere, *The Past Remembered* (4-part series).

Bob Gordon, *Magnolia Beach Memories.*

Mary Matsuda Gruenewald, *Looking Like the Enemy*, 2005.

Bruce Haulman & Jean Cammon Findlay's *Vashon-Maury Island*, published by Images of America, South Carolina, 2011.

Bruce Haulman's website, www.vashonhistory.com

Dr. Bob Norton, "Orchard Doin's" and other hand-outs to the VMI Fruit Club.

Pamela J. Woodroffe, *Vashon Island's Agricultural Roots: Tales of the Tilth as Told by Island Farmers,* 2002.

Marjorie Stanley, *Search for Laughter* (an Island memoir & oral history).

WSU Mt. Vernon Research Station's online information on fruit growing.

www.historylink.org (Washington State online history resources).

Index

To find names, look under People, Winemakers, or VAA Garden Hosts. Plants are listed under type, such as Annuals, Perennials, Vegetables, Native Plants. A plant vendor may be found under stores, garden centers, or nurseries; farms and flower vendors have own categories.

About the author

Karen Dale is a gardener, writer, Apple computer addict, and former oil painter. Born in Portland, Oregon, she has lived up and down the I-5 corridor of the West Coast all her life (excepting that one year in Alaska). She moved to Vashon Island with husband Bob Dale in 1995, living first on Beall Road a little south of the ruins of the Beall Greenhouses, and now above Shawnee Point overlooking outer Quartermaster Harbor. Her gardening blog for the Vashon Beachcomber can be found at http://blogs.vashonbeachcomber.com/gardenon.

To order additional copies of this book—

a) you can check any Vashon Island bookshop

b) you can email the author at karendale@centurytel.net

c) you can send a check for $30.00 per copy ($25 for book, $5 for priority mail) to—
   PO Box 13095
   Burton, WA 98013

   Specify—
   # of copies wanted
   Your physical & mailing addresses (they may be different)
   If there's a "Must Have Be" date

And thanks for reading Garden on, Vashon!

Notes